MW00831496

Courageous

WOMEN OF FAITH

BOOK 2

To contact Kathy or for more information email:

kathy.crockett@outlook.com

or visit

www.purehopefoundation.com

Copyright   © 2016 by Pure Hope Foundation

Cover Design - Nicole Fletcher

Senior Editor – Lindsey Holt

Supporting Editors – Dr. Lynn Huffman, Malissa Sheaffer and Calley Crockett

Formatting/Publishing Editors – Steve Crockett and Joe Setliff

Library of Congress Control Number: 1-3995258481

ISBN 978-0-9862533-2-4

So be strong and courageous! Do not be afraid and do not panic before them. For the LORD your God will personally go ahead of you. He will neither fail you nor abandon you.

Deuteronomy 31:6 New Living Translation

Contents

Introduction

Kathy Crockett

If you had told me years ago I would lead a book project where women shared stories of courageous faith I would have laughed. Maybe an academic article. Or maybe even some type of leadership book. Yet a book of stories from women? Not likely! I do get asked often how the Courageous Women of Faith books came to be so I thought perhaps you might like to know as well.

I've been blessed to meet a lot of people over the years from all walks of life. Whether a CEO of a billion-dollar company or an orphan from a third world country, I would find myself riveted by their stories and inspired by their faith through adversity. Often, I would write their experiences and the lessons I learned from them, in my journals. About a year ago, I sensed that the stories I am blessed to hear and collect show the powerful love of God and are glimpses of His miracles. These accounts need to be shared so others can be encouraged. This realization led to a challenging adventure of reaching out to authors, contacting editors, and learning about book publishing. It also taught me much about being obedient when you sense God asking you to do something. That pressing feeling that you should act. You can read more below on some of the details of how that played out for me and this series of books.

Early in 2014 I believed that the stories I had collected would make a good book. I could share my friends' stories and would have a cool gift to give others. My plan was to connect my friends with someone who likes to write and they would do the book. I gave the idea to several people. After a few months went by with no one really running with the idea, to my horror, I sensed that God perhaps was asking me to do the book. That was hilarious. I have no idea how to publish a book. I am not an editor or English professor. I had lots going on in my life with family commitments, work, and church. I was certainly not looking for anything else to do and knew I didn't have the capacity or space to insert writing and publishing a book. With a very lengthy list of excuses, I thought I was off the hook. It was ridiculous that I would do the book, right? Yet my mind kept coming back to the book over, and over, and over again. I finally relented and asked a few friends (via text, so it would be easier for them to say no) if they would write a chapter. THEY SAID YES! It was a strange feeling. glad they said yes, yet at the same time not quite sure how this was going to work. I told the authors to work on their stories over the summer (this was in April) and send me their chapters by the first of August, and we would go from there. I had NO IDEA what I was going to do with their chapters. I would figure that out as the chapters rolled in.

Fast forward to late July, I had not heard from any of the authors. I had not really checked on them either. We are all really busy right? I was frankly relieved. I had decided that perhaps the book would just wait until after my girls graduated from school (four years from then), and I would think about it again then. About that time, I went to a leadership meeting near Atlanta and meet up with my friend Ann White who I had told about the book. After a few minutes of light chit chat she asked me about the book. I told her that the authors are busy, I hadn't really heard from anyone. That even though I sensed that

God may have wanted me to do the book, it seemed that this is just not right for this season of life with kids, work, etc. She looked me right in the eye and asked me, "Kathy, so did you pray about this and feel like this is where God is directing you to go? Or did you just decide this on your own because this is going to be hard?" I decided right then that I was not really sure I liked Ann White. Do you have friends in your life like that, ones who hold you accountable to things? I had to admit that I had not been praying about it. I actually was avoiding discussing it with God in my quiet time. Avoiding that whole topic seemed to be working just fine until Ann pointed out the obvious—perhaps checking in with God and praying for direction might be a good idea. I still really didn't want to, yet I didn't want to be like Jonah and ignore something I sensed God was asking me to do. So I prayed that night.

By the next morning it was very clear to me that I was to do the book. I didn't hear a loud voice from God. It was more of a sense that I was to keep taking the next steps. So I called Ann before my meetings began at the conference and told her she had to finish her chapter (accountability back at ya). She said she could have it to me by September 1st. That sounded like a good date, so I told two other authors I saw that day at the conference. Turns out, they had been working on their chapters all summer and were good to go. Other authors told me the same. Then the sense I had to keep working on the book deepened into a pressure to work faster as August 15th rolled around. Meanwhile, another name kept coming to my mind, which I thought was strange because I thought I already had all the authors. Yet the name Joyce Carrell kept coming to mind over and over. She was the mom of one of my dear friends, Holly Morris, and was going through chemo treatments. I kept thinking I should wait, that it would be too hard to write a chapter right now. Yet her name was constantly in my mind.

I called Holly to ask if she thought it might work out to get her mom to be part of our book. She checked in with Joyce and sure enough she was game. It took a few days for me to connect with Joyce. I was busy getting kids back in school and getting ready for LCU Fall semester. It was a crazy time. Yet I just had to get on the phone with Joyce. We talked around August 18th yet it took me another week to get her specific questions to answer for her story. I almost decided to wait until after Labor Day to send them to her, yet my mind would not rest. I had to send them now. Joyce let me know she would work on the questions and other ideas she had and we would talk soon.

Little did I know at the time that Joyce would take an unexpected turn for the worse, and I would not get to talk with her again. She went to be with the Lord on September 6, 2014. It was absolutely heartbreaking. Yet Joyce being the beautiful, courageous, amazing woman that everyone knew her to be had worked on her chapter. She had a dear friend, who was also going through a battle with cancer, and they talked about the questions. Holly had gone to visit her mom, and they too were able to talk about the questions. Joyce shared things with Holly that she planned to share in the book. They had a very sweet time together. A precious 18-year-old LCU student, Libby Kirkpatrick, organized the content that we had from those sources, so we could include Joyce's chapter in our first book.

I was so grateful that I had responded to that pressing I felt. I was beyond thankful that Ann had encouraged me to pray about the book and ask for guidance and that God led me to reach out to the authors. I believe He went before me to make the book possible. He was willing to use me, His servant who clearly had no training in how to write/publish a book. It was ALL HIM.

The story of how we brought the book to market is also an interesting one. I will keep it short. I was still struggling wondering how in the world we would get this done. I was clueless on copyright, ISBN, book formatting, etc. I had some very gracious students and friends who donated their time to edit the chapters. Yet I still didn't know how we were going to get the book published. One night at our small group Bible study, I asked Joe Setliff, owner of a printing company, if he might know of someone who could help me. He just smiled and said, "Kathy you do know I help people with their books all the time, right?" Of course I did not know that. The funny thing was that I thought perhaps I had done all the hard work of getting the content of the book together and maybe God would allow someone else to take it from there. Since I was still clueless on how to do it and nothing was coming to me, I thought I was off the hook. Then in five minutes in my kitchen at small group Bible study, God took care of all those details. Joe walked me step-by-step through the rest of the process. And let me just say there were A LOT of steps. Joe was very patient with me, and I was so grateful.

I learned two huge things in this process along with thousands of smaller things. First, have people in your life who will make you better, to hold you accountable to do big things when you may believe it is too hard, and to cheer you on when you get discouraged and want to give up. I am grateful that Ann White was that person for me, reminding me to pray about the book before dismissing it. Second, do not ignore those pressings you feel to act. I am so grateful I was able to sense that yearning leading me to contact Joyce. The blessings I have received from being obedient to where God was leading me have been profound.

I want to thank everyone who purchased the first book and helped Pure Hope Foundation. We were deeply encouraged and even a bit surprised by the response we had to the first, which led us to work on the second book. Without all of you, this book would have never happened.

I also want to express my deepest gratitude to the authors. It has been such a privilege and honor to be trusted with their stories. They are very close to my heart. I have shed many tears and said many prayers as I worked with them to formally write about their experiences. In each chapter you will find a compelling story of hope that has risen out of tragedy, struggle, and pain. It took a great deal for each of them to share in such a public way. These are courageous women of faith. I know their desire is to offer readers hope and encouragement as we all walk together on this journey with our Lord and Savior Jesus Christ.

Shelley Fietz

Part of my routine at Lubbock Christian University is attending chapel on our campus, and this is where I heard Shelley share a piece of her life story. Her winsome way of sharing her struggles drew me into her world. I knew her story would be a great addition to our book. Even though I had never met her, she immediately said yes when I asked her if she would be game to be in our book. Within a few days, she drove two hours to meet with me so we could begin the process. Shelley's transparency and her tenacity to heal and save her marriage will encourage you. I hope someday you will also get to hear her speak– such a joy.

Messiah

Shelley Fietz

My husband found me early one morning, covered in vomit and passed out drunk behind the dumpster at the local Whataburger restaurant. We had an argument, I stormed out, and I had been gone all night. He received an anonymous phone call telling him where to look for me. I had no idea how I got there. Rock Bottom? I was there. A wife, a mother of two young children, a church member, a friend...and an alcoholic. *How did I get here?* Passed out drunk; addicted and depressed; living a double life filled with lies. *How did I get here?* My husband wanted to divorce me. How was I going to save my life, my marriage, my family? *How did I get here?*

How did my life get so screwed up? That is a valid question. I grew up in a church-attending family with one sister. We seemed to be a perfectly average family living a perfectly predictable life. In high school, I started dating and soon found myself in love with someone of whom my parents did not approve. We were very different. We were from different faiths, different races, and had very different families. They considered him to be a "bad boy" who got into fights a lot. Since my parents were so set against him, I fell hard for him. I spent every waking moment with him, many times by lying and sneaking around to see him. Two days before my senior year, we decided to spend the day hanging out separately with our friends. That night when we talked on the phone, I could

9

tell that he had been drinking. As usual when that happened, I silenced my phone when I went to bed so he would not be able to wake me by calling to talk all night long. The next morning, I awoke to numerous missed calls. There were a lot from him, a lot from his mom, from cousins, and from really random people that never called me. While I was getting ready to go see him for the day, a friend of mine called. She could tell that I had no idea what had happened. She told me that he shot himself and was in the hospital. I just hung up on her, thinking she was crazy. I went and told my mom what the girl had said. My mom's response was that I should call the hospital to see if he was there. They connected me to ICU, and I found out that he was indeed there.

So there I was, a 17-year-old girl, driving alone to the hospital to see if my boyfriend was dead or alive. The hospital hallways were crowded with friends and family. His sister came out of ICU to get me so I could go see him. He ended up dying that day. I was alone in my grief and had no idea how to cope with the feelings of guilt and loss. The girls at our high school who were from his family's ethnic community hated me and told me his dying was all my fault. I was terrified to go to school on the first day of my senior year because I was afraid they would hurt me. I joined them in placing the burden of his death on my shoulders, believing that it was all my fault.

For my parents, there was a sense of relief that he was gone. They did not want him to die, but they had always resisted his influence in my life. They had never liked him, and they did not like me being with him. So, as far as they were concerned, the problem was gone. He was no longer around to cause problems in our family. As you can imagine, I hated them for that. They did not let me grieve. I needed someone to hold me, love me, and to let me cry. I did not know how to experience this wave of grief and guilt. The walls of hatred towards my parents grew and grew.

I became the proverbial country song, "looking for love in all the wrong places." Instead of going to a counselor and getting healing, I turned to partying. When I was drinking and doing drugs with friends was when I "felt" loved. I felt like they could "see" me best when I did those things—a lie of Satan! Over the course of three years, I proceeded to give myself to any boy who made me feel pretty and loved. I completely lost my purity. Little did I know that what I did so flippantly back then would still affect me even to this day.

Ben entered the picture at this point. My family was thrilled; he was a great guy and he went to church. With Ben around, it was almost as if all the bad stuff from my life just vanished. We ended up getting married, and my life seemed perfect. He got a job as a pilot for an airline, which meant he would travel often. My plan was to have girls' nights out when he was away, to really still be able to enjoy my life the way I wanted to without him around to stop me. Those plans changed when I found myself pregnant with our first daughter. I was so excited to welcome my little friend! However, I did not realize my little friend was going to be so much work. I was alone with her A LOT! My "girls' nights out" soon turned into "me and the baby's nights in." I resented my working husband because he was gone so much. Re-enter Satan into my life:

he came in the form of alcohol. Of course, I did not think I had a problem. I would put my sweet baby to sleep and go sit on my back porch for a couple glasses of wine. Soon, the glasses became bottles, and the wine became hard liquor.

People started telling me that they were worried about me and they thought I had a problem. That really irritated me. My definition of an alcoholic then was someone who cracked open the bottle as soon as she woke up and then carried it around with her all day. No! That was not me. Yet, the truth was that once I started drinking, I could not stop. I was drinking to numb the pain from my past that I had never dealt with. I would get drunk and it would go away for a while, but it would just come back each time even stronger. During this time, our son, Jett, was born. Our marriage was miserable, but I lived thinking "Ben's not going to leave me. We have two kids. Who's gonna do all the laundry and buy all the groceries? We don't get divorced in our family."

Not only was I abusing alcohol and smoking cigarettes, I also began taking anti-depression and anti-anxiety medicines. I soon began blacking out on a regular basis. I would be "awake," walking, and talking, but I would not remember anything for hours at a time. Dozens of times, Ben would tell me about things I had done, but I did not believe him. I never remembered any of what he said I had done. He even tried videoing me and showing me what I had been doing in hopes that I would be shamed into changing my lifestyle. What I saw in those videos was awful, but I still felt no motivation to change. I had been telling myself that I was doing okay. I was keeping things held together; I only drank at night after my kids went to bed. They were never in any danger, right? Ben would ask me what I thought would happen if there was an emergency when he was out of town and I was passed out in bed?

Spiraling out of control, I was in deep depression. I never actually attempted suicide, but I wanted to. I was too scared and too selfish to go through with it, but I wished for a bus to come along, to hit and kill me so I would not have to do it myself. I believed that everyone around me would be better off without me.

One night, we got in an argument. It escalated to the point that I yelled, "I'm outta here!" and stormed out of the house. I used the argument as an excuse to leave, but all I really cared about was getting away to go drink. The last thing I remember was at 11:00 pm. The next thing I knew, it was 5:00 in the morning. I do not know what happened during those lost hours, but at 5:00 I woke up behind the dumpster at Whataburger, covered in vomit. I have no idea how I got there or who I spent time with that night. As soon as I tried to sit up, I saw Ben pulling into the parking lot. He was not happy! *How did I get here?*

Things finally came to a head in April 2011; Ben was through with me. Our marriage was in shambles. We hated each other and were merely going through the motions. He met with both of our parents and told them everything. I was given an ultimatum. I had destroyed relationships all around me. When I went and talked to my parents, they matter-of-factly reminded me that "every action has a consequence." I had dug my own grave and now had to figure out if I was going to lie there and die, or find a way to get out of it. At twenty-seven years of age, I was looking at the prospect of being a divorced, alcoholic mother of two young children. As I was talking to my parents, I kept hearing a name in my head... *"Patty."* Patty was a woman at our church who had a story of her own and had survived it, emerging both whole and healthy. I knew I needed to talk to her.

So, I called her up and met her at a park. When she told me about her life, I felt like she was the first person I had ever met to whom I could relate. She got me, and I got her. Addiction is isolating because it tells you that no one else can understand how you feel, think, or act as you do. I was amazed to finally be talking to someone who really understood me. It was the first time in my life that someone truly saw me. I knew that Patty had been where I was, so I told her every single horrible thing I had done in my marriage, things that no one else in the world knew.

Patty told me that God sent me here. That annoyed me—I believed God had been nowhere near me or my situation. She asked me if I was willing to get help. Finally, I was at a point where the answer was "yes." I wanted to get sober, and I did not want to lose my kids. Patty was the one who told me about Mission Messiah, a year-long rehab program for women. Many of the women are single mothers and are allowed to bring their children with them. Some who go there are under court order, some are homeless, and for most, it is their last chance at getting sober and/or staying out of jail. To be honest, I was pretty offended when she first told me all of this. It sounded like prison, and a whole year was way too long for me to be gone. I really wanted her to tell me that I just needed a couple of AA meetings and I would be good to go.

To be very honest, I consider myself to be a high-maintenance kind of girl. I did not like the idea of something messing with my scheduled life. I was a full-time hair stylist; I was completely involved with my kids' activities; I had a nail appointment every two weeks. I couldn't just leave! I knew in my soul that I needed a change, and Patty reminded me that there would never be a "good time" to go to rehab. No one ever looks at their calendar and sees a "free year" that they can take off.

So, Patty asked me to do two things: she asked me to pray about it, and she asked me to consider that it was the Lord who led me to seek help from her that day. Ugh! Pray? I had been raised going to church all my life, but it was just something I did, somewhere I went a couple times a week to tell everyone that my life was "just great." I struggled with God through all of this because I felt like he was nowhere. I would try to reach out to Him for help, but I did not feel like He was helping me at all. *How did He let all this happen to me?*

So, I went home that night to Ben, who was not speaking to me. That night, I became ill and the only voice I could hear was inside my head telling me to go wake up Ben and tell him that I would go to Mission Messiah. So, I finally did. He agreed that I should go, but I could not take the kids with me. He was ready for me to just be gone.

In the light of the next morning, I had pretty much changed my mind about going. Ben was on his way out the door to meet with Patty and her husband John to talk about our problem. At that moment, I prayed to the Lord—my first authentic, honest prayer in years. I asked God to please give me this chance; I asked him to save my family.

When Ben came home, he hugged me for the first time in forever, looked me in the eye, and promised to wait for a year before he divorced me, but only if I would go to the Mission.

This was my answer from God. I had to go. My life was about to drastically change. I was about to be revealed. I was getting ready to let a lot of people down. I put my life on shut down. I cancelled all my social media. That started everyone wondering what was going on. We decided it best not to respond to anyone either electronically or when they came in person to the house. I eventually sent out a mass text telling people that I would not explain it, but I was leaving in three days for a year-long rehab program. I asked them to pray for us, especially our children. It was awful!

I vividly remember how things were in our house for the last days before I left. I felt like I was going away to summer camp, but for an entire year. I felt such a heaviness! We told our four-year-old daughter, Madison, that I was going to where Jesus could teach me to be a better mom and wife. Our son, Jett, was only eighteen months old at the time. Leaving the two of them was the hardest thing I have ever done. It was just terrible leaving them, but I knew that they needed to stay home. This was MY problem and I needed to face it head on. Ben, who hated me at the time, chose to act in love toward me. He held me and let me cry. He slept with me in our room. He loved me more in those three days than he had been able to in the five years of our marriage. Ben is a private pilot for a family in the area where we live, and they were so good to him. He was totally upfront and honest with his boss about our situation, and they worked with him as he was being both Dad and Mom during that year. His boss firmly reminded him that family comes first. When Ben could not be with the kids, our moms took care of them. God was so good to us!

The Daily Schedule at Mission Messiah:

6:00 am: <u>Worship and Devotional Time</u>

If one person arrived even a minute late, everyone was required to show up 30 minutes early the next morning. This helped us realize that our actions affect everyone around us.

7:00 am-7:30 am: <u>Exercise time</u>

Many people will replace a substance addiction with a food addiction, resulting in a lot of weight gain.

7:30 am-8:15 am: <u>Get ready for the day and clean your room</u>

Each day there was a white glove inspection.

8:15 am-9:15 am: <u>Scripture class</u>

We memorized two verses daily until we were tested by reciting an entire chapter from memory. On the first day, the girl sitting beside me told me, "You can do this. I used to do crack and now I'm filling my heart with God's word. You'll make a 100." I thought she was crazy, but of course, she was right. By the time I left the Mission, I had memorized 7 books of the Bible: 1, 2, and 3 John, Galatians, Ephesians, Philippians, and Titus. It was such an amazing sense of accomplishment when I was able to recite large portions of God's word time and time again.

9:15 am-9:30 am: <u>Break</u>

We went to our rooms to see if we passed inspection.

9:30 am-11:30 am: <u>Class time</u>

We did Bible studies taught by a variety of women who would come in each day to teach us. We had usually 7-8 homework items to do every day. We were assigned everything from book reports to completing written Bible studies. The amount of class work that is done in the year at the Mission is equivalent to two years of college. It was very intense and I learned so much about God's word that year. There was never a time that I felt closer to God!

12:00 pm-1:00 pm: <u>Lunch</u>

After class, we were released to get ready for lunch. There was no "being served" at the Mission. We cooked, cleaned, and were responsible for all chores and maintenance done there. The food there was a huge struggle for me. We ate what was put in front of us, no more. There were no buffet choices and no menus to choose from. You got what you got, and that was it.

1:00 pm-6:00 pm: <u>Work time</u>

We worked long, hard hours.

6:00 pm-7:00 pm: <u>Dinner preparation and eating</u>

There were around 45 people to feed each day.

7:00 pm-9:00 pm: <u>Nightly Chores</u>

We were expected to treat the Mission as if it were our home. We were expected to take care of it. It may not have been the Ritz, but we kept it clean and very well-maintained. These chores would all have to be done before we could go to our rooms.

9:00 pm: Homework

At this time, we were sent to our rooms to do homework and scripture memorization. I would pray for supernatural sleep! Those days were so long and exhausting. I remember writing every night in my journal—some nights there would be tears coming down my face and dropping onto the paper because I was so lonely and so sad. Some nights, I would feel like writing cuss words all over my paper because I was so angry that I was there. However, other times I would be filled with so much joy and know that I was doing exactly what God wanted me to do. As hard as my days were, I never gave up. I kept trucking along, because God is a God of completion.

The year spent at Mission Messiah has four different Program Phases:

Iron Phase (1-3 months)

This was an on-site work phase. We did any maintenance that needed to be done on the buildings: washed the toilets, cleaned out freezers, washed out trash cans, cleaned the grout, organized the pantry, pulled the weeds, painted the walls, washed the windows, flipped the mattresses, repaired the doors, and swept, mopped, and scrubbed everything. The emphasis was not only on hard work; it was also on submitting to authority. We were expected to say "Yes Sir" or "Yes Ma'am" to whatever we were told to do. They were teaching us to not be so self-centered.

During this first phase, we did not really get to leave the Mission because they wanted to make sure we were stable enough to function before they sent us out into the public. A lot of women who come through this program have not been sober for years, and they have either been homeless or addicted every day of their life. This makes being around the normal, functioning public very awkward for them. It is necessary to make sure that the girls are staying focused completely on the steps toward getting healthy. The whole purpose for the Iron Phase is to stay on site and make sure everything gets done for the other people who live on the property. During the Iron Phase, residents emotionally become very close because all the women are together at all times throughout the day.

My first day, I was told I would be responsible for mowing the entire place, weed eating around all the trees, and then edging the entire campus. I was not meaning to be disrespectful, but I laughed and responded, "I don't really do yard work." The director kindly told me, "Well, now you will DO yard work. You will do it every day. I'll show you how to mow, if you don't know how, but this IS your job." So, for the next three months I was in charge of the yards there. At first, it was awful because my pride was so involved, but after about a week, I loved it. It was outside, and I could work totally alone. That was when I did my scripture memory work. Back and forth, I pushed that lawn mower as I laid up God's word in my heart.

While in the Iron Phase, I was also the cook. I was able to work on making the menu and had helpers to help prep the food and wash dishes. This was a great time for me since I love to cook. It was a great joy for me, coming from a family who loves to cook and to eat great food. Many of the women there did not have that background, so I really feel like I was able to bless them in that way. I turned up my praise music and had a blast making meals for everyone there.

Bronze Phase (3-6 months)

As you successfully spend more time in the program and learn to follow their rules, you are granted more responsibilities and privileges. During this phase, residents would stay on campus for the morning routine and then leave after lunch to go out and work in one of the two stores that Mission Messiah runs. "ZIP" (Zeal, Integrity, and Purpose) is an embroidery and printing store. "WOW" (Women of Worth) sells household décor and furnishings. All of the proceeds of these stores go to help fund the Mission.

After three months, if you have been following the rules, a 4-hour off campus pass is granted. I would always go see my husband and kids. So, as hard as the program was at times, I knew that every thirty days, if I followed the rules, I would get four hours just with my family and nobody else. Words cannot describe how precious those moments were for me.

Silver Phase (6-9 months)

The next phase shifted to full-time work mode. After the morning activities, I worked full-time from around 9:00-6:00 at one of the stores. I was also one of the two drivers at the Mission. We were responsible to make sure everyone got to work and to appointments. We drove those huge 15 passenger vans. When they first told me that I would be driving one of those things, I thought, "NO WAY!" After a couple of weeks, though, I really loved being the driver. It showed me that I was actually doing something right. I got to go grocery shopping and sit in the front with the air conditioner. That was a bonus!

This phase was a little harder because we still had to continue to do all of our homework and work all day off campus. Days would get long and my feet would get so tired, but it was really nice being in the real world and getting to be out with people. Some of my best days at the Mission were when someone from my church or one of my friends would pop into WOW and see me. God knew exactly when to do this for me. It would always be on one of those days I just did not think I could make it through another minute. Then, all of a sudden, one of my friends would be there to lift my spirits and encourage me to keep working and fighting for my family. It was such a great feeling and such a relief just to see people I knew. They would bring me a little news from home and, more often than not, a Diet Coke. I love Diet Coke so much, but we never had it at the Mission, so for them to bring me one was seriously one of the best days of my life!

The 4-hour pass turned into a 24-hour pass during Silver Phase. What a blessing it was to go home and sleep in my own bed! However, it made it that much harder to get in that car and drive back to the Mission. Those were the hardest days of all!

Gold Phase (9-12 months)

This last time period was fun because you knew you were almost done with the program. It came with a lot more privileges. Your daily routine was the same as in the Silver Phase, but the passes increased. Once a week, there was a 4-hour pass and one time in Gold Phase there was a 48-hour pass.

During each phase, there was still Bible study and memorization required, but our sole purpose during the last two phases was to work at the stores from 9:30-6:00. Many of the women need this training, not only in marketable skills, but basic personal skills as well. They have to learn how to relate to others, how to provide a welcoming atmosphere, how to greet, help, and check-out a customer. Many of these women have felony records (which makes it hard to get hired) and are able to continue to work at one of these stores after they graduate from the rehab program.

Routines and phases were all a huge part of my experience, and you have to understand what my days were like to understand my personal and spiritual growth. Let me tell you about my time at Mission Messiah:

Phone calls were very limited, but I was able to talk to Ben two times per week for five minutes at a time. My first

23

five-minute phone call with Ben was allowed two weeks after I arrived. Those were hard times, not only for me as I adjusted to life in rehab, but for Ben as he was now a single parent. Both of our moms helped to care for Madison and Jett, but Ben was really struggling. I had written him letters, but he had not responded. When it finally came time for our first phone call, I was over-the-top excited. He was not. I could tell quickly that he really did not want to talk to me. He was quiet as I talked, and finally told me that he was just busy picking up my mess. He knew that I needed to be there, but he was doing his job plus my job, and he was angry. We talked every third day for five minutes, and for many weeks, it was very clear that he was not really interested in how or what I was doing. After too many one-sided conversations with Ben, I completely believed that he would divorce me before my time there was over. A good friend comforted me by telling me, "Shelley, God did not bring you here to fail. You be obedient and God will work out the details. He will give you the desires of your heart, because He wants your marriage to survive. His plan for you is restoration!" Those were the words that I needed to believe in order to continue to be faithful. I returned to my room that night and began to pray these things over my life and my marriage. Restoration!

At two weeks, the kids were able to come and visit me for six hours. Many of the women there had their children living with them, and it was such a blessing for me to see mine, if only for a short time. I was going cold turkey from alcohol, prescription anxiety and depression medicines, and cigarettes. I was adjusting to a new life in so many ways: a new home, new responsibilities, new life-style in almost every aspect of my existence. I had never been an "everyday drinker," but was more of a binge drinker, so I did not really struggle with overwhelming physical withdrawal symptoms. As hard as it was to stay at Mission Messiah, I knew that, realistically, I had no other choice. Both Ben and Patty told me that if I decided to leave before the year was up, I could not come home or expect to receive any help from them. Ben was serious, he was giving me a year in rehab or he would divorce me. I knew the day I signed my paperwork to enter the program that God is a God of completion. I was determined that I would NOT quit.

Still, there were times that were really terrible. I was different than most of the other women at the Mission, and they disliked me because of it. I was the only one legally married. I made it a point to get up every morning and fix my hair and make-up—I just feel better when I do that. I had a lot of things that the rest of the girls there did not, items like hair products, my own bedding, and nicer clothes. Things finally came to a boiling point one day in the kitchen when I could tell that some of the women were talking about me. I was mad! I demanded that they stop being so mean to me. I told them that I was an addict just like them; I missed my regular life, just like they did; and I was trying to get my life back together, just like they were. After that, we were all able to share a little more mutual respect. I was eventually able to have Ben bring my hair tools and started doing the other girls' hair. That was a huge blessing! Many of them had NEVER had a professional cut or style. I was able to use my talent and profession as my "olive branch" to them.

At six weeks into the program, Ben and my parents were able to come for a visit. It was very awkward and strained between us. The kids were running around, and I had the feeling that I was on a blind date with a bunch of people around. Ben asked me what we did during the day and a couple of other very surface questions. It was a terrible visit. We, a stinking married couple, "side-hugged" when Ben left. What the heck!

Probably the lowest point came around seven weeks. I had already had a bad day, topped off by a bad phone call from Ben. Then, late that night, I was alone in my room, balling my eyes out before the Lord. I started screaming, "I'm so mad at You! I've done all this for you! I don't get to see my kids or my husband and to top it off, he still hates me! Was this in Your plan?" Then His voice came into my room saying, "You are trying to fix your marriage." I took that as a challenge. I got out a notebook and started writing. I wrote out every horrible sin, every struggle in my marriage, every time I drank until I passed out...I gave it all to God. "Here, You want it? You can have it! Fine, You want me to lay my life at Your feet? Ok, well show me that You are God and You fix it! Fix it all! I will meet You halfway, but right now I don't believe You."

I really feel like in that moment, God was thinking, "Finally! You are finally doing something about it! Okay, let's get to work." After that point, I really saw God working on ME. He was softening me. He was speaking to me. So at this point, I was doing great in my relationship with God. He was helping me in so many ways.

God always provided someone to speak His wisdom into my life just when I needed it. One example of this happened a few days before the second time Ben came to see me. I was trying to get him to come around to seeing things my way. A dear woman who worked at the Mission told me this: "Shelley, be quick to agree with your adversary. When you see Ben, be quick to agree with him. You are trying to defend your entire life, including the facts of all the horrible sin you have done. Quit defending it! You shouldn't defend it! You did it! All of it. You are already in trouble. That's why you are here. So, quit defending your life and lay it down. Listen to Ben and agree with him. Take yourself out of yourself and listen." She could not have been more right!

During week eight and Ben's second visit, I was walking him to his car to say goodbye. He had repeatedly told me that he was "fine" and to just worry about myself. He was still very aloof. I looked at him and simply told him that it was okay to be angry with me. It was like I had opened the floodgates and he started verbally throwing up right there in the parking lot. He yelled at me, "I am angry with you! I don't want to be married to you, and honestly, I hate you." By this time, girls from the Mission were walking up, and we had an audience to hear him scream, "I HATE YOU! I HATE YOU! I HATE YOU! I HATE YOU! I HATE YOU!" I had never had anyone tell me that before. Ben continued, "I want to divorce you. Actually, I think about it all the time that I can't divorce you while you are in this place and that makes me angry. I don't want to see you succeed because I hate you." He took a breath and threw his Bible at me, saying, "But this says that I'm supposed to forgive you. I don't want to and I don't even know what that looks like."

I think that was the first time I was able to listen and not interrupt him. Ben was getting to the point of breaking where God would be able to heal him. Before you can heal, you have to be broken. When he had finished yelling, I looked at him and said, "You are right. I did some awful things and I hope that you will someday be able to forgive me." I agreed with my adversary. "I promise that if you don't divorce me, I will work very hard. Thank you for being honest with me." Then, he drove off. Believe it or not, I was thrilled. That moment was real and it was truth. God can work with real truth.

Later that night, I prayed, "Lord, I know what you've done for me. Would You do that for Ben, too? Please just start speaking to him." I had so much confidence that God was working for our good and would continue to do great things. Ben was really struggling at that point. He struggled to forgive, yet he was also able to see just how many things I had been taking care of by myself with my job, our home, and our family while he was away travelling with his job. He got a taste of just maybe why I was always drunk when he got home. Honestly, as much as I did have a drinking problem, I did not let one other area slide. Even with a four-year-old, an eighteen month old, and a full time job, I stayed on top of our domestic life. Without me, he was responsible for taking care of everything. I had no doubt at this point that God was working and moving in our lives. I had no idea what the outcome would be, but I believed in God's power.

I received counseling as part of the program at the Mission, but a friend suggested that it would be helpful to be able to attend outside marriage counseling with Ben.

The director thankfully agreed to allow it. On the day I arrived, the director asked me what I wanted out of the program. I answered, "I want to learn to respect and submit to my husband. I have no clue what true submission looks like. Satan tells me that submission is bowing down to this man that I married, and I know that's not right. Shouldn't a marriage be hand-in-hand? I want to learn what Biblical submission looks like." Yes, I needed to get sober. I had an alcohol problem, but my marriage was also a problem. I think my addiction started with what happened to me in high school. I had never truly healed from that tragedy of losing my boyfriend, and I began trying to fill the void with alcohol, which lead to all sorts of damaging behavior.

In counseling, Ben and I had to talk about a lot of really hard things. I had to own up to the damage I had done. We had to discuss the situations that had caused all of the heart ache and try to tear down the walls of separation in our relationship. It was hard work! We are often asked if we would go through this trial again. Whew! There were some real rough patches with a lot of stickers in them, but yes—our family is worth the struggle.

At that point, we were very aware of the spiritual warfare that was trying to destroy the souls of our family. Ben was praying one night and felt like God was telling him that it was time to start forgiving me. He was not sure what that looked like or how he would be able to do it, but once he committed himself to the challenge of not letting the spiritual forces of evil win, Ben's heart began to soften toward me. He had good friends who were committed to fighting with him in prayer. They even came over one night and anointed every corner of our house with oil and prayed that our family would be restored and protected from the evil one. United in our fight against our common enemy, Ben and I were able to stop fighting against each other. Spiritual warfare is real and it is hard, but we knew that "The one who is in you is greater than the one who is in the world" (1 John 4:4).

I was three months into the program and had earned my first four-hour pass. Since we had been talking in counseling, I knew this would be a nice time together. Ben came and picked me up. We went to dinner with some friends and then went to spend some time together at our home. This was surprisingly hard for me. I walked into a house that had not been kept as I would have kept it for the past three months. It was a mess and just did not feel like my home anymore. At the same time, it was so good to be there with Ben that I really did not want to leave. The drive back to the Mission was really tough. When I made the comment that I wanted to come home, Ben unswervingly told me that I could in nine months when my commitment was over.

During my fourth month pass, I attended the funeral of the son of a dear friend and client. It was really hard to be back at my home church, for the obvious reasons, but also for the fact that unknowing people can make rude or thoughtless comments when it comes to rehab. It was such a weird feeling to be there with people who had not seen me in months. I felt like I was on break from prison or something. I wanted to wear a white shirt that said, "It's just rehab! You all have sin, too!" Even in this grief, God was good to us. I missed out on a lot of life while I was gone for that year, but all of the really huge events that would have devastated me to miss, God made it possible for me to attend.

The next month's pass turned out to be a forever altering one for our family. It was during this time that our third child, Mayson was conceived. Getting pregnant was <u>so</u> not on my radar at that time. First of all, Ben and I were only able to be together off-campus one time per month. My concerns at the time boiled down to restoring my marriage and not getting in trouble at the Mission. If I got a "pink slip," then I would get a visit taken away. I sure did not want that to happen!

So, a few weeks later, I was at work at WOW and one of my friends came in to see me. Before she left, she told me the great news that she was pregnant. We hugged and she went on her way. I got back to work dusting the store, and it occurred to me, "Huh! When was my last period? Have I even had one lately?" I couldn't remember! My mom was bringing me the kids that night, so I awkwardly asked her to bring along a pregnancy test. Just me and two kiddos in my tiny little room and BAM! Two lines. I was pregnant! At rehab!

When I called Ben, he was first worried that I would get in trouble for calling him without permission. When I told him that we were pregnant, he was so excited! Our biggest concern was not taking away attention from Ben's sister who was getting married soon. We in no way wanted to steal her thunder. I had a very strained relationship with both of Ben's sisters. They have a really close family, and I had done nothing but hurt him in their eyes. So, we kept our good news between us and our parents for a while.

However, one great blessing was that our little girl, Mayson, was prayed over every morning at devotion while I was at the Mission for the first seven months of my pregnancy.

At six months, I was able to have a 24-hour pass from the Mission. This ended up being around the time of Ben's sister's wedding. I was able to go home and watch Madison and Jett be the flower girl and ring bearer. It was a hard day, not being able to share our good news. I again felt out of place around family and friends, like I was the "get out of jail for a day" girl. It was hard being back at my house for the night, knowing I just had to turn around and leave again. I ended up having a total melt down the next morning over dirty socks. I felt like a complete failure because I was not there to take care of my family. That was a real low point for me. I had gotten a little taste of normal life with my loved ones, and I had to leave to go back to freaking rehab!

If I thought life at the Mission was hard and strenuous before, it became exponentially harder being pregnant. I was very sick during all of my pregnancies. But, at the Mission we had to operate on very little sleep. The schedule was very strict and there were hours of homework to do every day. I was exhausted!

I would go into the director's office deliriously tired and beg for a nap. I was weak and could barely see straight. He would tell me that I needed to push through it and pray about it. Ugh! A few days later I was laying in the shower, throwing up and balling. I asked God, "Was this really your plan?" I heard Him say, "Your spirit is willing, but your flesh is weak. No, Shelley, you can't do this alone, but you have Me. You are not alone." His peace returned to me. Did the circumstances go away or even get any easier? Nope. I was still tired and sick, but I knew that I could do anything with God's strength. I still got my homework done. I still memorized my scriptures.

I got so dehydrated one time that they took me to the hospital. I could not quit throwing up foam, so the director's wife stepped in and made sure I got medical care. They bent the rules for me after that and allowed me to have Gatorade and crackers in my room. Also, they began to allow me to get seconds at meals because I was pregnant. The other girls really hated me for that one!The months that I spent at the Mission were filled with amazing examples of God's provision for our family. He took amazing care of us through the brothers and sisters from our church. They loved and cared for our broken family in ways that I will never forget. There were times when Ben would come home and someone had mowed our lawn. Someone else would periodically bring groceries.

One of the hardest blessings happened just a few days after I left home. My daughter had her first-ever end of the year dance recital. She had worked all year to get ready for this recital. I remember being heartbroken at the Mission that day because I (the professional hair stylist) could not be there with her to help her get ready. I was so concerned about what her hair would look like. It seems a silly thing to worry about, but it was important to the two of us. God whispered to me that if I was obedient to Him, He would handle the details of my heart. There was a lady from our church who called Ben unprompted and asked if she could come over the curl Madison's hair. Even to this day, I tell this lady that she will never know what she did for me on that day when she took the time to curl a little girl's hair. I still have not been able to watch the video of that recital. It is just too painful, knowing that I saved our lives by going to rehab, but I still missed so much of their lives while I was away for that year—a whole year that can never be recovered. My daughter played soccer that year. I never went to one of her games. My son learned all that toddlers learn in a year without his momma to be there every day.

As always, God provided encouragement from where I least expected it. One day, while I was working at WOW, Ben's middle sister came by to see me. Our relationship had been strained for years. She once told me, years before, that I had ruined the family name by how I acted. On this day, she told me, "I'm proud of you. You being here makes me want to be different. Thank you for doing this." That was all she had to say! We are now so close! God is so good! Restoration can only come in God's timing.

Through the whole process at the Mission, I always knew that I was going to be able to win Ben back. I was never sure about whether his family would ever be able to forgive. Thanks be to God that the many family relationships which were damaged while I was drinking have been restored. Slowly, I saw God working on all of our hearts. Now, I am also on good terms with my other sister-in-law. We understand each other and give each other a lot of grace. My mother-in-law stepped-up big time and helped take care of the kids while I was away. My father-in-law shows me his love and acceptance every year by being one of the biggest donors to the annual Mission Messiah fund-raising golf tournament.

In that one-year period, I received two 13-gallon kitchen trash bags full of letters (probably 10-15 letters per day), and someone from church came and saw me every Sunday. Talk about seeing the Body of Christ! That was my fuel to make it through another week. I grew up at and attended this church my whole life and they were an amazing support.

About ten and a half months into my year-long program, I was working at WOW one day and the manager came to tell me that there was someone on the phone; she could not really understand them, but somehow she thought the call was for me. Now, remember, the rules were very strict; I could not even receive calls unless they were scheduled. I got on the line and quickly realized that it was Ben, and he was in distress. He has severe asthma and was driving himself to the hospital in the middle of a severe attack. He was crying because he really thought that he was going to die. When I got off the phone, I told them in no uncertain terms that I was going to the hospital to see my husband. They could kick me out of the program if that was what they thought best, but I was going to be with Ben. One of the house parents took me to the hospital. Upon arriving, I was told that Ben's pulse oxygen level was very low. Ben started giving me his final goodbyes, telling me the location of important papers, and reminding me to be more patient with our children. He really thought he was not going to make it, but the doctors were able to stabilize him enough for me to go out to the waiting room to figure out what to do. The Mission was still on my mind.

Would I be able to stay? I was so close to finishing the program, I did not want to quit now.

I was able to be with Ben during the whole nine days that he was in the hospital. We were in complete unity in our marriage during that time. It may seem strange, but I could not quit worrying about whether or not I would be able to go back to Mission Messiah and finish what I had started. I was so close to the year mark, and I wanted so badly to finish. I prayed a lot during that time with Ben in the hospital. The directors at the Mission were praying with us to determine what the rest of my time there would look like. Ben was still not doing well when he was released. When the Mission directors came to visit, they suggested that I return to the Mission with our kids. That did not set well at all, so we prayed about it, took it to our life group for prayer, and then to our church Elders. It just was not an option for us to expose our small children to the atmosphere at the Mission. I am so thankful that it is available for the women who need to have their children with them there, but we did not feel that it was right for our family. Ben and I were in complete agreement on this, but it resulted in my being dismissed from the program.

My early dismissal was such a blow. It was akin to walking across a graduation stage and someone jumping in front of me yelling, "Just kidding! Everything you've done means nothing!" I wanted to have my ceremony! I wanted to have the big cake that said, "Congratulations! You did it!" I wanted the Mission Messiah ring! I wanted to be able to come back and volunteer. As devastating as it was, I knew that the decision that we made was the right one. At the end of the day, only two things remained: the Lord and I were good, and Ben and I were good.

We had been in the hospital for nine days; I was seven and a half months pregnant; I was at home, having been kicked out of the Mission; Ben was still not well... What a roller coaster! Then, Ben relapsed, and we had to rush him to the hospital in the middle of the night. Ben had been telling the doctors during his previous hospital stay that he thought he had pneumonia, to no avail. Sure enough, when we arrived at the hospital, we had only been there for five minutes when he tested positive for full-blown pneumonia. His lungs were full! We were there ten days, and God led us to an amazing pulmonologist who helped to get Ben on the right medication.

Upon returning home from the hospital, we found out that our lease was up on our house, and we had to move. While chaotic at the time, it was truly for the best. That house was the scene of a lot of my bad choices over the years and held horrible memories for us. It was no longer my home in any way. I did some dirt in that house, and I wanted the blood of Jesus to wash away those memories to make way for new ones. I prayed for a new start, and the Lord provided. Once more, our prayers were answered!

As things began to calm down in our lives, the only nagging problem in my heart was the fact that it was March, and I had entered the Mission the previous year in May. I should be close to graduating. People would unknowingly ask about it from time to time, and I would just tell them that I was finished. It was such a disappointment to my heart.

A year later, Ben came in and told me to get dressed up because he got a babysitter and he was taking me out to dinner. This was such an out of the ordinary surprise that I asked him, "What did you do? What's wrong?" But Ben would not tell me anything. When we arrived at the restaurant, we were taken to a back room where all of the Mission Messiah staff, Patty and her husband, our families, and all of our close friends were waiting to celebrate with me. The Mission director addressed the group, explaining how he and I had a disagreement that resulted in my dismissal. He now believed that I needed to graduate from the Mission because I had earned it. They gave me a full-on graduation, complete with cake and ring. Everyone stood up and congratulated me. That was my closure! My completion! God provided just what I needed. The advice that my friend gave me had come true in hundreds of ways: "God did not send you here to fail." He has not failed me, ever.

The Messiah healed me. The Messiah restored my family. The Messiah gave me a purpose to help others find the hope and understanding that I received. I live with the belief that we should be real, authentic people. So many are waiting for a real person to come alongside them to listen, to understand, and to lead them to the One who can offer them restoration.

God is always ready to meet us. For so long, I wondered where He was. I wondered why He was not coming to me to bail me out of my struggles and sin. It was not until I was willing to meet Him, to surrender to His ways that my healing could begin. He says, "Draw near to me and I will draw near to you." All those times I struggled and felt unseen, He saw me. I believe that He was there with me, behind that Whataburger dumpster, waiting for me to come to Him.

God's version of my restoration looks so different than what I expected. I was hoping to just get sober. That was all I initially asked of God. Sobriety. As the giver of all good gifts, He gave me so much more—more than what I asked for or imagined was even possible. He gave me a life full of joy in the Holy Spirit. He gave me back my family. He gave me this amazing testimony to His great work in my life. He has given me so much fruit from my obedience, and all I ever asked for was to be sober. *How did I get here?*

Jesus the Messiah!

About Shelley Fietz

Shelley Fietz lives in Midland with her husband Ben Fietz. They have three children, Madison who is 8, Jett who is 5, and Mayson who is 3. They are all very involved in Golf Course Road Church of Christ. Shelley serves on the women's ministry team, and Ben helps serve with the teen challenge ministry. They both grew up going to church, and love that they can share that with their kids. Shelley enjoys shopping and loves to organize as weird as that sounds! The more organized and clean her house is the happier she is. She loves taking her kids swimming and they have found a new adventure—camping!

Lena Davis

Lena's family has gone to church with my family for years. One of our favorite things to do was go on family mission trips to a children's home in Mexico. I would hear bits and pieces of Lena's story and finally realized that I had never really heard all of it. She has lived a lot of life in her young years and experienced things I have only read about – escaping a country during a revolution, apartheid in South Africa, tragic loss of a spouse, immigrating to the US, becoming a Christian later in life, and more. Yet through all of this she has a joy and love for people and a huge servant's heart. Her witty sense of humor is great as well. I know you will enjoy this story!

A Blessed Life

Lena Davis

"May the favor of the Lord our God rest on us; establish the work of our hands for us—yes, establish the work of our hands." Psalm 90:17

It is interesting to me that others think my story remarkable. To me, it is just that: my story. Yet, I know that God has blessed me through each chapter, and amid my journey, He has shown me such favor.

It is amazing how a major event in my life, even one of which I have no memory, completely changed the course of my journey. As a very small child, I was a refugee. Our Portuguese family was forced to flee Mozambique, the country in which I was born. In the early 1970's, Mozambique was fighting for independence from Portugal (where my parents were both born and raised). The country won its independence after a civil resistance movement in 1975. It was then that my family fled to the neighboring Republic of South Africa and accepted political asylum from its government. I consider this "tragedy" one of my greatest privileges. I believe my experiences in an apartheid South Africa positively shaped my character and strengthened my resolve.

My parents were raised in Portugal by families of very modest means. As a result, neither of them were able to attend school. They briefly met while my father was home from the military for a two week break and were married by proxy very soon after that. My father returned to Africa and my mother had a small wedding ceremony without him. Imagine, a wedding with no groom! She then flew alone to Africa for the first time ever, to meet this virtual stranger she had married. I suspect that they were both running from the life they were dealt and hoping for a better future. To their credit, both parents eventually learned to read and write in both English and Portuguese. They worked hard and provided a life for their children that was far beyond anything they experienced in their early lives.

Sometimes, my children ask me, "If you are Portuguese and African, what are we? Are we half American and half Portuguese?" My answer will always be the same, "You are a child of God, thus a temporary resident of this world. However, if you must pick, then you are AMERICAN." They are free to include the tradition, foods, or thoughts of any culture that they deem admirable, but above all, they should be grateful to be an American. To be born into this country, in this day and age, is something for which we have enormous gratitude. I teach them that this gratitude demands civic responsibility in order to ensure that their children inherit the same blessings.

While my earliest memories of life in South Africa involve a peaceful existence—days spent on the beach fishing with my parents, or following hippo tracks along the rivers—that peace did not last. My days later transformed into many years of living in fear. As hard as it is to believe, South Africa remained deeply segregated until 1994, when it held its first democratic election. As unrest escalated into terrorism, we experienced bombings. Police brutality against the black people was an everyday sight. While the white government tried to build separate (but nowhere near equal) schools and hospitals, their efforts were often met by the burning of these new facilities. Talks of freeing Mr. Nelson Mandela seemed to only escalate the resolve of the black people to reform South Africa's antiquated policies. During my teenage years, I became involved in various leadership projects aimed at creating relationships between young black and white South Africans. Since all black people lived outside of town in what we called reserves, we had no relationship with any black people our age.

I distinctly remember as a young waitress in high school, my manager would send me to tell black people that they were not welcome in the restaurant. It revolted me, but I was never inspired to take a stand. Any talk against the status quo was always quickly squelched by my father, who in hindsight was probably fearfully anticipating another civil war. This would have most likely caused our family to have to flee for our survival again.

By 1991, my father was sure we were no longer safe in South Africa, so my family immigrated to Portugal. I lived there for almost one year, but I missed my beloved Africa so much. My constant crying eventually prompted my father to kick me out of his home. He told my mother to put me on the train to the airport and send me back to Africa. His harsh punishment felt like a dream come true to me. So, at 18 years old, with one bag and less than $100, I gladly left Portugal and returned to South Africa.

I quickly got a job and very soon connected with an old family friend, Ralston. Before, he had been much too old to be a love interest, but now at 19 and 23, the few years that separated our ages did not seem to be a problem. We quickly fell in love and were married within a year.

Ralston was fun, spontaneous, and compassionate. Even though he made twice as much money as we needed, he seldom had any. When I asked him what he had done with what we called our "pocket money," the answer was always similar: "I gave it to so and so." He lived life on the wild-side; he loved doing things like sleeping on the beach. He was happy when he was with those he loved and even happier when he could convince them to participate in some daredevil act. Ralston soaked up joy out of every minute of every day.

Ralston was a diehard Rugby fanatic—a passion he shared with his brother and his best friend. In August 1995, eight months after we were married, Ralston's favorite team was playing the Rugby equivalent of the Super Bowl, and the boys were fortunate enough to get tickets to the game. I was cheering for the only black man on the team. The boys accused me of doing that just because he was black. They believed he was added to the team just because Rugby was traditionally a white man's sport. Since Nelson Mandela had just been freed and elected president, many thought that Chester Williams was added to the team to appease the affirmative action advocates. It was not true; Williams deserved his spot on the team. The boys left early on the morning of the game for the two-hour drive from our home to the stadium. As I watched the game from home, I relished at how they would have to apologize to me when they got back. Williams was an excellent player who made significant contributions to the team's win that day. I made mental note of the game's end time and quickly calculated how long it would take them to return to me. I looked forward to feeding them dinner and joining their victory celebrations.

Of the three boys who travelled to that game, only Ralston was married. The others were not necessarily expected home at any certain time. Two hours after the time they were meant to arrive, having made all the excuses I could about how long it would take to leave the stadium and how they probably didn't leave right away because they were celebrating, I began to panic. I was working at a hospital at the time, and as a result, I was well aware of the procedures for locating someone who may have been involved in a car accident. Trying not to alarm the parents of the other boys, I decided to start the process on my own. I called a police station half way between our home and the stadium. The road between the towns was well known for ambushes and hijackings because it was a small, two-lane road with only one town in between. Most people did not travel at night, but being in your twenties makes you feel indestructible, so they had not worried about it when they planned the trip.

My call to the police station revealed that there had been an accident on that specific road. I asked about the number of people involved, but all he would tell me was that it only involved one car and that only one person was taken to the hospital. Again, my hospital experience told me that there could have been more people in the car, but they were taken to the mortuary instead. I had always considered myself an optimistic person, assuming things will turn out fine. This time, for some reason, I instantly knew Ralston was in that car. I started to sob uncontrollably and had a hard time trying to speak. The policeman asked me if I was alone. I told him I was. He then said that he could not answer any more questions. However, if someone else called with the license plate of the car I was looking for, he could confirm if that car was involved in the accident.

I decided enough time had gone by that even the parents would start to get worried. I first called the father of the boy driving the car. My distraught voice and the possible news must have really distressed him, for he angrily refused to give me the license plate information and told me they were probably fine. He would live to regret this mistake because his son was the only one who had not died at the scene. Had he taken me seriously, he would have had enough time to drive to the hospital and comfort his son while he died.

Still searching for answers, I called a family friend. He came over and assured me that our boys were probably safe, but that he would start driving the road to look for them. He asked me to call him when the boys arrived so he would know to turn back. He was as positive that they were fine as I was that they were dead. He arrived in time to the Stanger Hospital to see Jean-Luc alive for a few minutes.

Ralston and his brother had been sent to the mortuary. As I waited for my friend's return, my home started to fill up with concerned friends and Ralston's family. I distinctly remember each member of the family, head bowed, obviously praying. I wondered how God would solve this dilemma. Each of us was praying that the one we loved was the one that was in the hospital and not one of the ones in the mortuary. Ralston's father had died before we married, so the brother in the car with him belonged to his step-father. Was each parent praying that their son was the lone survivor? My worst fears were confirmed very late in the evening as my friend walked in the door without the boys. All I remember him saying was, "Jean-Luc died too." In that instant, I wondered if that was God's way of making it fair. Praise God, I know better now! None of our boys were taken by a God who delights in our pain or randomly takes lives. He was grieving with us and knows personally the pain each of us was feeling. Adding that pain to one more mother doesn't make this fallen world any fairer.

Just like that, in one horrible night, my eight months of marriage ended. Today, even knowing how very difficult the loss was on my twenty-one-year old self, I would marry Ralston all over again. Ralston loved me like I was his jewel. My favorite story that exemplifies his love happened one afternoon right before he died. The three boys called each other nicknames based on their favorite rugby players' names. Ralston's nickname was Joost. Joost van der Westhuizen was a rugby player who played as a scrum-half for the national team. He was a member of the victorious South African rugby team at the 1995 World Cup. (He was playing on the day Ralston died.) Ralston and I were walking along an esplanade one afternoon, in a small, neighboring town where it was very unlikely to see a celebrity. That afternoon, Ralston thought he saw Joost walking ahead of us. He had his back to us, so I was sure that it was just someone who looked like him. What would a Rugby celebrity be doing in this little town? I told him, "You're crazy that's not him." "Yes, it is!" he insisted. Finally, when I would not agree to run up to him, Ralston decided to call out his name and see if he turned around. Sure enough, Ralston knew his idol from the back. The real life Joost Van der Westerhuizen, was in Richards Bay that day. How does that prove how much Ralston loved me? Well, if I met my idol, I would introduce myself, tell him what a fan I am, and ask him a million questions, wouldn't you? Instead, Ralston grabbed my hand, ran up to Joost, and to my absolute embarrassment, said, "Joost, I want you to meet my wife." I am certain that man thought Ralston was out of his mind. Wouldn't, "Joost, I've always wanted to meet you!" have been more appropriate? Yet all Ralston wanted to do was introduce his young wife to his favorite celebrity.

After Ralston's, death, I was living alone. My family still lived in Portugal, except for a sister of mine who lived hours away from me. The finality of Ralston's death seemed impossible for me to reconcile in my mind. I worried about where he was and if we would ever see each other again. How would I possibly survive this? I began to rely on the people from the church Ralston and I had just started visiting. Neither of us were raised regularly attending church, but we felt ourselves drawn and had started going together. The church I attended took excellent care of me after the accident. If I did not come to church one Sunday, several of the members would come to my home as soon as it was over. I loved being alone so I could grieve, but those church members were determined to make that difficult. They fed me, checked on me, and held me accountable. Despite all this, I still had no real relationship with Christ. They were just good people taking care of my physical needs.

About six months after losing Ralston, I was lying in bed one evening, unable to sleep. It felt like I had not slept in months. Each day as I went to work and went about my business, all I ever wanted to do was come home so I could cry again. As I lay there, I felt the worst pain in my chest. It was a physical grief so severe, it seemed as if it would grant me my wish to die. Out of sheer desperation and pain, I climbed off the bed and went to my knees. I do not remember ever personally praying before that, but I heard someone say once that if you wished to live with Jesus, you should pray that and he would honor that desire. It sounded wise, so I obeyed. I stayed on my knees for a while, wondering what I should say. I knew for a fact that God would not give me what I wanted. What I wanted to shout was, "Give him back!" I was positive that would never happen, so what would be the purpose of a prayer? I decided to concentrate on the physical pain that I was experiencing. Knowing that the pain was a result of my grief, I wanted it to stay. I wanted to be miserable because it was proof of my love for Ralston. Could anything else honor Ralston's memory? Finding no adequate words and in desperate pain, I shouted out loud, "Please, please, please..." I have no idea how many times I shouted and then whispered that plea when I could shout no longer. What I do know is that the next morning I woke up on the floor, pain free, and having slept the whole night for the first time in months. I wondered about this God who listens to strangers. How did He calm me enough to sleep? Why did He care enough to do that for me in the first place? That very morning, I started my search to find the answers to those questions, and I knew exactly where to find them. The very hands and feet of Christ who had cared for my physical needs also deeply yearned to see me saved. I was baptized a short while later in a swimming pool with those precious souls rejoicing around me.

While Ralston's death definitely catapulted my desire to know the Lord, the truth is, all those years growing up in apartheid South Africa, I had been searching for the approval to do what I knew was right. Working in a hospital that served eighty percent black people, I was never asked if I could speak their language in order to be able to serve them efficiently. I was asked if I spoke the second official language in South Africa at the time, Afrikaans. I always assured them I was fluent in both languages even though I never needed any more than English to serve the few whites who found themselves too poor to use the white hospital. However, I quickly realized that what I really needed to speak was Zulu in order to get any information from the majority of the patients we served. The black people were always humbled at my attempt to speak their language. Almost every day, I was asked if I was a Christian. The truth is, I did not even know what being a Christian meant. Sometimes I would say yes, other times I would say no. In their eyes, only a Christian would desire to connect with them in their own language. The approval for doing what is right is seldom found in the world, but it is freely given from God: "But the fruit of the Spirit is love, joy, peace, forbearance, kindness, goodness, faithfulness, gentleness and self-control. Against such things there is no law." Galatians 5:22-23 NIV

I moved out of the home Ralston and I lived in while we were married when it became unsafe for me to stay there alone. My new home was in a closed community with a barbed wired wall around it. Even though we were living in what we called the "new" South Africa, there were no blacks who could afford to live in those homes. The only blacks who entered those gated communities were our maids and the "yard boys," as we called them. By then, I was strong enough to know that right is right even if nobody is doing it, and wrong remains wrong even if everyone is doing it. My maid and I would eat breakfast together on my veranda. I drove her to and from her bus stop and paid her a fair wage. Word quickly reached the other "Madams" as we were called. I was repeatedly reprimanded for allowing her to use my bathroom, eat out of my dishes, and ride in my car. The fact that humans can utter such nonsense remains a scandal to me, but I smiled knowing that against such things there was literally no longer a law—not in my saved heart, and not in the constitution. The Lord can redeem anything!

Ralston had a brother who lived in the United States. We had planned to come visit him and had both been working overtime to collect enough money to pay for a holiday in the United States. Ralston died exactly a year before the date we had picked. When that date came, his family encouraged me to make the trip on my own. I did not want to because it seemed so inappropriate to go on a lavish holiday a year after he died. They pestered me until I agreed. I planned to stay in Texas for a while and then head over to Portugal to see my parents. I arrived in Dallas, Texas and was immediately mesmerized by the enormous differences in this country compared to my home. Living someplace where every single thing was foreign was truly a sensory overload experience for me. Everything was interesting and everyone was interested.

I found a place where I became a novelty instead of a widow. Nobody knew my story in this new place. I could shop without people whispering about what happened. Plus, I could drive around without the constant reminders of what I had lost. For that moment, it was exactly what I needed: relief. I applied for a student visa when I reached Portugal and, instead of going home to South Africa, I came back to Texas. I called my sister in South Africa and asked her to please call my boss to tell her that I quit my job. I asked her to sell my house and my car, and then pack up all my things. I would come back when I was ready. There is a fine line between adventure and stupidity, and I am not sure on which side this decision would land. What I know is, that in Texas, I found a people who were loving and generous. There was no reason for this to feel like a mistake.

Two years later, I graduated from Paris Junior College and figured it was time to go home to start my life again. During a weekend trip with a friend, I visited Lubbock Christian University. I had no intention of studying there; my plan was to head home. Instead, I was offered a scholarship that I could not refuse and decided to stay two more years in Texas. In my final year, I met Todd at church. He was born and raised in Lubbock, Texas and was about as opposite from me (and Ralston for that matter) as he could be, but he had a deep love for me and a compassion for others just as Ralston had. We were married the month I had planned to go home after my graduation from Lubbock Christian University.

A few years later, we realized that we had something surprising in common. When Ralston died, Todd was living in Abilene and worshipping at Hillcrest Church of Christ. Hillcrest was the church that sent missionaries to South Africa during my Kindergarten year. They founded the church that served me after Ralston's death and later baptized me into Christ. By the time I joined that church, the missionaries were long gone and we had recently paid off our debt, becoming a self-supporting church. To mark that milestone, we had a celebration. The Hillcrest church celebrated alongside us from the States, they-marking work completed, and us-a work just beginning. We made a call to the States that evening and formally cut ties with our American sponsors. Todd was at Hillcrest celebrating and I was in Empangeni celebrating the exact same event. It's a small world, isn't it?

In 2008, Todd and I had been married for nine years and had two lovely children. Cameron was five and Annie was three. They brought us great joy! Our daughter, Annie started to do some strange things. In the middle of playing a game, she would stop and look confused almost as though she forgot what she was doing. She would occasionally run into things or stop in the middle of a routine action for no apparent reason. We chuckled about it most of the time, as though it was just part of her quirkiness. Of course, we did not realize, until those symptoms become more frequent and evident, that she was actually having seizures. By the time she was four and half, she had been diagnosed with absence seizures and had been under treatment with no success. Her neurologist moved through every drug known to ease this specific type of seizure for a whole year, but none did so much as even lessen the frequency of her seizures. Instead, they became more frequent, her side effects more disturbing, and our hope nonexistent. It was an agonizing year; her tremors were so violent on certain drugs that she could no longer feed herself, keep her legs still, or use her hands for just about any fine motor skill. We watched her go from a happy, thriving, young child to completely dependent on us for everything. With every new drug came the promise of success, but when all the known drugs failed, we were finally referred to a Pediatric Epileptologist at Cook Children's Hospital.

Everything her neurologist tried had failed, and in a very real way I felt like I, too, had failed her. As Annie's mom, I felt like I was the connection between her chiropractor, her naturopath, her neurologist and her pediatrician. We even went to New York to see a microbiologist and have her hair tested for toxicity by a homeopathic doctor. We spent everything we had on alternative remedies and tests. Still, I was unable to help her. I do not think I slept a whole night in an entire year. I diligently researched each new drug, each new possible cause, and each new natural remedy. My library became filled with books on epilepsy and the controversial ketogenic diet. All along, I continued to believe I could help find the cause and cure.

In my quest to find healing for my daughter, I neglected my own health and a nagging problem I was having. My right shoulder was causing me a lot of pain, and my arm was becoming weaker and weaker as the months passed. It was not until a few days before our first visit to Cook Children's Hospital that I realized the extent of my problem. I was trying to reach for something above my head and my arm would not move at all. The next morning,

I called my doctor to tell her I had a little problem. They told me I could have an appointment in two weeks. "Two Weeks? My arm is not working at all!" I complained. Hearing the desperation in my voice (as I thought of my upcoming appointment in Dallas and my arm not working while we were there) she offered me a cancellation she had for a routine physical. "I'll take it," I told her. "If I have to have a pap smear to get this arm checked, then that's what I'll do." I showed up the following day and had a routine physical along with a check of my arm. My doctor reported that the news about the arm was good, but there were more pressing matters, "It seems you may have neglected a bursitis in your shoulder for too long. That we can work on, but it's the lump in your thyroid that I'm very concerned about."

Meanwhile, Annie's appointment at Cook's did not go as expected either. I had hoped that a specialist would have been holding on to the missing piece of her treatment. Instead, he looked me straight in the eyes and said, "I am sorry, but I believe this is how your child will be for the rest of her life. There are a small fraction of children who for unknown reasons do not respond to the medications that help ninety percent of children with this type of seizure. It might be possible that she will out-grow this but it is very unlikely."

At this point, Annie required constant supervision. Her "absence seizures," true to their name, caused her to become "absent" for a few seconds or even minutes at a time. However, they did not completely stop her motor skills. For example, if she was riding her tricycle toward the road planning to turn onto the sidewalk before she reached the end of the driveway, a seizure would "zone her out" enough that her legs would keep peddling. At this point, her mind was not alert enough to make the decision to turn her steering. My daughter's condition was an accident waiting to happen. She also could not hear or speak while the seizure lasted.

Our Epileptologist felt that at this point there was nothing to lose, so he sent us home with one more medication to try. We agreed to try it, but there was no reason for us to believe this would make a difference when nothing else had. He warned us that this drug had serious potential side effects and was not commonly known to help this type of seizure. Taking this would also mean that she would need constant blood work to ensure that her liver was not being damaged with its use. He scheduled an appointment in a couple of months for an ambulatory EEG. They wanted to watch her for a few days and see if there was anything else wrong with her brain that was causing the seizures.

I remember the long drive home like it was yesterday. I kept hearing those words over and over, "She'll need special education. It's very unlikely she'll ever improve." Nobody had ever told us that before now. I held it together during the drive, but the moment I walked through the door a wave of deep despair caused me to burst into tears. I was completely overwhelmed and overcome with grief. My husband, Todd, found me in the room, sobbing. He looked at me and asked me what I was crying about. I do not break down crying often, so the scene warranted a lot more shock and concern. However, the tone of his question was calm and casual. As I looked at him in that moment, I realized that for a year, I had been harboring an enormous amount of resentment toward Todd for the way he accepted each blow we were dealt. He appeared to be completely unaffected by our child's prognosis. It was a true reflection of his "calm attitude" over the past year. He had not picked up one book, spent any amount of time researching on the internet, or sought out any new doctors. I felt sure that there was no way he could love our child and be willing to just accept this terrible news. I did not bother mentioning my feelings to him because I knew without any doubt what he would say: "You have to have faith in the Lord." Faith? I had faith for a year. I searched, trusted, and hoped. There was no time left for faith! It was over! She was never going to drive, be able to live alone, or have a normal life. There was no drug to even help her. Everything we tried was either useless or made things worse. What was there to have faith in? Every time I worried and Todd calmly went about his daily routine, we grew farther apart.

We started Annie's new medicine slowly, one small dose at a time. As for me, I was going through weeks of the battery of tests required to figure out that the lump in my thyroid needed to be taken out. The tests revealed that abnormal cells had been detected during my biopsy. There was no cancer, but those abnormal cells could eventually turn into cancer if we did not remove the thyroid. I had the appointment at Cook's for Annie's EEG coming up, so I chose to have my surgery right away. I wanted it to be done before we needed to take the next step for Annie. During the post-op discussion, my doctor assured us that the lump looked "good," and that he did not suspect it to be cancerous. Nonetheless, the nodule was sent to the

Mayo Clinic to be dissected and tested. About a week later, I was driving on the highway when the doctor called with my test results and told me that I had Medullary Carcinoma.

I walked into my home, got on the computer, looked up the diagnosis, read for about three minutes, then stood up and threw up. Unlike most thyroid cancers, this one likes to move into the bloodstream and spread quickly through the body. I remember feeling so alone. I certainly was not going to lean on Todd, the person who would simply assure me that God had this under control! So, the news of my diagnosis ripped open an even greater rift in my marriage. Please understand me, my husband is a good man. His "worst" quality is that he has only one emotion: CALM. I, on the other end of the spectrum, love all emotions: everything from peace to hysteria.

Before long, I had an appointment at Jo Arrington Cancer Center. I met with Dr. Shalaby, expecting to hear, "All is well. The cancer is contained. There is no need to be concerned." But the news was quite different. I would need another surgery. Radical Neck Dissection would clean out the lymph nodes around the thyroid. They would perform a CT scan to look for more tumors. This was based on the elevation of my tumor markers after the initial surgery. I would also require genetic testing to determine if I also had Multiple Endocrine Neoplasia Syndrome (shortened to MEN) which is often associated with this type of cancer. If I had this syndrome, my body would keep creating tumors for the rest of my life. The only thing that could make that news any worse was the realization that the syndrome is genetic, so if the results came back positive, I would likely have passed it on to my children. Whew! That was a lot of potentially devastating information!

The geneticist came in with an enormous stack of papers about MEN Syndrome. Considering the overwhelming number of challenges I was facing at this point, I politely asked her if she was positive I had the syndrome. She assured me that there was a chance that I did NOT, and that we would only know once I was tested. Considering all the certain problems I had to deal with, I felt like taking a stack of papers home to read about a problem I may NOT have was a futile exercise. There was no sense in borrowing one more problem. I felt like I had enough. My husband smiled, interpreting my refusal to accept the papers as an act of faith. Little did he know, with every added challenge, I was building up a wall and moving further and further away from him. I longed more and more every day for the man I had lost over a decade before and a continent away—the husband who wanted to introduce me to celebrities. He surely would have cared more for us. He would have grieved for his child. He would have known how being patient and faithful looked "reckless" to me. It felt reckless to leave our child's fate in the hands of strangers who did not love her or know her. Shouldn't love for our daughter require some sort of participation in her healing process, and even further, wouldn't it require some grieving? How could doing nothing at all possibly be helpful to any of us?

I had the second surgery on October 29, 2009. I went in with one vocal cord that had been permanently damaged during my first surgery. My voice had been raspy ever since my thyroid was removed, and the doctor assured me there was nothing to be done to repair the damaged nerve which controlled that vocal cord. I woke up after the second surgery and waited for the surgeon to come by. Instead, I got a surprise visit from my geneticist. The results were back early; I did not have MEN Syndrome. What a relief! If I was going to die, that was one thing, but passing on a genetic problem to my children was an added burden I just could not handle. As I thanked the geneticist, I realized something was different. My voice was perfect! How strange. My doctor had told me there was nothing he could do. When he came in the next day, told me the results were back already, and every lymph node tested was clear of cancer. Through tears, I thanked him for the amazing news and also for repairing my vocal cord. "What do you mean?" he asked. I said, "Listen to my voice, you fixed it." He just smiled and replied, "If I could fix that problem, I'd be a rich man. That wasn't me."

I went home the following day, ready to tackle my daughter and her new medication. I was sporting an enormous incision, all the way across my neck and up to my ear. (No problem! I "Frankensteined" it up for Halloween.) At this stage in Annie's seizures, my mother and sister had been recording every seizure she had so that we could determine if the medicine was helping, even just a little. Could we reduce the frequency from every fifteen minutes to once every hour? Even that would be a gift at this stage. After a couple of hours of being home, I asked to see the list of seizure times. Expecting to see a couple of pages of times, I was completely stunned when they told me that she had not had any seizures since the day before. Our last chance, no-hope medicine turned out to be our miracle drug! She did not have another seizure for the next five years.

Annie is almost eleven today. She regularly comes home with report cards that do not come close to reflecting the debilitating prognosis we were given when she was three. She is a smart, kind, and compassionate child who lives as if she fully understands the circumstances from which she was saved, despite the fact that she only vaguely remembers the experience.

What about me? Do I live like I understand from what I was saved? Do I live like I was given a second chance on earth? I honestly do not know. I wish I could say I do, but I know that I still fall short sometimes. I will tell you one thing that I do know, and it has taken me a long time to get to this point.

I am thankful to the handful of friends who held me accountable for my sin and refused to leave me in my despair. I am eternally grateful to the ministers at our church who spent endless hours counseling us. Through their love for us and the Lord, they were able to show me that I was suffering from something much more deadly than cancer; I was suffering from a cancer of the soul—one that was robbing me of the joy, peace, and calm that the Lord Himself gave me the day I was saved. In my grief, I lost sight of what I had gained. I learned a blessed lesson through that season: finding refuge in the Lord is a much mightier work of love than any number of hours of research and worry. Praise be to God for His mercy and His people.

The healing of my relationship with Todd was a long process of trying, giving up, trying again, throwing a tantrum, and giving up again. Sometimes we moved two steps forward, sometimes we went two steps backward. Every day, the Lord worked on my heart through the diligent mentoring of a dear friend and the repeated counseling from various ministers. The Lord worked to show me several small things that made a difference in my heart and gradually changed my attitude. The most unexpected realization was the fact that I constantly praised my son for the very same virtue that I hated in my husband. When my son was laid back and easy going, I called him a pleasure of a child. When my husband acted that way, I interpreted it as apathy. This revelation showed me that the sin was in my heart, not my husband's. God also showed me that the things I demanded from Todd were in areas where I was disappointed in myself for failing. The most obvious example of this was finding a cure for Annie. The more I failed, the more I expected Todd to provide the solutions. That pattern prevailed in every part of our lives: spiritual, health, emotional, and social.

At my lowest, I committed to the Lord that I would at least try to fight for my marriage. If our family did not stay together, I wanted to be able to say I did everything I could. I regularly asked the Lord to give me the desire to work for my marriage because I was too discouraged to feel like trying. A minister told me that if I tried, whether I felt like it or not, things would get better. He was right; the more I listened to the Spirit, the more it seemed like He spoke to me. I distinctly remember one day, after complaining for hours on the phone about Todd, the Spirit impressed on me, "You think he's so difficult to live with, how much fun do you think *you* are?" I was struck with remorse for the burden I was putting on my children, on my husband, on my family, and on my church. I asked the Lord to create in me a heart that would never again be a burden in search of my selfish gain. I continue to pray that today. The Lord can redeem anything—hallelujah!

Today, I am eternally grateful for the husband I have. I wish I was more like my faithful husband, Todd. I wish that my love for the Lord was unshakeable like his. Honestly, if my children were being raised by two of ME, they would be in bad shape. During the trials our family endured, I was too overwhelmed to appreciate him, but now, looking back, I can value his ability to remain calm amidst the trials of life. I used to long for what (and who) I had lost when faced with a crisis in my life, but now I am able to long for Christ instead. When I need a Christ-like example in my life, I do not have to look very far. He is the one sitting quietly right beside me, always calm and always faithful.

About Lena Davis

Lena was born and raised in Southern Africa, but she believes the Lord showed her special favor when he moved her to the great state of Texas. She lives in Lubbock Texas, where she met and married her better half, Todd. Her greatest pleasure is being called mom by Cameron and Annie. She loves to travel and do mission work overseas and locally.

Melody Young

When I saw that a "special guest speaker" would be coming to our church my curiosity was piqued. Little did I know my socks would be blown off by Melody Young and her story. Melody is a beautiful young woman and, as I heard her story, she became even more beautiful to me. Her ability to share the reality of her disability and the struggles she has will touch your heart. Then at the same time, you will be encouraged with her faith and her family that sees her through. She is a feisty fighter – not only for her own challenges – also for her kids in their challenges. I think my favorite part is the love story with her husband who has walked right beside her on this journey. Get ready to be blessed!

Melody in 2000

A Broken Body to Heal a Broken Spirit

Melody Young

Let me paint a picture for you. I was active all of my life. I started playing softball at age 4, added on basketball in middle school, and then cross country in high school. I found confidence in my abilities as an athlete. But sports were not my only talent or passion. I played the flute in the school band, eventually even becoming the Drum Major both my junior and senior year. I thrived socially, being awarded everything from Homecoming Queen to Miss New Caney High School to female athlete of the year. I even got selected to sing the National Anthem at a Houston Astros baseball game. My whole life was right on track. All of my successes gave me great confidence in myself and in my abilities. I had everything going for me: talent, beauty, and popularity. Then my whole world came crashing down on me.

In 2000, right before my senior year of high school, I began having some weird physical symptoms. It began with bad aches and pains, especially in my knees and ankles. As my senior year progressed, my wrists and hands started to slightly swell. I did not really notice, but people around me began to comment on it. Soon, my hands and feet began swelling after every practice and game. I would have to ice them down to keep the swelling at bay. Since I had been on the varsity teams for cross country, basketball, and softball since my freshman year, we were hoping that the symptoms were a result of normal athletic wear and tear.

After my problems continued, my mom finally decided to take me to an orthopedic doctor. His initial question to me was, "Do all the girls on your team complain like you do?" I was shocked and frustrated, but we figured that I was probably just over-doing it in practices. However, the pain was beginning to affect my performance. I just could not play or run like I once had.

Right after graduation, I got engaged to my middle school sweetheart, James. I vividly remember the day the arches in my feet really started hurting—we were out shopping for flowers for the wedding. I have not been the same since that day. We soon began to realize that something was terribly wrong with my body. Pain became a constant presence in my life. I could not even brush my teeth without it. I would have to lift one arm with the other arm just to do something simple like turn on a light switch. I was losing the ability to do everything I had been able to do for myself.

As I approached my freshman year in college, autumn of 2001, we had a series of frightening misdiagnoses from Rheumatoid Arthritis to Scleroderma. My family and I began sending out emails asking for prayers as the situation looked more and more bleak. Each doctor's visit made us increasingly discouraged, but we tried to keep our faith. For example, the doctor who diagnosed me with Scleroderma gave us no hope. He handed my mother a pamphlet without saying a word. The first line of it explained the devastation of Scleroderma and listed various misdiagnoses. When we got a positive lab report, James made the comment, "That's what we've prayed for." The doctor's response was, "Well, whatever makes you feel better." His condescending response to our faith-filled answer made it clear that this was not the physician we needed. So, we continued our search.

In the meantime, James and I were attempting to "carry on" life as usual even though we still had no idea what was really wrong with me. He was physically carrying me to class on his back because I was struggling to walk. Even then, he was my rock and encourager. James has always helped me to stay on my path. He physically did everything for me that I wasn't able to do for myself.

We finally found a doctor in March of 2002 who was a gift straight from God. I believe that God made sure that I went to Dr. Thomas because I had been meaning to cancel that particular appointment, but I forgot. After it was too late to cancel, we decided to go ahead and go. We were amazed at Dr. Thomas' willingness to do anything to get to the bottom of my mysterious illness. She went so far as to get out her old medical text books and flipped through them for two hours: asking questions, actually listening to me, reading for a while, and then flipping pages some more. Each time we reached a dead end on a possible answer, she would press on undeterred, looking for more information. She finally settled on Eosinophilic Fasciitis. It is an auto-immune disease, which oddly enough was listed in a Scleroderma pamphlet we were given as a "possible misdiagnosis." I went through another series of lab tests with good results, only this time Dr. Thomas noticed something. This was something the other doctors did not see, or maybe just did not check. My eosinophils (a type of blood cell) were up 20% from where they should normally be, but mine were actually on the way down from where they had been. She also explained that had this disease been caught within about 6 months of its onset, the symptoms could have been reversed with steroids. This was beyond frustrating! I had been to a doctor well before the 6-month point, and had simply been asked, "did ALL the other girls complain this much?"

As we tried to process the frustration of the missed opportunity to live the life we had in mind, at least now we had a diagnosis! I was put on some strong medication for precautionary reasons. However, there was really nothing that could be done. The damage to my physical body was complete. I had faced the full gamut of the disease without medication. This was an unexpected challenge. We were planning to get married in a few months at that point, and this "precautionary" medication could cause severe birth defects. (Not something we wanted to be faced with during the onset of our married life together!)

On June 29, 2002 I married the most amazing, loving, selfless man who knew good and well that I was not the same person that he fell in love with in 8th grade. We had no idea where my disease would take us, and we had no idea how I got it. However, he was willing to take on this journey together, regardless of the challenges that lay ahead of us.

Despite the series of bad news during this time, we received great news the week of our wedding: I had normal blood work; praise God for that! Little did we know, the outward physical changes from the damage done to my joints were only beginning.

There were only about 200-300 cases of Eosinophilic Fasciitis in the U.S. at the time, and we struggled to define what had caused my problems. It was suggested that it could have been caused by a traumatic head injury I sustained when I was 3 years old, an old epidural hematoma that could have just manifested itself in this way. It can also occur from overuse of a certain vitamin. I did pop a lot of vitamin B12 while I played basketball, but we found out later that it was not the cause. Stress can even play a part—there were any number of stressful situations I experienced in high school that could have caused it. It just all seemed so random. I was extremely frustrated with the whole situation. Looking back, I realize now it was at this point that my journey really started.

By the time we got my blood work back from the last doctor's testing, my eosinophils in my blood had attacked all of the fascia tissues (connective tissue covering and binding together muscles) in my body, resulting in scar tissue in my muscle fibers. Now scarring is a good thing if it stays where it is needed, however, scar tissue is a really sticky substance. As my body compensated for the pain, my joints settled into unusual positions. Over time, as the scar tissue continued to settle, my hands and arms locked into place depending on the activities for which I used them the most.

In retrospect, looking back on how I reacted to the illness, diagnosis, and resulting consequences, I can clearly see that anger was my first overwhelming emotion. Why? Why did a God that I grew up loving and believing to have so much mercy and so much grace let me suffer so much when I had done nothing to deserve this? I can remember screaming in my thoughts to Him, *"Why are you doing this to me?"* I was extremely angry for a good two or three years—honestly, I was just down right mad. As a result, I did not really even talk to God much during that time. I would go to church, get convicted of my bad attitude, but then shut Him out just as soon as I walked out of the church building. I did this because I was so mad and so afraid of facing the truth.

I will admit now that I was expecting Him to work a miracle of healing in my body. When I did rarely talk to Him in prayer, I demanded that He take my illness away. *"Just take it away! I'm tired of dealing with it. I'm tired of hurting!"* I simply wanted to return to being who I was "before." So, the only prayers I ever prayed were out of anger and pain. I begged Him to make it stop, but it did not stop. There was so much more to the story that I did not know about at the time; I had a lot of maturing to do. While I was desperately praying for a cure, my mother begged others to pray for me. After becoming a parent, I can now imagine what she went through watching me suffer. It occurs to me now that God willingly did the same when He watched His child suffer on the cross. The journey out of my pit of bitterness came about because through all this time, we were faithful in going to church services. Our preacher gave a lesson one Sunday morning out of Matthew 6:27 where Jesus asks, "Who of you by worrying add a single hour to your life?" Everyone had been telling me that I needed to stop worrying and let God have my burden. That is a lot easier said than done, even under the best of circumstances! However, this was a real turning point for me. Not only had friends and family been saying, "don't worry," but now I could see it written so plainly in the Bible. The message God had been trying to give me was now so clear, "Trust in ME!" At that point, I realized that I had to quit being scared. I was being controlled by my terror of the unknown. *Was I going to live to see 30? Would I be in a wheelchair the rest of my life? Would I be able to have children? What was my quality of life going to be?* These were the things I was worrying about. I now had a diagnosis (what I had been asking for,) but when I got that answer, I wanted more. I wanted to know how everything would end. Would I ever be able to love myself again? At the time, I did not like who I was. I wanted the "old me" back, the "me" who could whup up on someone on the basketball court. I enjoyed that! That living was fun! However, this "new me" who had to have someone to do almost everything for me was painful and humiliating!

So, as I began to make that transformation from anger to acceptance, I had to make the hard decision to accept the fact that I would never again be able to do so many of the things I loved to do. Yet, these things that I loved were all things that served ME. God was slowly shifting my focus to others. The transformation was a slow, painful process. I guess it had to be so I could learn from it.

My husband would tell me, "You can't change what has happened to you. You have to make the best of it. Do you understand the opportunity that God has given you to help other people through your struggles?" I was slowly starting to accept the facts, but I still had a lot of vanity. Vanity and pride are the top evils that I battle on a daily basis. Every time I made progress accepting that I would live in pain, I would run into someone from high school who remembered me and identified me for my athletic abilities, my musical abilities, my looks, and my Homecoming Queen status. When they saw that my "identity" was gone, I feared that I had become a "nobody." That scared me. I did not want to be a nobody.

The choice I had to make at this point was either to roll over and die or choose to love God through the life He gave me. The first decision would have stolen the opportunity for anyone to learn from my situation. The latter would mean that all of my struggles would not have been in vain. Thank the Lord I was surrounded by people who uplifted me. My husband, my parents, even my in-laws were amazing; they all just kept throwing positivity toward me. It seems I was able to catch some of it! God was in control whether I liked it or not. Eventually, I started to come back out of my shell. I had not really smiled for at least two years. This was such a personality shift for me. Before this happened, I had once been given the nick-name "Smiley" by an umpire I saw at multiple tournaments for a few years. I had temporarily allowed this disease to take away my true identity—not the identity my old successes had given me. As I was losing pieces of myself, of my identity, I had to replace them with something. Over time, I chose God.

It was hard—really hard! I was a selfish person. I liked ME: I liked my talents; I liked being good at things; I liked the applause. However, I was not doing anybody any good, except myself. That had to change. The strong sense of my own power and ability to take care of things myself was replaced with an amazing peace that came from trusting in God as my strength. It has really just been within the past few years that I have understood and accepted the fact that I am actually in control of nothing. I graduated from college in 2005 and began my teaching career in New Caney ISD. I have now been there for 10 amazing years. I got pregnant during my first year of teaching and gave birth to our baby girl, Jewls, in 2006. Although I felt wonderful during my pregnancy, it was not until years later that my husband and mom admitted to me they were afraid I would not live through childbirth.

We had our second child, our son Preston, in 2009. Despite my body's diminishing abilities, I felt amazing during both of my pregnancies. The reason my body felt so good while I carried my babies in-utero was because of the increase in elastin during pregnancy. However, during the post-partum times, this extra elastin in a woman's body goes away and the pain in mine returned with a vengeance. As I compensated for the pain while caring for my babies, I altered the way I physically did tasks (changing diapers, holding bottles, etc.) As the pain would slowly subside, the changes I made trying to compensate for pain started to show as they permanently reshaped my body. My left hand's fingers had drawn upward from holding a baby, while my right hand and wrist had curled inward because of writing and other tasks. The post-partum weeks were very painful for me as the elastin came and went and my hands worsened. The damage that was done to my joints during my illness is irreversible. I understand now that this condition is the material with which God has to work with in my life and the lives of my family members.

On a day-to-day basis, my husband and kids help me out in huge ways. James brushes the back of my hair every day, puts my socks on every morning, and takes them off every night. Most nights I struggle to take my shirt off, too. I cannot put on jackets or straighten my shirt once I get wrestled into my clothes. The sweet fiancé who would knock on my door every morning in college to make sure I got to class is the same man who still serves me every day, even after 13 years of marriage. He does for me what my body will not allow me to do for myself. He is the definition of a faithful man!

My children are now old enough to help me, too. So, when James is unavailable, I will ask one of them to assist me. Sometimes they will pick things up when I drop them or even open jars when I cannot figure out a way. They do not always jump at the opportunity, but I believe I am giving them opportunities to practice serving others.

A few years ago, I went to a foot doctor who helped to change my life. This doctor shaved down calluses that had previously been very painful, and finally helped me find orthotics which allow me to be a mom and housewife at the physical level that I have always wanted. I can now be on my feet for a much longer amount of time. Because of these changes, I can vacuum, clean the bathroom, dust, do dishes...and yes, these are blessings! All these tasks I previously avoided because I could not stay on my feet long enough. Some jobs I avoided because I was simply afraid to fail. When James started graduate school a couple of years ago, I found that he was not able to keep up the house work as well without assistance. One day, I got tired of the mess and decided to just go for it. I conquered my fear and realized that not only could I do it, but my feet were holding up, too! I still get a pass on the laundry duties because I cannot reach into the washer and dryer, but I am now able to contribute to the simple tasks that keep our house running smoothly.

My husband and I continue on this journey together, learning about God through His word. One of the most recent things I have come to realize is that since my life situation and disability is what God wants for me, then I want it, too. After all, I want what He wants, don't I? You need to understand that I say those words with my teeth clenched because my body hurts so badly. The physical pain is so real, and the longing for the person I was can be tempting. I have to ask myself daily, "Do I really want what my Father wants?" What else is there? To relinquish control is a constant battle. I will most likely have to make the conscious decision again, but it brings me such peace.

Letting go of the control you think you have (but really do not have) brings peace.

Like Paul, who prayed in 2 Corinthians 12:8, "Three times I pleaded with the Lord to take it away from me." I have begged God to take this pain away from me. We all have things in our lives that wear us down, things we just want God to take the struggle away. It would make life so much easier, wouldn't it? I have prayed that prayer many times. Yet, as I grow in maturity in Christ, I am able to understand that in my weakness, I find His strength. When I had my whole body, I had nothing. When my body became broken, I gained everything. I tell my students, "You might think I'm crazy, but I thank God for my disease. It is a blessing because it keeps me in check." I believe that God allowed me to go through this trial to help me.

Just a few months ago, my husband reminded me that the Holy Spirit is talking to me, but I cannot hear Him if I am not listening. In the midst of an argument I was having with my husband one night, I was sobbing in frustration about why I had to allow my disease to affect every aspect of my life both physically and emotionally. Suddenly, the most overwhelming peace came over me, and it was like God was telling me, "I allowed this disease because I love you." God allowed Paul his "thorn in the flesh" because He loved him and because Paul needed it. "In order to keep me from becoming conceited, I was given a thorn in my flesh," 2 Corinthians 12:7 NIV. This is MY thorn, and I need it, though for so long why I needed it was beyond my grasp. If this is what God wants for me, then I need to embrace it. I do have to remind myself on a daily basis that it is okay. God will be glorified. This is okay for me to deal with, and God will meet me here. My life is not about me anymore. I have to intentionally choose my mindset on a daily basis.

I lost many abilities as a result of this disease. Basketball. Softball. Playing the flute. (Thank the Lord I have not lost my ability to sing, because that is my worship.) The things that I have gained are harder to see, because they come from the inside.

I know that my children are stronger because they have a mom with a disability. Little did we know, we would be rearing a young daughter and son who have both been diagnosed with Type 1 Diabetes two years apart. This was very difficult to accept and embrace, but I realized quickly that this experience expanded my purpose. All of my physical and emotional struggles through the years were "training" me for this race. God trained me to run this race with my daughter and son, who (like me) now have a life-long, never-ending struggle. I can help them work through the emotional burdens that come with the physical changes and struggles they will face. When they feel like they are at their wits end, I can confidently say, "No, it is not fun, and yes, it is frustrating – but God is in control and you're going to be okay." All the physical pain, all the mental stress I have braved, all the thought processes and grieving that I have dealt with over the past 14 years have finally had a purpose I can visibly see, and that purpose came in the form of my own children. They don't have to wonder and go through their struggles without somebody who "gets it." I have faith that my struggles will help my children get through their own hurdles they will confront. I am thankful for my disease. I thank God that he allowed this trial to strengthen me, to refine me. "I have refined you, but not as silver is refined. Rather, I have refined you in the furnace of suffering" (Isaiah 48:10 NLT). I can be of help to them in time of need as they go through the emotional process of a life-changing condition.

"Anyone who meets a testing challenge head-on and manages to stick it out is mighty fortunate. For such persons loyally in love with God, the reward is life and more life." James 1:12 MSG. I am so thankful that we are able to "stick it out" with God as our mighty helper. I am thankful for each day that He gives me the opportunity to love Him and to love those around me. I am thankful that He chose ME for this life.

About Melody Young

Melody Young has two beautiful children – daughter Jewls who is 14 and son Preston who is 9. She and her amazing husband James live in the Houston area in the great state of Texas. Melody has been a middle school teacher for 11 years. They are very involved in their wonderful church participating in Leadership Training for Christ. As a family, they anxiously anticipate the annual Family Camp weekend in June where 20+ families fellowship through games, devotionals and food. Outside of church, Melody loves spending quality time with her family on camping trips to the beach and soaking up some sun.

Leanne Harris

Leanne and I have attended the same leadership conference for years. I have enjoyed getting to know her and our friendship is a blessing to me. Her heart for helping and serving others is such an inspiration. I have been the recipient of that encouragement many times— she has helped me be brave. Leanne's story highlights the very real challenges and deep blessings that come with having a child with a disability. Leanne's ability to face those challenges with courage and perseverance makes me love her even more. She is a wonderful wife, mother, and friend.

Entering Grace—A Faith Expedition

Leanne Harris

I met my husband, Glenn in East Texas at the Tyler Jr. College Radiology program in 1979. He was my supervising student leader, a year ahead of me in school. We were friends first, dated for a couple of years, and then got married. I quit my job to stay at home when our first child, Amanda, was born. Although I was a stay-at-home mom, I did a few things on the side to earn a little extra money. One of my jobs was driving a school bus early in the mornings and again in the afternoons. The bus that I drove had some kids with Down syndrome on it, and I remember thinking it was the saddest thing I had ever seen. They were in a group home, were not well-cared for, and were very low functioning; it wrung my heart with compassion for them.

When Amanda was two and a half, we decided it was time to grow our family again. We were delighted when I got pregnant just as planned. Throughout my pregnancy, I felt very good. After a couple of ultrasounds, the radiologist (a good friend of ours) confided in Glenn that he did not think that I would carry the baby to term because I had something called a blighted ovum. They did not tell me any of this, and my OB never mentioned it either. Yet, my condition did not affect the pregnancy, and I did carry the baby to term. Based on later ultrasounds, our physician told us we were going to have a very healthy seven-pound baby boy. We were so excited.

Toward the end of my pregnancy, we sold our home and moved into a rental house because we were low on money and the addition of a child would increase our expenses. One evening as I was painting the new house (which was actually an old house) I noticed that the baby was not moving, so I called my doctor. He had me try a few home remedies to get the baby moving, but there was nothing. He asked me to come in the next day. He said all was fine and the baby would come any day now. The next night, I felt my contractions starting, so I woke Glenn up and told him it was time to go to the hospital.

When I got to hospital, they put me on monitors and discovered I was in true labor. My labor pains were extreme, but when they examined me, I was only dilated to a 1. I had a successful, natural childbirth with Amanda, so we knew something was not right for me to have that much pain so early in the labor process. It was determined that the baby was in distress with a dropping heart rate. They immediately began prepping me for a C-section when the baby's heart completely stopped on the monitors. Everyone jumped into action, but for me, it felt like they could not move fast enough. The doctor had just barely arrived and the nurses were in the middle of shift changes. They struggled to get the wheels unlocked on my bed so they could wheel me to the operating room. They finally got me rolling down the hall toward the OR, and Glenn was following right behind me. We were both horrified; the baby was dying inside of me and there was nothing we could do. When I got into the OR, I could hear trays flying and people scrambling to get instruments out to operate. The nurse was putting my catheter in place, and I was trying to scoot my pregnant self over onto the operating table. The anesthesiologist handed me the mask and asked me to hold it while he got the drugs mixed. Just as I was finally drifting off, I was jarred back to consciousness by three tugs so strong they lifted me off the table like something was pulling me from above. The doctor actually had to cut into me to pull the baby out before any of the anesthetic had the chance to fully set in and before they could give me an epidural. He had to pull extremely hard because all my amniotic fluid was gone and the uterus was crushing the baby—they call that a dry birth. I was rising off of the table because of the strength of his pulling. It was a very rough delivery.

Nothing about the birth of our second child went the way we expected. The first surprise was that our baby was a girl instead of a boy like our doctor had predicted. Secondly, and even more shocking, was that our new baby girl was smaller than anticipated, and she was not "normal." Glenn recognized it immediately when he saw her and began to weep. I asked him, "What is wrong?" And he responded, "Our baby has Down syndrome." I could not believe it. "No, she doesn't. That must be the lady next door's baby. I am only twenty-eight; there is no way." Glenn said, "No, honey, she does." I responded, "I don't believe you. Bring her to me." So they brought her to me, and all I remember thinking was how beautiful she was with her blue eyes and her little pink hat on her head. If she turned her head a certain way, I could see why they said she had Down's, yet I still refused to believe it. The nurses showed me the indications: her fingers turned in a certain way, the speckles in the irises of her eyes, and the larger space between her big toe and second toe. I could see what they were talking about, but it was all so surreal, it was just unbelievable. To me, she was simply a beautiful baby girl. We named her Angela Christine, which meant angel of Christ.

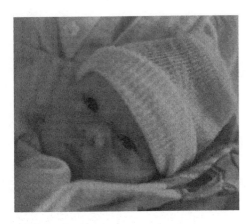

The next few days seemed like a nightmare. My parents walked in to the hospital with blue balloons and gifts for our baby boy. When we told them about Angela and that she had Down's, my dad passed out right there in the postpartum area. The nurses had to put him up on a stretcher, and my parents turned around and went home. I was worried that my parents might not accept this disabled child. However, they showed back up at the hospital the next day with smiles on their faces, ready to be grandparents to Angela and supportive parents to me.

Then, the next few days were full of managing Angela's medical care and my medical care without Glenn or my mom at the hospital to help me because they were finishing up our move back at home. I was on pain meds and very sore from my rough delivery. Well-meaning visitors would come by, look at me, and say, "I am so sorry." I did appreciate them coming, yet it was so hard having those conversations over and over again.

While I was in the hospital, I did not even know who had Amanda in their care. She would come to the hospital every couple of days with different families. The church did such a beautiful job of taking care of her and our family. People gave money and prayer support and filled needs we did not even realize we would have. It was simply amazing; I cannot imagine having to go through something like this without our friends and a church community to support us.

I was in the hospital for a week. Two men from our church offered to help Glenn finish up our move. We had not planned to finish our move until after Angela was born, so I had not even finished packing up our boxes. The church just responded incredibly: two guys turned into many, many people. Twenty trucks showed up at our house, and people packed everything for us, cleaned up, and unpacked after the move. One day during that week, my nurses told me I could take a little break from the hospital and go home for dinner. So, they loaded me up in the car in the summer heat and took me to our new (old) house. I felt horrible. The heat and the car ride made me nauseated, and I walked into a house that did not feel like home to me yet. I will never forget walking into my little rent house. I was so grateful for all that everyone had done for us, but I walked in and everything was all wrong. The air conditioner was not working, and our belongings were in the wrong places and some things were even broken, I missed my other beautiful home. After only thirty minutes, I realized I needed to get back to hospital. It was the first time I realized my need to be with my daughter. In the hospital, all I wanted was to get away, but once I was away, I realized I belonged at the hospital with Angela.

I stayed in the hospital for a couple more days. I was absolutely exhausted from all the visitors and conversations about her care, so I mostly slept. They would bring Angela to me to nurse, and then I would just sleep some more. Of course, nursing was difficult because she had low muscle tone, so that was quite an ordeal. In the hospital, I rested as much as I could because I knew the rest would stop when I got home. I was right; when I got home, I had a two-and-a-half-year-old daughter who also needed my care, and Glenn had to go back to work. Glenn's mom was such a huge help at that time. I went around the house trying to find where people had put things (for example, I found garlic in the linen closet.) It was a crazy time, but I was overwhelmingly blessed by all the visitors and meals.

The day we took Angela home, our support system was strong and waiting to hold us up. Angela was already fiercely loved by so many friends and family. In some ways, bringing Angela home was joyful much like bringing any child home, but in other ways, we grieved the death of a dream for a life our baby girl and her sibling would never have. We were moving forward with no idea what the future would look like. Thank God for the precious friends that pointed out how special Angela would be. Honestly, we do not know what the future holds for any of our children because we are not in control. In those days of uncertainty, the scripture I clung to was the story of the disciples asking Jesus if a young boy was born blind because his parents had sinned. Jesus' response was beautiful: *"Neither this man nor his parents sinned...but this happened so that the works of God might be displayed in him"* (John 9:3.) I clung to that response and held it in my heart. I told myself, "God is going to use this. It will glorify him and grow us."

After a few days, we were re-admitted to the hospital and Angela was given a diagnosis of a minor heart defect. Then, as time went on, Angela's diagnoses became more of a reality. The genetic testing results we received a couple of weeks later were very emotional for all of us. They predicted she would live but that she would have a horrible existence. Our pediatrician was a good friend of mine and we had kids the same age. She wept for our family and the thoughtless things people would say to us. People would ask her, "Patty, aren't you going to have Leanne admit that child to the Denton State School?" She compassionately told me, "I can't believe people are saying that." Glenn and I even had people ask us if wanted to keep Angela. Our response was always, "Of course we want to keep her!" Even years down the road, I would have people call me saying, "I hear you are the mom of a mongoloid child. I am so sorry; how do you cope?" It was shocking to discover that antiquated ideas about Down syndrome from over fifty years ago still existed. Most people's mentality about our situation was so discouraging. God always provided even though Satan was attacking our family from every angle possible. We were not taking care of our own health due to the stress. Glenn felt that God was punishing him for things he had done wrong in his life. It broke my heart to see him think and feel those things.

My initial response was, "Lord, how could you let this happen?" Over time, my attitude shifted to, "Lord, just use me." That perspective helped me get out of the funk I was in. Angela's therapists told me things I needed to be doing to stimulate her, but I resented others telling me how to play with my baby. I wanted to focus on loving and caring for her without having to act like her therapist. Eventually, my mindset became "We will do all we can to make this child as strong and independent as possible, whatever it takes." It took Glenn about six months to realize that this was going to be a blessing from God and not a curse, and of course, Angela being so stinkin' cute helped that realization. Angela's doctors and other parents told us to enjoy the first year with her because after that, her whole life would be about services and therapies. We took their advice and soaked up every moment of those early days.

We did choose to start with some therapy and needed surgeries right away with Angela, which left us very little time to process. I read every book I could get my hands on, and got in touch with as many therapy services as I could. We joined a program called ECI (Early Childhood Intervention) and it turned out to be an amazing resource. Through ECI, therapists would make visits to our house, and I received immediate resources and support. I started going to conferences right away. I am a networker, so I wanted to meet people who could help us.

It took some time, a lot of time, really, to see this as a blessing for our family. I eventually became an advocate for other parents. I would visit new parents in the hospital who had babies born with Down syndrome, some of whom were considering giving up their baby for adoption. I never judged those feelings; I understood them all too well. I would tell them they could certainly do that, but I would also encourage them to walk forward on the path God had chosen for them. I would tell them that I had no idea what the Lord had in store for me and how I would grow as a person from having Angela. When you wish for everything to be normal, you can wish away special blessings that come to your life from the circumstances you have been given.

Angela's development was delayed, but not a lot. She was rolling over on time with the rest of her age mates, and she walked at ten months. Her teeth were very slow coming in, which worried us a great deal. Our lives became a constant routine of going from therapy to therapy, but Angela grew up fearless. It was not long before she would just toddle off anywhere I took her. Everything was a great adventure! She got lost at VBS one time because she disappeared to go exploring. We fell more and more in love with our little adventurer. When she was preschool age, we got Angela enrolled in an early intervention campus. It was one of the best things we were able to do for her; she learned amazing skills like sign language. By the time Angela was four, she knew over four hundred words in sign language. Those teachers pushed her and me and I am forever thankful.

During Angela's toddler years, Glenn and I wrestled with whether or not to have another child. We knew that because we already had one child with Down's, the odds of having another child with Down's was higher. We knew others with two Down's children in their family, and the thought of it was very frightening for us. Eventually, even with the additional risks, we decided we did want another child. We knew it would ease the burden on Amanda to have another sibling who would help care for Angela one day. Once we were pregnant again, my OB/GYN reminded me there were tests we could run to make sure this baby would be okay. I told him, "It doesn't matter if everything is okay because I am going to carry this baby no matter what. Regardless of what the tests might show, we are going to keep and love this baby and do the best we can with what God has given us."

Angela was two and a half when John was born. John came early, unlike Angela who was right on time, and it was another painful, traumatic delivery. It was difficult having much of our family in health crisis at the same time. While I was in the hospital having John, my mother was in the hospital recovering from an intense shoulder surgery. My dad was actually dying, although we did not know it at the time, but he died weeks later. So, at one point, John was ambulanced to Ft. Worth to the Children's Medical Center, I was in Denton Regional Hospital, my mother was in a Lewisville Hospital, and my dad was sick and trying to cope. It was horrible. Again, I went through another extremely dark, depressing time, thinking, "Dear God, how am I going to function? How can we pay these bills?" I did not know what was up and what was down. But as always, God continued to be faithful and provide what our family needed, one day at a time.

Not long ago, Amanda was looking at pictures of our life during the kids' early years, and she noticed a few things.

The first thing she told me was, "We were loved so much by you both." We have countless pictures of me reading to our kids, rocking them, wrestling on the floor, and playing with them on the swing set. There are pictures of all the fun birthday parties and all the other events from their childhoods. The second thing she noticed was, "Mom, you were tired!" I said, "Yes, for sure!" There were days I just did not know how I could keep going, but somehow, God gave me the strength and we were so grateful for the help my sweet parents gave us. The third thing she noticed was that our house was always a mess. Again, I could not agree more. The five of us lived in a tiny, 1200 square-foot rent house. Money was so tight in those days. There were days I thought we would not make it, and then people would leave groceries on our porch. God always timed these blessings perfectly. I gave up every possible luxury I could. I remember at one point praying, "Lord, I have given up so much. I don't need my nails done or the gym; please just let me keep getting the newspaper." It may sound silly, but I loved coming home on a Sunday after church to read the newspaper and nap. Yet God gently showed me, "No, you don't need that either." So I gave up my newspapers, too. Let me tell you how sweet God was to me: a few weeks later, a sweet woman across the street came over and said, "I don't have time to read all these newspapers. Can you just come get my newspapers and take them over for me and put them in the recycle when you are done?" From then on, those newspapers were like manna and quail from Heaven. Eventually I had way too many, I was reading history, not news! How like God to give us more than we need.

When Angela was about five or six, we found out about a list that she needed to get on for funding. The waiting list was about fifteen years. So, we did everything we could to get her on that list to get access to resources. This would help with rent and a staff of support people. With the help of the Texas MHMR (Mental Health and Mental Retardation) agency, we knew we needed to get a financial planner who could help us navigate the unique challenges of having a child with Angela's condition. I will never forget sitting down with the financial planner. He drew out what our finances looked like and what it was going to cost to care for Angela. It was clearly a mismatch. He was really hard on us. He said, "If you guys were to die today, Angela would be put in foster care and here is what she would not have: dental care, shoes, clothes..." and he went on and on. Glenn and I went home devastated. I cried for three days. We had done everything we could do to care for this child, yet it felt like we had done a horrible job. I called the financial planner and told him, "I can't believe you were so insensitive to us. Do you have any idea the heartache that it is to do what we are doing?" And he said, "Yeah. So, are you going to do something about it?" He made me so mad. As it turned out, that was his MO: to get you mad enough to spur you into action.

So, that is what we did—we began to act. I am forever indebted to this man who cared enough to tell us the hard truth. We put together a financial package including a letter of intent. When something happens to us and Angela gets transferred to a guardian, all her preferences are in place. We basically arranged things so that her lifestyle will not change even if we are not around to provide for her. We got her funding arranged in a trust and in our wills. I planned her funeral, I put her records in order, we stated our preferences from church to being scared of thunder storms to ice cream and puppies. It took years, but it is done, and we can sleep at night knowing we have done everything we could not only for Angela, but also Amanda and John. Through all our work on this, I learned that many parents were unaware how much work it would take to provide for their children. Parents would say to me, "I wish my child could have what Angela has," and I would tell them they could. Yet they would say, "I am not sure I want to do all of that; it is a lot of work." We were always working hard to fight for Angela's rights and to find resources for her. It was a constant battle of advocacy.

Angela was involved in Special Olympics and was very active and healthy. She never had any life-threatening surgeries, which is very common with children with Angela's health challenges. We did have a few of the typical, common surgeries like umbilical hernia and getting tear ducts built, but nothing life-threatening like a heart surgery. I started looking for nutritional supplementation when I found Juice Plus+, the company I partner with today. We saw great improvements with things like sinus infections because her immune system was functioning better. I worked hard to help Angela be her best. I treated her like my other kids in many ways with discipline. We tried hard to keep things in balance so that her siblings did not feel like she was getting all the attention. She had a chore list just like Amanda and John, and she had a very typical upbringing through elementary. We advocated constantly throughout Angela's education so she could thrive in a normal classroom with other children without an aid. She did great; she did have a modified curriculum, yet it worked. In school, it was not the kids who were scared of Angela, it was their parents. I took Angela to friends' homes so they could know how to treat her: do not bribe her with candy or appease her with food, just treat her like other kids. We created a Circle Of Friends group and it was a blast. I educated nurses and teachers at school on how to work with Angela, and she was able to thrive in that environment. We did everything that is regular for an American family together. I fondly remember looking into to the backyard at all of the kids on the trampoline and in the sandbox.

However, all hell broke loose when Angela started middle school. We simply could not accept the type of education she was getting, which was nothing. It was an undesirable school district situation. I went to a conference with the Dallas Autism-Down Syndrome Society. After only half a day of the conference, I came home and told Glenn, "We have three choices. We can sue the school district and pray that things change in Angela's lifetime, we can pretend like we don't care that she is not receiving the services she needs, or we can choose to move to a school district that is already providing the services she needs." Really, for us, there was only one choice.

So, the next week, we put a for sale sign in the yard of the house we had just remodeled. We ended up in an apartment in another town and started all over for Angela's education. John and Amanda were such troopers to make the sacrifice of leaving their friends for Angela's sake. It paid off—she was in a very good school district all the way through high school. However, it got harder and harder as she got older. High school hallways are a cruel place even without a disability. I prayed fervently that God would protect her and intercede for her and that people would be favorable toward her, love her, and protect her because she was so vulnerable. I will never forget going to lunch with her one day in high school and following her as she was navigating the high school hallway. Angela is a little, short thing, and she worked hard to get through all the big football players and big people around her. She would sit at the lunch table by herself, and when the bell would ring, she would go the bathroom and lay her backpack down where people could take things out of it. Then, she would be late to class, get a tardy slip, and be punished. It just broke my heart. Angela brought out the best in some special people though, and it was a delight to watch them rise up to step in and lead and protect.

There were countless heartbreaking moments like that—watching my child just continue to push through despite all the obstacles in her way. Angela just wanted to be loved and accepted. She was a cheerleader in middle school, and she always modeled such good behavior. That is why it is so important for these kids to be in a regular classroom. They model what they see, and if you put them in a classroom with kids that are disturbed or have horrible behavior, it pulls them down. Over the years, I coped by being active and engaged. I fought for awareness and better treatment for Angela and other children like her. Whatever next seminar or speaker was coming to town, I was there, and I was bringing other parents. I ran in circles with other moms who had children with disabilities. I started a special education parent-teacher group, and I was very involved in community.

I was a pioneer. I was held up as an example by our special needs financial planner because we were willing to do whatever we could do to care for Angela in the event that we passed away early. We made sure that our other kids would also have what they needed for themselves and for Angela. We prepared Angela to be in group home settings. Employment-wise, she has two jobs. She is also highly involved in Special Olympics. We pushed and pushed to prepare her to be at her utmost in case we are ever not here to care for her. If that were to happen, the more skills she has, the easier it will be for her to blend in and have a productive life.

Angela has changed all of our lives. When Angela was first born, I worried for my oldest, Amanda, and what it would mean for her. She was always going to have this stigma of having a mentally disabled sister. To Amanda, however, it was just normal life. Of course, there have been times she wished for a normal sister, but Angela made Amanda who she is today. Amanda was always a great big sister, and she grew up to become a speech pathologist assistant. She works with kids with disabilities and is a wonderful advocate for them. John, although he is the baby of the family, grew up to be a big, strapping Marine and a Texas State Trooper. I am sure John was teased at times about his sister, but he always defended her and he is still fighting for justice today.

When John was growing up, his friends would spend the night with us. One time I was driving a group of them in the car and one of them said, "That's so retarded." I looked back at him and said, "Do you mean that is like being mentally slow?" He said, "No, that is not what I mean." I told him, "Well that is what you just said. Angela is mentally slow, so she is what is called "mentally retarded." That kind of hurts my feelings to hear because she is bright and doing the best she can with the package God gave her." I could tell John's friends had never thought of their words that way. They loved Angela and would never want to say anything to hurt her. We were constantly teaching people to love Angela and helping them be sensitive to the language they used. To this day, John's friends are still fond of Angela and are kind and protective of her. It has been so sweet to watch.

The divorce rate among couples with a child with a disability is upwards of 80%, so Glenn and I knew we would have to be very intentional about our marriage. In the early days, Glenn was working two jobs because money was so tight, so we really only saw him four days a month the whole time the kids were growing up. We always worked opposite shifts so one of us would be with the kids. Angela had ten surgeries by the time she was ten years old, so we pretty much lived in doctor's offices and at therapy. As hard as it was to find time together, Glenn and I worked hard at our marriage. We were determined to push through this and be better at the end—not just to survive it, but to be better as a family and to encourage others. One of the things we did was escape to a marriage retreat once every couple of years. As the kids got a little bit older, we took weekend trips together to get away and decompress. It was never anything fancy because we had so little money, yet we knew that it was very important that we kept our marriage first or we could not take care of our kids.

This is what I would tell anyone who might be struggling with marriage or with your kids with disabilities: put God first, then your relationship with your spouse second. Glenn and I were highly involved in our church, we participated in Bible studies, and we sought out mentors who could encourage us in our relationship through this journey. I would not trade anything for the spiritual partner I have in Glenn. He loves his kids so much, is such a good husband for me, and is such a servant-hearted man. He gives unselfishly and he never complains. Living with Glenn and Angela has been so transformational for me because neither of them really gets angry. They are peaceful and loving, and they have changed my life simply because of who they are and how they love me, unconditionally.

What I have I learned about myself? I am tenacious, but as hard as I fight, I cannot do this on my own. I have to have help around me, and I must always rely on God. This journey has stripped me of my pride and forced me to lean on God and the help of his people. I have come to see that so much of what we value about people is in what they can do, but I am learning to focus on who people are at their core and not just what they can do. Angela deserves everything to be done for her that can be done because she is God's child, not because of anything she can or cannot do.

Most days, I carry on with courage and passion in my heart. Yet there are times when Satan comes to attack me with "What ifs." What if we die and Amanda and John move far away? Who will care for Angela? What if I am not caring for Angela as well as I need to be? What if someone hurts her or she gets lost? She does not complain, so I would not know if there was something wrong. When Satan attacks me with these fears, I cling to God and his promises. Yes, I have wrestled with God over this, but He has always been faithful. When in a trial like this, you can either let adversity cement and strengthen your faith, or you can allow it to make you bitter and cynical. The outcome is your choice. Rather than letting this trial turn me into a hateful, resentful person, I choose to let this journey purify me and refine me, drawing me closer to Christ and making me more like him every day. It brings me joy to use what I have learned to help others, so I continue to actively advocate.

Today I am thankful that as a National Marketing Director with the Juice Plus+ Company, I have the time and financial freedom I need to bring Angela on vacation with us, take her to lunch, enroll her in camps or attend a doctor's visit. When she was nineteen, Angela moved out to live I a group home with three other girls. I am very thankful for the great people who care for her. She comes home most weekends and calls every day. However, there may be a day when she would need to come back home full time. Who knows what can happen? But I am trusting God already has it handled.

One thing that is really important, when you are describing someone who has a disability or a disease is to put the person before the condition. Instead of an asthmatic child, you have a child with asthma. I do not have a mentally disabled child; I have a child with mental disabilities. The person always comes first because the disability does not define them. Many scriptures have spoken to me and changed me, but one that stands out to me comes out of Proverbs 31: 8-9 NLT: *"Speak up for those who cannot speak for themselves; ensure justice for those being crushed. Yes, speak up for the poor and helpless, and see that they get justice."* To me, these verses became my charge and my commission: I have been called to open my mouth and defend the rights of Angela and others like her.

When I hear people say that they just pray that their child is born normal and healthy, I think to myself that they might be praying away a transformational life experience. God's perfect will for us may not look perfect in our eyes. God does not allow accidents; everything has a purpose and a plan. Angela has brought about sensitivity in all those who know her. Amanda now works with kids with disabilities and loves to call and talk to Angela. John loves coming to see Angela, and he and his new wife, Lyndsay, spend time with her whenever they can. I work as an advocate for a cause I never knew anything about before we had Angela. Glenn speaks to every parent he can that has a child with Down syndrome to encourage them. Our family, our marriage, our lives have been completely transformed. Angela inspires people to look past the surface to get to know what is underneath: kindness, humor, gentleness, and beautiful, unconditional love. My—who would we be without Angela?

About Leanne Harris

Leanne Harris is a woman on a mission. She has been the wife of Glenn for 34 years now and still learning to be a mother of three great adults.

Leanne's background includes work as a Radiologic Technologist in the Emergency Room, owning a mobile imaging company, and Nuclear Medicine working with patients who had cancer. She retired early from "Sick Care" and is now thrilled to serve as a National Marketing Director with own her own Juice Plus+ Franchise focusing on "Well Care."

Her desire is to help others to rise up into the greatness which they were created for. Leanne loves people, gardening, good food, exercising, reading, personal development, music, worship, advocating for people with special needs, traveling and hanging out with her family.

She is an acclaimed nutrition nerd and documentary junkie after her experiencing her own huge health transformation. She loves traveling the US to deliver her motivational lectures.

Leanne's passion is to meet others where they are on their journey to better health, spiritual well-being, and financial independence, helping them achieve their goals and dreams, which is only possible through God!

Sara Eggleston

Sara and I both own a wellness franchise and became friends over the years. Yet, it was not until a devotional where Sara was speaking that I learned about a very difficult season of her life. I had never really known someone who had been in the witness protection program before. As I learned about what she had endured it made me love and respect her even more. She is another example of how God walks with us through tough seasons of our journey and helps us overcome.

On Eagle's Wings

Sara Eggleston

My life can be described as "before" and "after." The "before" involves twenty years of darkness, terror, and despair. I lived through every single one of my worst fears: disappointment, unfaithfulness, dishonesty, embarrassment, poverty, illness, failure, and loss. Living in the "after," I look back at those years and I know the only reason I survived was because God was faithful to walk through the darkness with me, though I could not see Him at the time. Even when I may not have felt close to Him, when I tried to do it all on my own and drifted away from Him, He never left my side. This is my story of overcoming terrible things, things I would never wish on anyone, yet it is also a story of redemption, hope, and restoration through my savior, Jesus Christ.

Before: Blind Love

I picked up the lingerie that did not belong to me off the floor and instantly had a sick feeling. I had just been carried over the threshold of my new home, just three days after our wedding, and found it in our bedroom. When I asked my husband, he told me it must have been from the people who had lived in our home before us. He gave me that smile I could not resist, and I was so in love that it did not occur to me to doubt him; his explanation made perfect sense. I had married a wonderful man who was a Christian, who loved people, who had a charismatic personality, and who came from a wonderful family. Of course the lingerie was from the previous residents, what else could it be?

My husband and I met in high school. His grandparents went to church with my family. The first time we saw each other, we had an instant attraction; I fell madly in love. For a while, my parents were concerned I would marry him before I even finished high school, but we waited until we got into college. While we dated, I noticed a few things that unsettled me a little. He was very showy, he was careless when spending money and he drove recklessly. He also seemed to have a constant desire to get away, which displayed itself when he decided to join the service instead of going to college after high school. He made this choice without even discussing it with his parents or me, his girlfriend. I thought his actions were a little unusual for such a big decision, but despite the unease and the worry I felt, I loved him so much that I ignored those feelings.

Because my husband was in the army, our first months of marriage were spent living in a small apartment near Fort Bliss in El Paso, Texas. As the months passed, I continued to have unsettled feelings about this man I had married. It wasn't long before my husband bought a car and a television that we could not afford. I was surprised because we already had a car that was paid for. More often than not, we did not even have enough money to buy groceries at the end of the month; we certainly could not afford payments on a car and a television. When he made decisions like this, I tried to respect his role as the husband and not make a fuss. I occupied myself with housework and continuing my education, still believing that everything would be okay. One Sunday, an elder at the church we attended approached me and told me that my husband had stolen money out of the collection plate. I did not believe him. There had to be some mistake. I asked my husband, he denied it, and I believed him. The blinders of my love for my husband kept me from seeing the evidences of the weak and corrupted character of the man that I had married.

After a few months, my husband was transferred to Fort Dix, New Jersey. I had a big decision to make. Should I go with him to the east coast, or should I stay and finish up the college education that I had started before we married? It was a really tough decision, but I ended up choosing to stay and finish my degree. In retrospect, I see that my decision stemmed from my God-given and parent-instilled intuition and perception. Without my education, I would not have been able to support myself through the chaos that lay ahead of me. I lived with my in-laws who I grew to love dearly, and I became particularly close to my mother-in-law. She was wonderfully good to me and taught me a great deal. I stayed in touch with my husband through phone calls several times a week, but we did not see each other much during that time. One night, I received a phone call that shook me to my core. My husband told me through tears that he had gotten drunk and been with another woman. I was heartbroken and devastated, but I loved him so much. I told myself he never would have done that if he had not been drunk. I decided to forgive him and believe him when he said it would never happen again. I hung up the phone shaking. Was I crazy? Was it my fault because I did not move with him when he was transferred? His betrayal was a deep wound, but what could I do? He had asked for forgiveness, so I put it out of my mind and moved on, placing the blame on the effects of alcohol rather than on his true character. During the two years my husband was in New Jersey, I finished my degree and became an elementary teacher in Abilene, TX. When he finished his tour of duty with the Army, he joined me there.

My husband's continuing irresponsibility and irregular patterns of living were getting worse, and my eyes were beginning to open to his dual personality. His deceit only continued to grow. Around me, he acted like the charming, protective, Christian man with whom I had fallen in love. Because of his high intelligence, he could spout my values back at me in a way that made me feel guilty to have ever questioned him. When I found *Playboy* magazines under the seat of his car, he claimed that a friend had left them there. I got turned away at the grocery store when the manager told me that we had bounced several checks. I was no longer allowed to make purchases by check. I was horribly ashamed and mortified. I left the groceries on the counter and went home only to find that our water had been shut off because of another bad check. I could not comprehend how this had happened. I had learned at a very young age the importance of stewardship and how to balance a checkbook. My husband and I had a joint bank account at the time. My checkbook showed that we still had money in the account, but he had concealed several bounced checks from me. Extremely angry, I confronted my husband. He denied knowing that we were out of money. I felt helpless. I chose to accept his word because my only other alternative was to leave him, and I could not bring myself to give up on him.

Before: Living in Fear

As things began to fall apart for us financially, I lived in a constant state of shame. I had been raised in a home where we trusted each other and followed through on our word. I was so embarrassed to be viewed in the community as undependable. I lived each day in shame, disgrace, and fear; I lived each minute desperately asking God to show me what to do. The kind of life my husband's actions immersed me in was so shameful and opposite to the life I had known growing up that I just felt dirty. Life used to be stable, truthful, and trustworthy, but it had become unstable, untruthful, and untrustworthy. Some days I was *so* frightened and burdened that I would have to pick up my legs with my hands just to put one foot in front of the other.

Then, in the midst of all that chaos, I became pregnant. Instead of it being the joyous news that it should have been, I was overwhelmed with fear because my teaching job was the only thing sustaining our family financially. In those days, you could not start teaching a new semester if you knew you were pregnant. I was terrified that my principal would find out. My husband did nothing to ease my worry or the financial burden; he never gave any thought at all to our finances. Fortunately, my principal liked me and did not want to lose me. When I had to resign at mid-term, he found a friend to fill in for me with the understanding that I would try to come back and teach again.

The night my daughter Camille was born, her lungs collapsed due to asthma. For a while, it was uncertain whether or not she would even make it home from the hospital. All of the fear I had been living with was nothing compared to the terror that I would lose my daughter. Day and night, I carried the burden of the fear that my baby girl was going to die. We set up a device where I could hear her sleep, and I kept it hooked to my body, but I was afraid to go to sleep in case she stopped breathing in the night. So, I stayed up every night, sewing, cooking, and cleaning. Most nights I only got two or three hours of sleep at most. Camille's fragile hold on life was more terrifying to me than if my own life was in danger. I loved her so much, and I felt so helpless to save her. She was the most precious thing in my life, but I could not even enjoy the days that she was well because I was always anxious about her becoming sick again, which she always did. She had thirty-seven trips to the hospital before she was five. Every time, I was so afraid that a check would bounce without my knowing, that we would get to the hospital and be turned away because we could not pay. That was a constant, nearly immobilizing fear for me.

I was frantic and did not know where to turn. My life was in shambles with an irresponsible, unfaithful husband and a sick baby. I felt the weight of the world on my shoulders. I was about to go crazy. I had always worked to be a good person, good wife, and good mother, but nothing was working. I was not depending on God. I did not understand that bad things happen to good people, yet God is still in charge of it all. It is not a matter of our control, but His, and it is not a matter of how good we can be on our own, but of how good we are because He is our good Father. In the back of my mind, I knew these truths, yet my focus continued to be on what I could do to regain control and change things for the better.

I walked through the stages of grief during that time. I denied the truth of the corrupted man my husband was showing himself to be. I negotiated with God to turn my husband's life around. I became depressed to the point of despair. Acceptance did not come for many years. Each time something bad happened, I would think, "Oh, I can't believe it. I can't handle this. I can't stand it." The pain overwhelmed me. To this day, I still feel physically ill when I remember the pain.

Our finances continued to worsen until my husband decided to run away from his problems. I received a call that my husband had attempted to commit suicide. They had pumped his stomach and were keeping him in a hospital. My father-in-law went to get him, because I could not leave the baby or my job. My husband was put in a psychiatric hospital for treatment, but the doctors could find no reason to keep him. His IQ was so high that he was able to fake emotions and give the correct answers. When he was released, he seemed to be better for a while. Then the next catastrophe struck.

I will never forget the scene. Camille was in the oxygen tent at our house, trying to recover from another severe asthma attack. The police came to my front door. They told me that our Chevrolet Impala had been abandoned on the edge of town and there was blood all over the inside of the door. My husband had disappeared. News reporters were hot on the heels of the police, wanting details about the shocking news I had only just received. My precious mother-in-law came over to watch Camille so that I could go to work. I had to keep my job now more than ever. Not to mention, staying occupied was the only thing that was keeping me sane. I knew if I got to school, I would be with the children and I would be safe. Pictures of the abandoned car were all over the news, and I had constant waves of fear and shame wash over me from the public spectacle. My husband had left me behind to clear up his debts, sell our home, and take care of our child. No one knew where he was. I had a strong feeling that he was alive and simply avoiding his responsibilities. The police had discovered a letter in the abandoned car from my husband to me. He wrote that he had been unfaithful to me from the beginning of our marriage, and he told me I was free to get a divorce. However, I only got a legal separation. Deep down, I still felt there must be something wrong with me that had caused him to be unfaithful.

My dad kept a tiny, old trailer close to the Abilene Christian University campus for students to use for living quarters. Fortunately, at the time, the trailer was unoccupied. Camille and I moved in after the house sold. Though the trailer was a godsend, during that time, I lost touch with the God who had sent it. I felt He had abandoned me. I had a sick child, a husband who had disappeared, and no money. I continued to be absolutely terrified that I would take Camille to the hospital and they would refuse to treat her because I had not paid my bill. So, most months I tried to pay our medical bills before I purchased food.

In the midst of that darkness, I came across some books that helped me to begin to make sense of the mess in my life. That search soon led me back to the Word of God. I began to pray, asking God why he had forgotten me. As an answer, God sent me one of the greatest gifts of my life. One night after putting Camille in bed, I sat in that little trailer house asking God to show me that He loved me. In my mind, I heard these words: *Go call Laura.*

Laura was a former college friend of mine whom I had seen at church the previous Sunday with her handsome husband and three precious children. I remember thinking how lovely it was that she had such a stable family and such a nice spouse to help her. I argued with the voice in my head, saying, "It's past 10 PM already, it's too late to call." But, the voice would not stop. When it got past 11 PM, I rationalized, "I cannot call Laura this late, for sure. Besides, I do not have her phone number." Suddenly, I remembered the Old Testament story of Samuel and how God spoke to him in his sleep. So, I gathered my courage and called my sister-in-law, who I knew would have Laura's number. I wrote down the number and went to bed. After that, the voice became a tremendous pounding in my mind to the point that I simply had to call. As I dialed her number, I waited with my anxious apology ready and waiting to give. When I began to apologize for calling at midnight, Laura burst into tears and sobbed into the phone. She told me that her husband had left her and their children, and since 10 PM she had been clutching a butcher knife, ready to slit her wrists and kill herself. She said, "I have been praying since then that someone would help me and give me a reason to live."

There was no denying that God had answered both Laura's prayer and my own. He showed me that he loved me more than I could ever imagine by trusting me with another person's life. Yet, I almost had not listened. As the days ahead got worse, I often looked back on the night when I heard the voice of God, and that memory reassured me that he would see me through. Even though my faith wavered and needed to be bolstered in the years ahead, I never again doubted that our God is real, or that He is able to deliver those who are his own.

After being missing for over a year, my husband resurfaced and wanted to reunite. I was not surprised at his sudden reappearance; I never thought he was truly gone. I wrestled with anger and frustration. I had finally reached a place of peace and order in my life, and here was my missing husband: back out of nowhere and wanting to come home. I had no feelings of forgiveness toward him, but I trusted that God would once more provide what I needed for the situation. I came across a story of a woman whose husband was unfaithful, and she shared words of wisdom that had come to her from a counselor: *I will to will the will of God.* Those words struck home with me and started me on the path toward forgiveness. I wanted the will of God above all else in my life.

Like Gideon in the Bible, I asked God for multiple signs, telling myself I would only reconcile with my husband if they came to pass. One "fleece" I laid before God was that we would be able to move out of our tiny trailer house into a home where we could start fresh as a family, and He provided that for us. I waited until my husband had a stable job, and had gone back to school to finish his studies. I did not tell my husband the changes I was waiting to see in him; those "fleeces" were between me and God. When I saw those things occur, I felt at peace to begin our reconciliation. Against all odds, I still loved my husband, and it was hard for my heart to accept the truth I knew in my head.

After that, we moved to Dallas, and I had hopeful expectations that the best was yet to come. The reign of terror came into full control of our lives, however, when my husband became a witness to an interstate crime that involved the Mafia. Camille and I were put into witness protection with only enough advance notice to pack one suitcase. Our beautiful home was confiscated due to unpaid back taxes, and we were on the run, being moved from place to place for our protection. I was numb. Yet, I felt a deep sense of peace and total trust in the protection of God. I remember thinking that if the secret service had not been able to prevent President Kennedy from being assassinated, there was really no way they could protect us. Our only hope was to rely on God, and I clung to that knowledge.

That year was filled with events more horrible than I could comprehend. I was called by the FBI soon after the protection program began. "Your husband has been beaten," they said, "and is in a hospital in Oklahoma." I was flown to see him. Seeing him beaten beyond recognition filled my heart and life with even more fear. I could only imagine what might happen if the same people who had done this were to find Camille or me. A few weeks later, my mother-in-law was murdered and my father-in-law was shot twice. I had come to love my mother-in-law so much, and her loss was devastating. She had been one of my best friends during the early years of my marriage to her son. She understood my concerns and was willing to listen and love me without defending him. I attended her funeral with an FBI agent by my side. My father-in-law was later accused and convicted of her murder, and he was sent to prison for life. The jury believed that he had lost his mind because he had lost all his money by investing it with his son. To this day, I do not know if he did it, or if the Mafia killed her. The timing of it all was very suspicious. As I wrestled with my grief over my mother-in-law, at times I wished my husband was dead. I did not want to kill him, but I just wanted him to not be able to use, manipulate, and hurt any more people. I wondered to myself, "Why does he keep living when his wonderful mother is dead?" I was so confused and hurt.

My only option was to fall back on what I had been taught as a child. The only thing that is absolutely trustworthy is the Lord and His Word. At night when I was alone in the dark, I would whisper Psalm 23 to myself. I clung to the stories and encouragement of scripture. I found courage knowing that "God hath not given us a spirit of fear; but of power, and of love, and of a sound mind" 2 Timothy 1:7 KJV

Finally, my husband gave his testimony in court, and the pressure lifted. Apparently, a hit is lifted when a person is no longer in danger of giving information concerning those who committed the crime. The Lord put peace and forgiveness into my heart, enabling me to let go of my hurt and anger when we reunited as a family. We settled back in Abilene, and I enrolled in graduate school. I sold real estate on the side to supplement our income while I was in school. My husband became involved in construction, but was unable to make the money that he desired. However, he still tried to live the life of a man with money. He continued to have numerous affairs, and was even reported in the newspaper as having witnessed a robbery while he was in a hotel with his "secretary."

We moved to Houston, and once again, I was the one providing for our family. As my teaching career was progressing, my husband's health was regressing. He was deteriorating emotionally, spiritually, mentally, and physically. Unknown to me, he was an alcoholic and drank vodka all day, every day. Again, looking back, it is shocking how much a person can hide even when you live with them. Perhaps my heart did not want to know what my eyes could not miss.

As a result of his lifestyle choices and the traumatic circumstances with his family, my husband ended up in the hospital with some very serious surgeries. He spent almost a year in the hospital in intensive care. I was an assistant principal in my school district at this time. Every morning, I got up at 4 AM to go check on my husband in the hospital. I was back home by 6 AM to get Camille and myself ready for school. Soon after my husband was released, he had a heart attack and had to undergo a quadruple bypass surgery. Once more, the terror of unpaid bills, my husband's unemployment, and the struggles of daily life threatened to overwhelm me. I got a second job on the weekends selling women's shoes to help pay rent and buy our essentials.

Before: Bold Spirit

One Sunday afternoon, I cast myself down on the floor of our den in deepest despair and prayer. I called my dad and told him that I did not think I could keep going. He said, "You know, Sissy, I've been worrying about that." He told me that he had talked about it with his best friends just that morning. I hung up the phone, embarrassed and frustrated that my mental health was the current topic discussed by my dad's friends. I got on my knees and said, "God, I will make it. You've shown me I could make it this far. I will make it; with your help, I'll make it." As a result of that prayer, I began to feel the strength and power of God entering my body in a fuller way.

A few months later, we had to move again because our leased house had become too expensive for us to afford. We were barely settled into our new house when a police officer came to my door with a notice that my husband had been apprehended and taken to the city jail. I drove downtown to the jail and asked what the charges were against my husband. I was told that he had several unpaid traffic tickets that gave them the right to pick him up, but that he was suspected of heading a white collar crime ring involving lots of "money deals" in the area. I told the district attorney that if he was guilty, they could keep him. I strongly suspected that he was, but I doubted that he would ever be convicted. I had always believed in him and tried to trust in him, but I was at the end of my rope. I did not believe that he would ever change. The bail for his release was several thousand dollars that I did not have. I asked the district attorney to allow me to see him, promising I would not get the bail money from my father if I thought my husband was guilty.

When they brought my husband out to me, all I could see was the devastation of a life that could have been great, the destruction of our marriage, and the living death of a father to a child. I saw twenty years of misery, courage, and failure all mixed together. I realized the only things I had to show for twenty years of hell on earth were our beautiful daughter and what God had made of me using

His potter's hands. This would have to be enough—and it was. All that my husband wanted from me was a cigarette and for me to get him out of jail. This really was the end.

When I returned home from the jail that night, fourteen-year-old Camille asked me, "Mom, why don't we get a divorce?" Hearing that wisdom from my own child moved me to action. I called my older brother and asked for the name of his friend who was an attorney. He called his friend, and the divorce proceedings were started immediately. The next day, I discovered that my husband had somehow managed to get into my bank account that I kept separate from him and that all my money was gone. Checks used to pay our essential bills like rent, water, and electricity were bouncing, so I had to borrow money from my parents. I felt like the storm was finally over, but I knew that the consequences would continue beyond the storm. My parents had to help me pay off my personal debts, and I had to file bankruptcy to cover debts that my husband had accrued without my knowledge. I watched the effects of these events on my daughter as she grew up. She is strong and successful, but I can still see the scars of the pain that she endured all those years.

I had a friend tell me one time that I should have given up on my husband the moment I found signs of infidelity in the first week of our marriage. I wondered to myself if that friend might not have been one of the ones who would have condemned me if I had given up so soon. Anyone looking at our lives from the outside could easily say that I was foolish to have endured so much for so long, to have undergone so much upheaval. In some respects, that may be true. However, I see that God was working on my heart and molding me into the person He wanted me to be. I became a better person through those twenty years; I became a person who knew I had to depend on God rather than myself. When I finally left my husband, I knew beyond a shadow of a doubt that there was nothing else I could do. With God's help, I had done everything I could to encourage my husband to change. My husband chose never to make that change.

After: Living in Victory

At that point in my life, it dawned on me that many of the things I feared the most had happened to me. I was broke, broken, divorced, and devastated. But with God's help, I had survived. In my early adult life, I feared having a husband who was unfaithful, being embarrassed and written about in the news, being without enough money to pay medical bills, and having a husband who committed a crime and went to jail. I ended up living all these things. I experienced the fears that all single moms do. I was afraid of not being able to fill the roles of both parents, I was afraid of not being able to make ends meet financially, and I was afraid of being alone. I did not want to be single; I loved being married. The greatest gift on earth is being married to the right person, yet the greatest sorrow is being married to the wrong person. There are worse things than being alone.

From the ashes of my life, the Lord began to rebuild. There were many things for which I could give thanks. I had a beautiful, intelligent daughter. I knew, if she was all I had, that the pain had been worth it. There were other good things, too. God had molded me and made me into a new person who was learning to depend not on her own abilities, but on what He could do and had already done. He walked beside me as I walked through the valley of the shadow of death, and led me into green pastures and quiet waters. Through God, I went from living in fear to living in victory.

I was single for a year before I met Frank. He was the 39-year-old bachelor who taught the singles class at our church. He had spent most of his life focusing on his career and simply had not met the right woman yet. After I met him, I still had doubts—you cannot live through the hell I experienced for twenty years and not have doubts about getting into another relationship. Yet, his commitment to his word stood in stark contrast to the deceit to which I was accustomed; his word was his bond. He shared all the same values and character of my family, and he quickly became an important part of it. Frank built his own relationship with Camille and loved her as his own. She loved him in return and asked him to adopt her after we were married.

Our life together has been one of joy, which is the way a marriage should be. We have dealt with our fair share of hardship, yet through it all, there was always joy. Frank is such a faithful servant of the Lord and loves me in such a beautiful way. He also is a wonderful father and now grandfather to Camille and our grandchildren. Coming from twenty years of deceit and terror, I found in Frank rest, trust, and security. I look at my life, and I see "before" and "after," I see despair and joy, I see emptiness and abundance. But through it all, I see the unending faithfulness of God. He is my story of redemption, hope, and restoration.

Frank and Sara

Sara's daughter Camille and her family

About Sara Eggleston

Sara is a native Texan who has moved from the country to the big city. She graduated from Munday High School and from Abilene Christian University with a bachelor's and master's degrees in education and administration.

Sara lives in Houston, TX with her husband, Dr. Frank Eggleston. Sara and Dr. Eggleston are National Marketing Directors and speakers for The Juice Plus+ Company. They have one daughter, Camille, who is an attorney and law professor at Texas A & M University. She lives with her husband and three children in College Station, TX.

Sara taught in Abilene, TX, for 10 years before moving to the Houston area where she was a principal for 20 additional years in two different schools in the Katy Independent School District. She has received numerous awards for excellence at the regional, state and national level. Sara was presented the Alumnus of the Year award in Education from her alma mater, Abilene Christian University in 1995. During Sara's distinguished career in education, she taught teachers, administrators, and businesses.

Sara has also been a life-long learner of God's Word. She has taught Bible classes and conducted Biblical retreats her entire adult life.

Sara has a book, On Eagles' Wings, that was published in late February, 2011. The theme of Sara's life is to give and serve others. Both she and her husband want to pass that love of service on to others by modeling it themselves. Her book can be purchased on Amazon.

Arlita Winston

I met Arlita at a leadership retreat in 2010. I was instantly drawn to her beauty and also how Christ seemed to just exude from her presence. We got to know each other even better as we became involved with the non-profit Pure Hope Foundation. Arlita is a gifted story teller. I found myself often riveted by memories of her life she would share. She also is one of my spiritual mentors who I long to learn from and model. Her knowledge of scripture and love for Jesus Christ is inspiring. I remember a time I was wrestling with a decision and shared it with Arlita. I had an executive coach tell me that if I could get more comfortable in my own skin perhaps my business would grow. I shared this with Arlita and in her gently – yet firm – voice she said, "Kathy, I believe that perhaps you should consider becoming more comfortable in His skin, and all the other things will come to you." That one statement was so wise, so focused, and blessed me richly. This is just one example of so, so many of how Arlita's love and wisdom have made a difference in my life. She and her husband Joe are so precious to me. I pray that you will be touched in a profound way by her story.

Bound Together

Arlita Winston

The rugged scenery of the Northeast Coast excites me. Its beauty envelops me as I drive. I am on my way to see my lifelong friend, Elisabeth Elliot. She has always been "Betty" to me. Our time together is so precious. We are continually amazed at the riches our friendship has brought. Just thinking about how we met as young mothers makes me smile. She was ten years older than I. We had an instant bond, like two magnets snapping and connecting. We had each other in gales of laughter talking about similar school experiences and sharing other life stories. Yes, we were deeply drawn to one another. I have often wondered why. Perhaps one reason was because we both had experiences working in a foreign mission field. We both knew we were willing to give up our lives and sacrifice everything while serving God, but there was more. Memories and stories told to me come flooding back as I drive.

In the beginning of 1939, I was just a baby. My family moved to the Dutch colony of Sumatra in Indonesia to begin missionary work. We docked in Tokyo, took a train to Kobe, Japan, and waited for a steamship to Sumatra. On the train, there were German soldiers in full uniform, coming to train the Japanese army. A foreboding of war settled in my family's hearts, yet they had peace about the work they were about to begin in Sumatra. The next year, my parents continued to hear rumblings of attacks in many of the European countries. They experienced great sorrow and concern as they thought of dear missionary friends in Europe. Were they dead or alive? Perhaps Japan would invade Sumatra and our family would be sent to internment camps.

Then came the fateful day: December 7, 1941. Our family had a short wave radio that received news from San Francisco. On this particular day the announcer's voice was crisp and urgent. The family gathered around the radio. "The Japanese have attacked and bombed Pearl Harbor..." We also heard that the Japanese paratroopers had landed on our island, Sumatra, to the north of us. The refineries of Standard Oil and Shell Oil were ablaze. The government had taken all the Dutch men into the army to fight against the Japanese. Our family was in grave danger if we remained where we were.

News of the invasion and warning from the Dutch officials filled the following days. Spies were already imbedded in the town and would know if we tried to hide in the jungles. The invading army was steaming down the Malaysian Archipelago, and we were destined to be either killed or interned in concentration camps. The head of our mission, Dr. R. A. Jaffray, sent a message to the missionaries in the island, "Get on your knees and ask God whether you should stay or go. Then, no matter what happens, you will know He will be with you." Mother said, "Absolutely we are staying! We will not leave our sheep!" My father and Uncle Hubert said, "You go to bed, and we will decide!" Oh, that was so like Mother! I could just imagine her eyes flashing. And I could also picture my dear Daddy and Uncle quietly taking the reins and making the final decision. You see, not long before this, my Auntie had died in childbirth leaving my mother with six children under the age of nine to "mother." Our two little families were like one now in the jungles. As they were praying, a knock came on the door. A small group of Kubus stood there with eyes large with alarm. "You must go! Please, you must. We can retreat into our jungles, but you must leave!"

Daddy awakened Mother. "I'll help you get the children ready. Pack only what we can carry." We travelled five hundred miles from Jambi in Sumatra to the island of Java, where the ambassador helped our family. He advised us to take a train to Surabaya and look for a ship there. To leave from Java was too dangerous because there were enemy submarines in the sea. Upon arriving in Surabaya, we discovered there was a ship, the U.S.S. *President Madison*, in the dock. It had sailed from the Philippines when Pearl Harbor was bombed and was refueling.

We had no money, but through the graciousness of the Embassy and the US Consulate, the shipping company guaranteed our fare. We cabled home that we were evacuating and requesting funds. Special contributions were collected in the U.S. to cover the $3,000 that was needed to pay for our journey. Boarding the ship on December 28, 1941, we pulled out during the night to avoid being attacked. This was the last passenger ship to pull out of the harbor. We learned that three of the ships that left just before us had been sunk. Within hours, all remaining foreigners were rounded up and interned in Japanese concentration camps.

In the early morning dawn, families stood together on deck with our life preservers. We would wear these all day long, every day. Staring at the ship's wake, we saw that it did not form a straight "V" shape outlined with waves. Daddy checked his watch. Three minutes in one direction, and then the ship shifted its course. It zigzagged in another direction for three or four minutes. This, too, would be the daily regulation. Sometimes it plowed through the seas going north, but then it would go south, east, or west. How would the captain and the officers find their way through a pathless sea?

Hours became weeks. Mother settled into a daily schoolroom routine with us, teaching us every day. Nevertheless, we remained on alert always as submarine alarms went off frequently.

Cape Town was a very brief stop. No one was allowed on shore. The ship refueled, renewed supplies, and took on more food for the long trip ahead. We were also assured this time that we would be part of a convoy. We could see it forming in the harbor. However, for some inexplicable reason, the *President Madison* was not ready to leave when the convoy left. Everyone felt such disappointment as we watched those ships gather and sail out together. Later, we learned that submarines had attacked and sunk the entire convoy.

After that, we were in the Atlantic Ocean and faced a new enemy. Instead of fearing attack from the Japanese, we feared the Germans. Day after day, we zigged and we zagged, 4 degrees one way, 3 degrees another, coming finally into Port of Spain, Trinidad, at the northeast corner of South America. Once on shore, there would be a short respite from the tensions. This was a British city with traffic, people, and parks—order, beauty, and peace of civilization.

Leaving the Port of Spain, and going through the Caribbean, more wreckage of torpedoed ships floated on the water. Sirens continued to wail day and night. The passengers raced to the lifeboats, interrupting "normal" activities. By then, we had been on board the ship three months. We sandwiched the frightening times with school classes, shuffleboard, table tennis, and visiting with the other passengers. Finally, the last night before we came in New York, we heard that two ships had been sunk very near where we were. The *President Madison* neared the New York harbor but stayed out in the ocean that last night. We were told we would land in the morning. As the sun began to rise, the *President Madison* slowly and silently passed the Statue of Liberty. No one cheered. No one laughed. No one wept. All were numb.

Newspaper headlines in New York announced, "Ghost Ship Arrives!" No one knew we were still afloat. It was March 28, 1942 when the family walked off the gangplank. We had made it back to America. Money was wired to us and over the next weeks we made it to California, where my parents continued in ministry. We had experienced first-hand what it meant to rely totally on the Lord for everything, even our very lives. Yet, it would not be the last time.

Our family went back overseas in 1948 to do mission work in China. As we were arriving, many missionaries were fleeing because of the unrest the country was experiencing. Chairman Mao was moving his troops closer to the Chinese capital. Newspapers screamed of war. The "bamboo curtain" was beginning to fall. Driven by a Divine urgency, Daddy preached the good news to thousands before it was too late. One of his means was through a radio station that reached deep into China. In May of 1949, we watched Shanghai fall to the Communists. For weeks, I had "lived" in the role of Queen Esther. A group of missionary children had been putting on plays for the community. Our parents felt this would help us to keep our minds focused on God and His character. My sister had become weary of my role playing, and accused me of acting like a "princess." "No," I would answer. "I am a Queen!"

I have such vivid memories of one particular night. I was ten. It was the night the communists entered our part of the city. Our windows were heavily draped to prevent light getting out as a target for bombs. That evening I knelt on the floor next to the great big radio, listening to reports on where the Communist army was and where they were headed. "Daddy, they are just four miles out of the city now." We had just finished supper and knew we would probably die that night. Daddy gathered us all together – I will never forget—I can see that room to this day: my mother great with her sixth child sitting next to a coffee table with a magazine featuring Princess Elizabeth. She was holding Prince Charles on her lap, his white, embroidered christening dress flowing over her royal blue gown. I thought to myself, "Why, I am a princess...a daughter of THE King, and I might be seeing my King tonight!"

Daddy gathered us all into the living room. We sang, had our regular prayers, and read Scripture. Then he wanted each of us to pray. All I could think of were Queen Esther's words when her nation faced annihilation, "We have come for such a time as this. If we perish, we perish for thee, Lord, for we have come for such a time as this." Surely my sister would laugh now, when I prayed Esther's words, but they filled my heart and my mind. After our devotional, we were tucked into bed and fell fast asleep. The next morning devastation surrounded us. In some areas of the city horses were sawn in two and stacked like sand bags. Dead bodies were everywhere. Soldiers, some as young as early teenagers, filed out of the apartments where they had been hiding, and a white flag fluttered from the windows. Shells had hit everything around us, yet our home had not been hit. We knew God had spared our lives. Very soon after that, they moved us into a compound where we lived under "city arrest."

One year later, we were allowed to evacuate, this time to Japan. It was the early spring of 1950. We were shipped out on an LST, a large, barge-type naval landing craft used to transport men, weapons, and supplies straight to shore. In our case, it had been used to transport cattle, and straw and dung were still on board. We chugged along until we got into international waters. Around 4 o'clock in the morning, we sighted the U.S.S. *President Gordon* with the enormous American flag painted on the bow. It felt like all of America had come out to rescue us! Our small LST bobbed about on that big, dark ocean, but the lights from the steamship lit up the sky. A cook with a high, white hat stuck his head out of a porthole shouting, "We have hot cocoa for your kids!" There were so many decks on that grand ship; it had to have been at least 50 feet above us. Once our LST was securely tied to the main ship, a rope ladder was then lowered for us. We grabbed the ropes, one in each hand, and placed our feet on "steps" holding the ropes together. With the turbulent sea, we climbed careening this way and that while being cheered from the top decks. I kept my eyes fixed steadily on my sister's feet above me. Daddy carried wee baby John. Mother came behind him with 2-year-old Paul. Andrea took 6-year-old Hubert's hand, and I held tightly to 4-year-old Stanley. Thinking about how we climbed the unsteady rope ladder helping the young children makes me reel—I know now there were angels surrounding us! As we landed on the deck, the captain and the first mate met us. They looked at our family, and in astonishment said, "Haven't we seen you before?" Here was the very same captain and first mate who had rescued us from Sumatra! Later, when they dropped us off in Japan, the captain said, "Well, I hope we don't have to rescue you from this country also!"

Years later, my mother asked me, "Arlita, do you know what held us steady the night the Communists came in and Shanghai fell?" I said, "No, what would that be?" She said, "It was your prayer. 'If we perish, we perish for thee, Lord, for we have come for such a time as this.'" That story and those words have been such a deep part of me. It reminds me of how God uses children, how he grips the hearts of young people and gives them purpose. My siblings and I were an important part of Mother and Daddy's work.

But now I see the sign "Strawberry Cove." I am near Betty's house. I pull out of my reverie. We have shared many decades of friendship and memory-making together. My mind shifts from my childhood memories to the stories she has shared with me over the years of her experiences as a missionary.

I knew about Betty long before I ever met her. She was ten years older than I, and a beloved alumna of the same school I attended -- Hampden DuBose Academy. As students, we knew first hand of her mission work as a single woman, and then heard of her work with her husband, Jim Elliot, and their baby, Valerie. Betty and Jim were both alumni of Wheaton College in Illinois where they fell in love. One of my favorite stories of the two of them is the night they sat together in the moonlight in a quiet cemetery talking of their love for one another. As the moon climbed the sky, it slowly threw the shadow of a cross dividing right between them, as if to display the central importance of Christ in their relationship. They would be single for five more years before they were married and traveled to do mission work together. In January of 1956, my senior year, in an assembly we were alerted to pray fervently for the Elliots. Jim and four other men were missing. Their small plane had gone down. I stayed up all night with some of the faculty and Mrs. DuBose, praying, waiting for word about the five men. Little did I know; I would someday marry into a family who was like kinfolk to the family for whom I prayed. A few days later we were told of the tragedy. Jim Elliott had been speared to death by the very Indians they were trying to reach. The following year, October 1957, we were astonished to hear that Elisabeth and her toddler daughter were going to live with the Indians who had killed her husband to share Christ with them.

Then I actually met Betty herself. It was only a few years later. Strangely enough we were friends instantly, and before long we became "soul-mates." Some saw Elisabeth as being stern, unapproachable, and even perfect. I knew a different Elisabeth. For more than fifty years, she became my closest friend. She had been held up as a model for me by Mrs. DuBose, and I wanted to become that, but knew it impossible. Together, we discovered how the God we both believed in was truly personal and wanted us to know Him. We had separate paths, to be sure, but we walked together in a deep friendship, corresponding, telephoning, sharing our hearts, and talking about God.

One day, she told me her side of the story which had been written up in *Life Magazine*. Photos taken by Cornell Capa were splashed over the many pages for the world to see. We talked over the kitchen sink as we washed and dried dishes together.

She began by telling me that, during her time as a missionary in Central America, one thing after another seemed to go wrong. Before she married Jim, Betty was a missionary who lived with the Colorado Indians in Central America. Diligently and painstakingly, she tried to understand their language. She ended up developing an alphabet that could be used to translate the Bible into their language. After almost a year of this work, she moved to Ecuador to marry Jim and join in his work with the Auca Indians. About a month after her move, she was taking a trip in the mountains. Her work was carefully protected in a suitcase and tied down—along with squawking caged chickens, baskets holding vegetables and fruit, and a variety of tied bundles—with ropes on top of a bus. The road was narrow. The terrain was steep. The bus careened around a corner. Suddenly the ropes broke. Chickens, fruit, vegetables, and her suitcases tumbled down the mountain sides—all of her work, the precious papers and documents of the Colorado Indian alphabet, nothing could be recovered. Gone.

Another day, she heard gun shots. She ran out to see an Indian painted in red war paint. Her translator lay dead on the road at her feet, his brains spilling out on the ground. There, lying in front of her were the words that she needed!

Then she talked to me of her grief and loss when her husband was killed. As she stood at the kitchen sink drying the dishes that I was washing, she began reliving that time.

"It was Monday January 9, 1956, which began as a fairly normal day in the routine of our work. Jim and some of the other men had flown deeper into the jungles to try and make contact with the Auca Indians, as they had done before. It was common for the men to be gone for a few days at a time. I received a call letting me know that the men, who normally checked in, had not been heard from since the previous day at noon. A search party was formed to go look for them.

"That was the first moment I knew that anything was amiss. A verse God had impressed on my mind when I first arrived in Ecuador came back to me suddenly and sharply: *"When thou passest through the waters, I will be with thee, and through the rivers, they shall not overflow thee..."* Isaiah 43:2 KJV. I went upstairs to continue teaching my

Indian girls literacy class, praying silently, "Lord, let not the waters overflow.

"A couple of hours later, they relayed to me that the plane had been sighted from the air. All the fabric on the wings had been stripped off, and there was no sign of the men. Right away, the authorities were notified of the five missing men and a ground search began. All the wives and the children gathered together in one location waiting for news. On Wednesday, we received the first reports that they had found a body. Then, another. Once again, God, who had promised grace to help in time of need, was true to His word. None of us wives knew who these bodies might prove to be, but we did know "in Whom we had believed." His grace was sufficient.

"As we waited on more news, children played, babies were fed and bathed, the members of the Rescue Service came and went, and one of the wives maintained contact on the short wave. Meals were somehow cooked and served, visitors greeted and informed us of the latest word, and prayer went up to God continually. "

The blow was crushing to her. All you have to do is look at some of the *Life Magazine* pictures as she is listening to the news coming in on that radio to see that. She recalled those moments for me that day in the kitchen as the two of us were alone, and our hearts were bound together as I lived it with her.

Most people don't know that she felt like a total failure. What was missing? "Arlita, I was lying in a hammock in the jungles, turning these events over in my mind. 'God!' I cried. 'You've allowed all of it to be destroyed! I've given you my life. Three years...gone! Why am I even here in the jungles?! '" She had been reading Isaiah 43 , and came to verse 10. *"You are my witnesses,' says the Lord, 'and my servant whom I have chosen **that you may know and believe me and understand that I am He.**'"* "Arlita," she told me, "I need to know His character and His ways, so that I am not shaken." Those words were a turning point that changed her forever. She would never need to ask "God, why?" For He was "Lord.

Betty talked of going back into the jungles, to the very people who had killed Jim, and how Valerie was part of her and part of Jim. She knew that she would take Valerie to go back in and finish the work Jim had started. It reminded me of what Paul says to Archippus in Colossians 4, *"finish the work that God has given you to do."* That is how Betty saw it. It is also epitomized in one of her favorite poems drawn from a sermon by Ugo Bassi. (Someone took his sermon and made it into poetry.) It was one of Betty's treasured possessions. She gave me a very old, marked up copy. One of the stanzas is:

"Measure thy life by loss not by gain,

Not by the wine drunk but by the wine poured forth.

For love's strength standeth in love's sacrifice;

And whoso suffereth most hath most to give."

She learned to know His character! And those words summed up her perspective. They had a resounding echo in my own heart. That day in the kitchen, as Betty quoted the poem to me, I knew it was the way she lived, and certainly the way I wanted to live!

Betty was a complex person. Despite the depth of grief, she experienced in that time, she also experienced a level of joy and exuberance that few understand. A rather officious woman once demanded from Elisabeth Elliot, "Who IS the REAL Elisabeth Elliot?!" to which she replied, "May God protect me from ever knowing!"

When she went back into the jungles, she went with focus and with purpose. With her face set like a flint, she took little Valerie to complete the mission for which Jim had given his life. In her mind, what did it matter if she was killed? So was her beloved Jim. The most important thing was that those people needed to know God loves them. So, the sacrifice of her life certainly was nothing greater than what Jim had given, and it most certainly was nothing greater than what Jesus had given in order that we might know. She did not count her life for anything. At the same time, she lived exuberantly and passionately. She could throw her head back and laugh a deep, resonant laugh. Quick to see the humor in so many things, she would sparkle as she communicated with her eyes to those close to her.

One night Valerie, age three, was squatting beside the fire and asked if one of the tribesmen was her daddy. "No," her mama replied, "these are the men who killed him." "Oh," said little Valerie. That was all. In those six words Betty, so direct and true, began teaching her child forgiveness. I watched her live forgiveness to the end of her days. Her biggest wonder of all was God. And her most favorite book in all the world was the Bible. She loved words, but in the Bible's Words she found power that changed her life. She learned the power of forgiveness.

Betty had a brilliant mind. She was a superb debater in college. She was a fine linguist, a writer, a musician, and a lover of knowledge. She was well equipped to be a missionary, to do something big for God! But was that enough?

Some years later, after we first connected, I was able to walk through an exciting time with her when she fell in love with Addison. She was so startled that anyone would look at her and notice her, which I found amusing because I always thought she was beautiful. When she fell in love with Addison (Ad), my husband, Joe, and I saw her eyes take on new sparkle. I watched years of stress, strain, and loneliness disappear. Here she was in her 40's, and he was 64, yet Betty and Ad were love birds. To our delight, they spent one of their honeymoon days with us in our home. She moved to the North Shore of Boston when they married, and of course we visited them many times.

The few years Betty had with Ad were magical. Then the awful news came of his cancer; those were heavy days. She kept him right at home, nursing him and caring for him to the very end. The days and nights were long. One story she loved to tell me was about a time she was up in the middle of the night, mopping up vomit with her hair damp and straggling. The room was filled with the stench, and as she was mopping it up, she felt like she was an old hag. Ad looked up from the bed and said, drawing out every syllable, "You...are...simply...glorious." His words touched her to the core. She described this incident numerous times with such wonder. Betty thought Ad was what Jim Elliot would have been like if he had lived to be that age.

Ad and Betty had opened their home to boarders who were going to a seminary nearby. Two students lived with them, Lars Gren and Walt Shepard. Interestingly enough, those two later became very important in her life: one, her third husband, and the other, her son-in-law. Both were helpful in the last days of Ad's struggle with cancer. Ad passed away before they celebrated their 5th anniversary.

After Ad died, Betty was content to stay single the rest of her life. Yet, both God and Lars had other plans. Not too long after Ad died, Betty's daughter, Valerie, married Walt Shepard. Betty did the arranging for the wedding alone, feeling the anguish without Ad by her side. Valerie wore Ad's mother's Edwardian wedding gown. The day of the wedding, it was a beautiful scene to watch Lars step in to support Betty in overseeing the reception. It was clear to me that he was in love with her, but Betty seemed not to notice. If she did, she certainly kept it to herself. Lars stayed right by her side taking care of so many things the father of the bride would have done. Everything went smoothly so Betty would not have to worry. To me, that event was such a lovely picture of how deeply Lars cared for Betty. He was watching over her and caring for her. Lars gently and persistently pursued Betty's heart as she grieved and healed. Over time, he wooed her and won her with his love and care. They moved to "Strawberry Cove" by the sea, and were married for 38 years.

Betty and I were both captivated by the sea! There is a large picture window in their living room looking out over the ocean. Above the picture window is a wooden plaque that says in old English lettering, *"The sea is His, and He made it" Psalm 95:5 KJV.* He made it, He owns it, and He rules it! We often talked about God's strange ways, and how inscrutable they are. *"His way is in the sea, and his path in the great waters, and His footsteps are not known,"* the Psalmist says. *(Psalm 77:19)*

One tranquil day at the end of the summer, she and I went swimming off those giant rocks. We chose a wide, flat rock, and grabbing onto the thick ropes of seaweed, we slipped easily into the sea. Gorgeous! Invigorating, like a sea of icy ginger-ale!

Buoyed up by those great waters, I began singing a line from a hymn above the noise of waves, *"Oh, the deep, deep love of Jesus, vast, unmeasured, boundless, free!"* She sang back exuberantly, *"Rolling as a mighty ocean in its fullness over me."* I picked up the next line, *"Underneath me, all around me, is the current of Thy love,"* and she finished the first verse with *"Leading onward, leading homeward, to my glorious rest above!"*

The waves began kicking up. She knew the signs better than I and motioned me back to the flat rock. With great difficulty, she hoisted herself up with the ropes of seaweed. It was my turn now. Wham! A wave slapped me off course and then another one. The rock was really far from me now. For the first time that day, I was scared. She was scared. And then I felt the thrill of the ocean's power lifting me up with a great swell toward the great rock. I grabbed for the seaweed. The swell cast me right up onto the rock! Shaking, we scrambled back up towards the house. Climbing the hill, we told our husbands only how exhilarating it had been!

One night, very late, she telephoned me. She had a front row seat by her picture window overlooking the ocean and "The Perfect Storm" of 1991. Her description is engraved on my memory. "Waves, terrifying! Like great stallions, fiercely pounding up the rocks to the highest cliff, their white manes thrashing wildly in the wind!" She was in awe of the raw terror and violence of the waves, and exulting in God's beauty at the same time. Those waves trampled down mansions that night. Somehow her "Strawberry Cove" was spared. We talked about *"His ways in the seas...His paths...God's ways!"* (Psalm 77:19). The oceans—changeable, ungovernable, vast, unfathomable, terrible, overwhelming—and yet our God has the ruling power. In the very next verse, the Psalmist describes God as a Shepherd leading his flock: "Thou leadest thy people like a flock by the hand of Moses and Aaron" (Psalm 77:20 KJV). Sheep like still waters, not troubled oceans, and the Great Shepherd cares for his sheep.

What kind of God do we love? A passionate, jealous God, with a fierce love that can sweep us into His safe arms. Betty couldn't be moved by the terror of night because she knew a fiercer love, a more passionate lover, God Himself who would move all of heaven and earth to woo and to win. She could rest in His love...underneath her, all around her, in the current of His love! There is a small, 2-letter word: "So." We take little thought of it. "For God sooooooooooo loved the world, that He gave..." passionately, fiercely, so that the earth shook!

Lars loved, supported, and encouraged Betty. I remember one time, Betty and I were praying about some problems Lars was having with his eyes. Betty was not moved to tears easily, yet this day as we spoke, she wept and wept. She asked me, "How in the world will I continue my ministry without Lars?" Lars stood in the gap and helped Betty in immeasurable ways with her ministry. It was common for them to travel to a different location each week across the country and sometimes in different parts of the world. Lars organized all the engagements, travel, locations, and details. He coordinated all the arrangements for publishing her books and selling them at events. Their relationship was one of deep dependence on each other. Betty's ministry would not have been possible without the devotion of Lars.

I pull up to Strawberry Cove and park along the curved lane. Lars immediately welcomes me, and leads me into the room where she is sitting, watching out their big windows overlooking the ocean. "Hi, Betty," I say softly, kneeling down close to her.

The dementia came on gradually. She was frustrated when she couldn't "find the operative word!" Growing up, Betty was never at a loss for words! Then a line from a familiar poem would disappear. She couldn't remember a familiar friend's name. Then came the day when she was given a diagnosis by her doctor. That was the day she and Lars were coming to see us, but first she had an appointment with her doctor before they left Boston. They went straight from the doctor to the airport to catch their plane. When they arrived at our home, Betty grabbed my arm, "Arlita, I must talk to you alone." Lars and Joe were still unloading the luggage from the car, so we went upstairs to my bedroom. Those following minutes are deeply ingrained in my memory. Taking a deep breath, she told me, "I have just been diagnosed with New-onset Dementia and Alzheimer's." I felt my heart break for my best friend. There was nothing for us to do but hold one another and weep.

The news weighed heavily on our hearts. Joe and I were the only ones, other than Lars, who knew at that point. Betty's diagnosis was not public knowledge for quite some time. To walk with Betty through this disease over the years was a difficult, and trying journey, but one I would never give up. We walked through endless valleys and climbed impossible mountains through the years of her dementia. For years after her diagnosis, Betty remained quite capable. However, as time passed, I remember going to a number of conferences with Betty. Sitting on the front row I would fill in the gaps when she would forget. Frantically she would look down at me for the "operative word" or the missing phrase from a hymn or poem. I watched her feel lost and confused, and I treasured the privilege of being with her to reassure her.

Betty's dementia brought us even closer together, in another dimension, than we had been before. I went to visit her frequently, and she would come to stay with me. We spent countless hours going through her journals and sharing our hearts with each other. I gradually saw her mind slipping away. She was the first to recognize it; she would tell me of bewildering things that puzzled her. She had walked off the stage in the middle of a speech before she had finished, and didn't understand why Lars was upset and insisted she return to the podium. She was sensitive to God's leadings, so it discouraged her when she could not remember. A part of her was dying. She knew it and could do nothing about it. She was puzzled and perplexed, yet she also accepted it with grace. Her acceptance and my acceptance helped to forge an even deeper friendship for us. We could look in each other's eyes and know what the other was thinking.

We got to a time where Betty could no longer string words into a sentence. She would look earnestly into my eyes and know that somehow I understood her as she babbled. I understood her heart. I would respond, helplessly asking God to show me how. She would laugh or scowl at the appropriate times in our conversations. Then came the times when she did not understand at all. How I longed to talk with my dearest friend like we did in our younger days. I would instinctively pick up the phone to call her, and then remember she would not be able to talk. I grieved for my friend. I grieved for the loss of what had been. Yet, I loved and cherished her for the time we had left.

Every time I visited her, knowing her mind had not been with us for quite some time, I had a particular request for God. Would He give me a "window of grace" where I could communicate with her? If it was just a few minutes, or if it was an hour, I prayed I could connect with her and that we could understand each other. During my visits, there were plenty of times I knew she was not with me. Yet, every single time I was with her, it was not long after I arrived before I knew she recognized me. He gave us that small window of time where we would connect.

God answered my heart cry, and I knew intuitively I had gotten through to her, and she to me.

Physically, she remained rather strong! She could pull my arm with a strong grip and lead me to the door. She wanted to walk! "Outside!" she would point. One time I couldn't get her to come back home so we simply sat on the side of the road in the dirt. Eventually, maybe half an hour later, she let me help her to her feet and we walked home. The most important message I wanted to get through to her was that I loved her, everything was going to be all right, and that God was good. I promised her we would take care of her Valerie and her grandchildren, all was well and she could rest in that knowledge. I also regaled her with funny stories and things we had shared through the years. She may not have understood those stories, but it did my heart good to relive them. Yet again, I was so grateful for our times of connection; they brought peace to my heart. How I knew when she was aware of me, I am not really sure, but the rest of her family would tell me she had not been like that since the last time I visited.

Betty is gone now; she finally went to be with the Lord after 10 years of battling Dementia and Alzheimer's. We had wept together when she first told me about her diagnosis. However, we both had a deep understanding that God was working his purposes out. As we had so many times before in our lives, we found encouragement from the words of St. Julian of Norwich: *"All is well, and all is well, and all manner of things shall be well."* Deeply embedded in my heart is that God overcomes evil with good. The primary prayer in my heart when Betty told me the news was, "God, will this give You glory? Will this give You pleasure?" Yes, we all prayed for her healing. We also had times when we prayed for the Lord to take her; it was just too much for her to bear, for Lars to bear, for us to bear. Yet, the Lord did not choose to take her right away. In my heart, I said, "All right, Lord. There must be something else very important to You going on here. What is it?" Whether I prayed to God about healing her or taking her, there was only one thing left to realize; God had a greater purpose in mind and it would bring greater glory to him. So in my heart I said, "Yes, Lord." Betty also prayed, "Yes, Lord."

Amy Carmichael wrote, "In acceptance lieth peace," and those words remain engraved on my heart. God is good. We may not understand his plans, but God's purposes are going to be fulfilled. In that understanding, my heart comes to rest. Am I in anguish? Yes. Do I grieve? Yes. Yet I never felt compelled to ask, "Why, God?" Instead, I asked, "God, what can I learn from this? What can Lars and Betty learn from this? What can I learn about You in this situation?" I experienced similar thoughts when my mother was dying and I was nursing her. I carry with me a deep, underlying belief that God is always good, and He knows what He is doing. He had purposes to fulfill! What remains for me is to learn how I fit into that plan. How do I make things joyful and pleasant for my dear loved one going through this trial? How do I grasp the hand of my Lord so that what I am doing is as if my Lord is doing it? And of course, God is really the one doing everything, isn't He?

I think about the sea and what it meant to Betty, and then I remember how God used the sea in my own family's life. We escaped death and crossed through treacherous waters safely only by the grace of the Lord. The sea is unchangeable, ungovernable, unfathomable, terrible, and overwhelming, yet the Lord has a ruling power over it. In the same way, he rules over our lives even when we are overwhelmed by the waves that toss us to and fro. God was faithful to Betty when her linguistic work was stolen from her and gone forever. He walked her through losing not one, but two husbands. The way God leads his children through the stormy seas of life to peaceful waters brings me to tears.

Frequently, Betty and I spoke about God's strange ways. We searched out the character of the Lord. I miss my best friend every day. I miss watching her trust God with complete abandon, following in obedience wherever He led her. But when she died, she handed the baton to us, cheering us with that deep warm laughter: "Learn to know Him. Trust Him. Now obey Him!" We can choose to run our race wherever He calls us—through jungles or across stormy seas, sometimes in spectacular ways, and sometimes rather ordinary. She would want to remind us, especially when we have forgotten, that we are loved with an everlasting love, and "underneath are His everlasting arms."

I spoke at Betty's Memorial Service. I wish I had remembered the poem that we both had loved so much written by Amy Carmichael. I think I would have simply stood up and quoted it, and then sat down. The words described my best friend.

Fire Words, by Amy Carmichael

"Oh God, my words are cold:

The frosted frond of fern or feathery palm
Wrought on the whitened pane –
They are as near to fire as these my words;
Oh, that they were as flames!"
   Thus did I cry.

And thus God answered me:

"Thou shalt have words, but at this cost:
That thou must first be burnt –
Burnt by red embers from a secret fire,
Scorched by fierce heats and withering winds that
   sweep
Through all thy being carrying thee afar
From old delights. Doth not the ardent fire
Consume the mountain's heart before the flow
Of fervent lava? Wouldst thou easefully,
As from cool, pleasant fountains, flow in fire?
Say, can thy heart endure, or can thy hands be strong
In the day that I shall deal with thee?

"For first the iron must enter thine own soul,
And wound and brand it, scarring awful lines
Indelibly upon it; and a hand
Resistless in a tender terribleness,
Must thoroughly purge it, fashioning its pain
To power that leaps in fire,
Not otherwise, and by no lighter touch,
Are fire-words wrought."

Editor's note:

Arlita found the following poem by Archibald Marshall, tucked among Elisabeth's things. She said it was well-worn and seemed to be well-loved. We do not know at what point in her life Elisabeth came across this poem; it could have been after Jim was killed, or it could have been later in her ministry. What we do know is that the words of this poem spoke to Elisabeth's heart and later to Arlita's. Our hope is that they will speak to your heart as well.

All that We Loved in Him is Living Yet

All that we loved in Him this shall remain – smoothed from each wrinkle cleansed of each stain

All of the earthliness now fined away

All the heavenly purged from the clay

From the frail mold of this mortal set free

All that we loved in him ever to be

All that we loved in him all this shall last—though from our dull earthly sense he has passed

Years had been added more peace to his face—strength serenity grace unto grace

Though from our dull earthly sight he is gone—all that we loved in him this will live on

All that we loved shall live

Only the best

He has but laid down his weapons to rest

He has put off the armor of strife—faithful to death God hath crowned him with life

Purified glorified – fit to the sky – all that we loved in him never can die."

About Arlita Winston

Arlita grew up in a missionary family living in Sumatra, China, and Japan. She came back to America for her formal education and married a medical doctor who is also the son of missionaries to Belgium. In 1965, Arlita and Joe sailed with their children to Hong Kong to help set up a mission hospital for refugees pouring into Hong Kong out of China.

Now after 58 years of marriage, 5 grown children, 28 grandchildren, and 9 great-grandchildren, she finds she is living in a world no more secure than when she was growing up. She is convinced of God's love and His ability to take the worst and turn it for good and His purposes if we will cooperate with Him. Giving other women this hope has been one of the reasons for teaching Bible studies and speaking in Women's Conferences and Retreats.

Arlita lives in Moorestown, New Jersey where Joe has recently retired from 54 years of Family Medicine. She has been a frequent guest on Elisabeth Elliot's nationally syndicated radio program, "Gateway to Joy." She has also done six thirty-minute television programs on women as Mothers, Wives, and in Society for 3ABN. She is a National Marketing Director with The Juice Plus+ Company.

Note from Kathy Crockett regarding Arlita's chapter

The story of Arlita's father's life is chronicled in great detail in her book *Heart-Cry*. Much of the content in this chapter related to her family's work in Sumatra and escape from the Japanese in December 1941, as well as them being in Shanghai when the Bamboo Curtain fell, was taken from her book. I highly recommend you read her book as we were only able to share a sliver of the wonderful story. You can purchase the book at Amazon or on Arlita's website www.arlitawinston.com

Specific contents related to the details of the days after Jim Elliot's death and Elisabeth waiting to find out the news were a mixture of memories Arlita had of stories Elisabeth shared with her and also the books written by Elisabeth Elliot, *Through the Gates of Splendor* and *The Savage My Kinsman*. We were only able to include a tiny amount of the richness of the story. You will want to read even more. Books by Elisabeth Eliot can be found on Amazon or www.elisabethelliot.org. *The Savage My Kinsman* not only shares about Jim's tragic death yet also includes details on how Elisabeth decided to go and share Christ with the very people who killed her husband, taking along her 18-month old daughter Valerie with her! Numerous pictures are also included in this book to give you an even clearer picture of Elisabeth's love for these people and her Lord and Savior.

Lindsey Holt

I have had the privilege of watching Lindsey Holt grow up. I remember being in a Bible study with her mom during a time when her sister, Lauren, struggled with her health in high school. Her dad taught our Bible class at church for a while. This family is dear to me. Lindsey was an English major at Lubbock Christian University who offered to help edit the first *Courageous Women of Faith* book. Her talent for taking raw, voluminous, transcribed material and weaving it into an inviting, accessible story is distinctly special. She is not afraid to go into dark places with authors who have stories with pain, suffering, and heartache. She takes those hard stories and draws out the hope the authors have in Jesus Christ. Without Lindsey, there is a very good chance a second *Courageous Women of Faith* book would never have been published. I was able to lean on her heavily with editing responsibilities which allowed me to work with authors in getting details of their stories and bringing the book to the marketplace. I could not be more proud of Lindsey for her hard work on our books – but more importantly for her courage to share her story that evolved after the publishing of our first book. She now has an even deeper connection to our authors. She is quite a remarkable young lady.

I Will Still Love You

Lindsey Holt

I grew up in a home that was in many ways very normal, but in many ways very special. I have two wonderful, loving parents who taught me from birth about the Lord and demonstrated his love to me daily. My mother is gentle, compassionate, and creative. My father is full of faith, wit, and wisdom. I have an older sister, Lauren, who loved me fiercely, fought with me and for me, played pretend with me for countless hours, shared her paper dolls with me when forced, let me tag along with her and her friends, paved the way for me in everything, and taught me everything I needed to know about whatever the next step might be in my life.

When I started the seventh grade, my sister was a sophomore in high school. A few weeks into the school year, Lauren became very sick and could not get well. The days turned to weeks and the weeks turned to months. My parents searched tirelessly for answers. The doctors could not figure out what was wrong. When their solutions did not help her, several even went so far as to suggest that Lauren was making it up or exaggerating her symptoms for attention. Meanwhile, my parents and I witnessed Lauren growing weaker daily. As a twelve-year-old, I watched in horror as my big, good, strong, brave, capable sister wasted away in front of my eyes. She constantly dealt with excruciating pain, could not keep food down, and became so weak she could hardly walk.

Finally, after a year and a half of searching, my family found answers at the Mayo Clinic in Minnesota. Lauren was diagnosed with Adolescent Autonomic Dysfunction, a chronic illness. She bravely faced her life ahead with the news that, while she could not be cured, she could be treated to get her symptoms to a manageable level and hopefully live a somewhat normal life.

Over the next several years, I watched Lauren courageously battle through each day, determined to live and to live well. Don't get me wrong—she had her moments. We all did. There were times of tears, of crying out in frustration and desperation. Yet, in the moments where the pain was great and the discouragement was greater, I watched my family members consciously choose to cling to God. One time in a dark and weary moment, Lauren said, "I'm just stubborn enough to not let go of God!"

How profoundly incredible, right? I'm telling you, I have special people.

Like anyone's story, the years that followed in my life were filled with seasons of sorrow and seasons of joy. Each of these moments deserves an entire chapter of their own, but I need to briefly mention them because they shaped and molded me into who I am today.

When I was a sophomore in high school, my mom's sister unexpectedly passed away from a stroke. Our families were close, and we still grieve and miss Denise to this day. I know my pain was nothing compared to that of my mother grieving the loss of her sister or my cousins grieving the loss of their mother, but it was my first, real encounter with grief. I vividly remember after receiving the news that she was gone, my bewildered, aching, fifteen-year-old heart whispering, "I still love you, God." I anchored myself in those words in the season of sorrow that followed Denise's loss.

My senior year of high school, a season of joy arrived when I fell head over heels for a boy in my youth group. Heath was handsome and quiet and funny, and I went around with my head in the clouds and a goofy grin on my face for weeks after he told me he liked me. I had no idea I had just started dating the young man who would later become my husband. Heath was so intentional with how he treated me and others that I could not believe I was the one lucky enough to get to date him.

Getting to leave high school behind and embrace college was so exciting for me, but then again, I would say leaving high school is probably a relief for most people. I threw myself into all sorts of activities and programs at Lubbock Christian University and was happily wrapping up my first semester of college when a season of sorrow struck me again. On November 4, 2011, my best friend and mentor from youth group, Anabel, was killed in a bus accident. I was devastated. Anabel had faithfully walked with me through more than one season of sorrow in my life, and she was the kind of friend who filled my life with joy, laughter, and Christ. Anabel was an adventurer, and with her, I felt braver and fuller of life than ever before. With her sudden loss, that fullness was snatched away, and I was shaken to my core. I was with Heath's family when we heard about the accident, and I clearly remember Heath holding me up and supporting me when my knees buckled at the news. In those immediate moments of heartbreak, I recalled my silent prayer years before when we lost Denise. It was a little harder to say this time because my heart still bore the scars from its last season of sorrow, but silently, my heart called out to God, "I still love you."

With Anabel's loss, I felt a drive to carry on her legacy. I wanted to be with people who knew her, and I wanted to talk about her to people who did not know her. I wrote about Anabel and spoke publicly about her impact on my life as a way of keeping her with me. I wanted to love on people and change people's lives the way she had changed mine. Going back to school and participating in all of my activities was straining, and I often slipped away to go cry, but I continued to put one foot in front of the other. Eventually, although my heart never stopped missing her or feeling the weight of her loss, I looked up to see that time had somehow passed.

2013 and 2014 were whirlwind years with seasons full of joyful chaos. Heath was studying abroad in Spain in the fall of 2013, and although I was completely sappy and pathetic about how much I missed him, I was unbelievably busy helping Lauren plan her wedding. She met her husband, Trent, in the Praise Choir at LCU, and they started dating right around the same time Heath and I did. Because Lauren was a teacher, the best time for their wedding turned out to be during Christmas break. Heath came back from Spain just a few days before the wedding, and I spent the weekend of the wedding living somewhere in between so busy I could not even think straight and somehow frozen in time, removed from the scene to soak in the awe of such a holy moment surrounded by such wonderful people. Lauren was glowing and radiant at her wedding, as every bride should be, and Trent cried when she came down the aisle. During the ceremony, I kept sneaking glances at my favorite groomsman, Heath, thinking it would not be long before it was our turn. It was perfect in every way.

In the early spring of 2014, Heath and I got engaged. We had known for years that we wanted to get married, but we had decided to wait until we were close to done with school. Unfortunately for my poor, sweet parents, we decided on another December wedding. Bless their hearts. Exactly one year after Lauren and Trent, one day before their one-year anniversary, Heath and I got married on 12-13-14. It was a joyful and blessed day, and we were surrounded by all the people we loved most. The only bittersweet taste to our celebration was the people we were missing. Heath had family members who had passed away or were too sick to come. I missed Denise when I looked out at the faces of my family, and it was painfully obvious to me that Anabel was not standing up with me as one of my bridesmaids. Even in the midst of all the joy, those absences were not unnoticed. Yet, we found little ways to be sure they were all remembered and included in the celebration with us, and the day was as beautiful as we could have ever hoped.

Spring of 2015 absolutely flew by. We were newlyweds, rapidly approaching college graduation and the need for jobs. I also spent every day of that semester begging Heath for a puppy, so it might have actually dragged by slowly for him. Lauren and Trent had moved to Artesia, New Mexico just a few months before our wedding, but we would all get together for family dinners whenever they came into town. Finally, graduation, jobs, and a puppy arrived (in that order.) We took a family weekend getaway to the mountains in the summer, but that was the only family vacation we were able to take because of our work schedules.

By the time the fall of 2015 arrived, I was weary and in great need of rest. I was recovering from two solid years of wedding planning (one for Lauren, one for me,) and a whole slew of life changes that hit me all at once. As exciting as all of those changes were, I was more than ready to slow down and be refilled. As the holiday season approached, I eagerly anticipated the upcoming time with our newly-formed family of six.

Early November of that season marked the four-year anniversary of the accident that took Anabel's life. On the day of the anniversary, I went with Anabel's mom and another dear friend to visit the crash site of the accident for the first time. Never in a million years would I have dreamed I would have the courage to do that, but God had worked four years of peace and healing into my heart to prepare me for those holy, tear-filled moments. That day, as hard as it was, gave me good peace with which to enter the holiday season.

As we prepared for the holidays, my heart was joyful at the promise of being with my family. The week of Thanksgiving arrived, and I was shopping and baking and packing like crazy. We were headed down to the Houston area to meet with my dad's family at a ranch. Tuesday afternoon, I got off work, and Heath and I hit the road to go as far as Abilene for the night. We were set to stay the night at my mom's parents' house, where we would meet up with my parents and Lauren and Trent. We planned to carpool together for the rest of the drive on Wednesday. I packed music for the car, thinking about what my sister would enjoy hearing. We were all a blur of phone calls, texts, and plans. Heath and I left town before my parents or Lauren and Trent, so on our way, we pulled over and stopped at Heath's hunting lease. As we got out to walk around and check the feeders, I felt my heart fill with peace. It was completely dark, but the huge, West Texas sky was lit up by the moon and thousands of stars. It was stunning. I took a deep breath, and Heath and I paused for a moment to soak up the still beauty. I remember thinking it was the most peaceful I had felt in a very long time.

We got back in the car and I called my sister to tell her we were getting close to Abilene. We talked about which rooms we were going to sleep in for the night and how to get into my grandparents' house without waking everyone else up. We laughed and talked about how we were going to fit all of our luggage into one vehicle. Then we said we loved each other and said goodnight. Heath and I arrived in Abilene before anyone else and went straight to bed to prepare for our long day of driving the next day.

I woke up the next morning to the sound of someone knocking on our bedroom door. My first thought was that it was still late at night and somebody else had just arrived. Then, my head began to clear, and I heard my parents calling my name through the door. I got up, opened the door, and saw my parents with a look on their faces I had never seen before. I felt fear begin to stir in my stomach and rising up into my chest. "Is something wrong?" I asked, feeling I already knew the answer. But nothing—nothing—could have prepared me for the words that came next. "We got a call from a State Trooper. There has been an accident. Trent is in critical condition, but Lauren didn't make it."

Just like that, in a single moment, she was gone. We had no chance to say goodbye, no chance to prepare ourselves, no chance to even pray for a miracle or a different outcome. All I can remember is shock, confusion, disbelief, and a huge, gaping hole through my middle that I could physically feel. Someone, I honestly do not remember who, helped me walk down the hallway to the living room where we could all sit together. Words, information, and facts drifted into my ears about the accident from my parents, but they barely registered. I was keenly aware of my own beating heart when somewhere else on a highway in Texas there was a precious heart that ceased to beat. It was as if my heart pounded stronger with the loss, making me painfully aware that I must go on living despite what was suddenly missing in my life. With each second, my heart, soul, and very being simply pounded, "My sister. My sister. My sister."

Of course, in those first, raw moments, what immediately came to my mind were the promises I had made to God when we lost Denise and then when we lost Anabel. I knew Satan was waiting for me to respond, almost as if he was saying, "How about now? Do you still love Him?" I did not dwell on it for long, but I knew that moment was crucial. Through tears and a broken heart filled with hopelessness and despair, I made the conscious decision that I would not give Satan this victory over my heart. I felt anything but victorious in that moment, but I knew that God was. I silently cried out to God with all the determination I could muster, "I. Will. Still. Love. You."

I do not have a lot of visual memories for what happened next, but I have a lot of sounds I remember. I heard my grandparents weeping as my parents broke the news to them. I heard my dad in the next room, calling his siblings one by one (there are seven) to tell them what had happened and why we would no longer be joining them for Thanksgiving. I heard my mom on the phone with Trent's parents and friends back home, trying to sort through the stories to find out what had really happened and how Trent was doing. I heard phones ringing, feet shuffling around the house, voices in hushed tones, and the occasional quiet crying.

A few hours after we got the news, a small handful of my dearest friends in all the world called me one at a time and wept over the phone with me. A few hours more, and my phone began to go off with text after text after text. There were hundreds. I read them all-every single one of them-on our drive back home to Lubbock. It kept my own thoughts at bay.

Getting in the car to go back to Lubbock was heartbreaking. We should have loaded up in a car full of laughter and family to go celebrate a holiday of gratitude. Instead, we somberly loaded up to go home, quiet, lonely, and heartbroken. I hugged my parents tightly before getting in the car, the idea fresh on my mind that I could just as easily never see them again, just like I would never see Lauren again. I was terrified to be in the car. I was anxious. I was numb.

In the car ride on the way home, I wept for the first time. This was not the soft crying I did at my grandparents' house; this was gut-wrenching, heart-ripping, soul-searing wailing. Have you been there? That kind of weeping pulls the anguish from the very depths of your being and slowly, violently, painfully pours it out of you. Only when you finish, the anguish remains. And the deep weariness sets in. From the earliest moments of this tragedy, I remember feeling a bone-crushing weariness. I alternated between thinking, "It can't be true. There has to be some mistake..." and thinking, "This is the burden I will have to carry for the rest of my life. There is no relief anywhere in sight." The rest of my life had never seemed so hopelessly long, even in light of how fleeting life can truly be. It seemed my lot in life was to be the one left behind to grieve, hurt, and try to carry on.

We had to get back to Lubbock before the close of the business day so my parents could go to the morgue and sign to have Lauren's body moved to a funeral home. The next day was Thanksgiving, and we would not be able to do anything because of the holiday. Legally, those actions were Trent's right as Lauren's husband, but Trent was barely clinging to life, unconscious of what had happened, so the responsibility fell to my parents. Even amidst my own blinding grief, my heart was overwhelmed again and again with sorrow for Trent. The doctors were working frantically to save his life and piece his body back together, but if he managed to survive, he would wake up to a broken heart no surgery could ever repair. I could not bear the thought.

When we arrived back in Lubbock, my parents went to take care of business and then to the hospital to check on Trent. I simply went home. I was not ready to face people yet, and I was sure there would be plenty of them gathered at the hospital. I walked into our house and put away the groceries we had packed and prepared for Thanksgiving. Even that simple act was a painful reminder of how differently my day had turned out than how I had planned it. I sat on the bed in our bedroom with the lights out, staring into the quiet darkness, feeling small, alone, and scared. Heath came and sat with me for hours, just holding me in silence.

I cried some and spoke occasionally. When the horror of reality and my anguished thoughts would begin to crowd in on me, I felt like I would suffocate. The only way to keep true insanity at bay was to take deep breaths and pray this simple prayer again and again in my head: "Abba Father, have mercy on me." Slowly, as I breathed and prayed, I felt space begin to clear around my mind, protecting me and pushing back the mental attacks of Satan. Before we went to bed that night, I told Heath, "Tomorrow morning, I'm going to wake up, I'm going to remember everything that has happened all over again, and I'm going to start crying. I'm going to need you." His faithful, steadfast response to me was, "I'll be here."

Thursday morning, Thanksgiving Day, I woke up and immediately began to softly cry. All I had to do was speak Heath's name and he pulled me close, whispering, "I'm here." There are many horrific scenes I have burned into my memory from the days following the accident, but that beautiful memory of Heath being the physical hands and feet of God for me in that moment will always shine through the despair. After a while, when my crying continued, Heath broke all the rules we had ever established in our house and brought our dog, Darcy, to be in bed with me. My sweet, seventy-pound baby gently cuddled with me while I cried—again, a sweet moment in the midst of great sorrow.

We went over to my parents' house around lunch time. Sweet, precious people had sent us food for a Thanksgiving meal, but I could not eat anything. I was not able to eat for a week after Lauren died; every time I tried I felt sick. So, my parents, my husband, and I sat down on Thanksgiving Day to plan my sister's funeral. It seemed like a horrible nightmare that we were spending our holiday like that, and I just kept expecting to wake up from it all.

One of the worst things about losing a family member is the fact that the time when you have no desire to do anything is the time when there are a million and one things to do: the decisions, the expenses, the funeral plans, the burial arrangements, and the list goes on. My parents took care of everything with the funeral home and cemetery. I felt very helpless at times, but I tried to find things I could do to help. Six months after I graduated college with an English degree, I found myself putting it to use writing my sister's obituary. I sorted through a lifetime of pictures, my life and my family in pictures, to pull together a slideshow for Lauren. How do you even begin to simplify a loved one's life into a ten-minute slideshow? All of it—spending Thanksgiving planning a funeral, writing my twenty-six-year-old sister's obituary at the age of twenty-two—just seemed so horribly wrong. It felt so upside down and cruel that it could not possibly be really happening. And yet, it was.

My family agonized over every decision we made, not only for ourselves and our grief, but because Trent was unable to make these decisions for his own wife. He was still unconscious and unaware of what was happening. We wept at the knowledge that he would wake up and everything would be over and done. I stayed away from people other than my family as much as possible. If I was not helping my parents make arrangements at their house, I was at home sitting in silence and stillness. Only a tiny handful of my closest friends came to see me, but other than that, I was alone with Heath and Darcy. It was so strange to me, because with Anabel's loss, I craved company. With Lauren's loss, company was the last thing I wanted or needed. It was simply too much for me. It almost hurt twice as much because now I had lost a best friend AND a sister. I could not even bring myself to go up to the hospital to see Trent until Friday or Saturday because I knew I would have to face the public.

When I finally did go, Trent was completely unrecognizable. He was so swollen and bruised and stitched up, I never would have known it was him. Seeing him made my stomach drop, because it made me think "If Trent looks like this and he lived, how much worse must Lauren have been?" But those are the kind of questions that can torment you and bring harm, not healing, so I pushed it away. We had to be careful what we said in Trent's room, because he was still so close to the edge of death that if he heard something about Lauren, they said it could be harmful for him. All I could do was sit and hold his hand and tell him how glad we were that he was okay and that we were praying for him. I told him with silent tears streaming down my face how much we loved him and wanted him to get well. As I watched him cling to life, all I could think about was how fiercely Lauren loved him. If she could have asked me one thing, I think it would have been to love on Trent and take care of him.

Friday was filled with more funeral plans and arrangements. Different things were important to different ones of us. My mom wanted to see Lauren, but my dad did not. I was relieved when they felt differently because it allowed me to feel free to choose what was best for me. I wanted to remember Lauren full of life, so I chose not to see her body. It was important to my mom that we have a visitation, so even though I was trying my hardest to stay away from people, we scheduled one. It was important to me that we have Lauren's service after her burial. I wanted to end on a celebration of her life. The way we practiced giving and taking during those days of planning has served us well down the road of this grief journey. We each grieve so differently and need different things. It is so important to remain mindful of our differences and allow grace for each other. Some days you say, "This is what I need right now," and some days you say, "I may not need this, but you do."

On the evening of Black Friday, when the rest of America had spent the day shopping, I spent the evening shopping with my mom for clothes for my sister in her casket. I almost could not do it, but then I remembered that Lauren trusted my fashion advice above anyone else's, so I wanted to help pick one last outfit for her. We chose blue, Lauren's favorite color. She always joked that her whole wardrobe was blue, but blue brought out her beautiful, sparkling, smiling, blue eyes, so why would she need to wear anything else?

Saturday passed, and then Sunday. We were not ready to go to church on Sunday, but we worshipped and poured our hearts out at home as a family. Every spare minute was filled with pictures and phone calls and receiving visitors as they came to bring gifts and love on our family. The house filled with food and flowers and cards until we ran out of room to fit it all. And at the end of every day, I wearily escaped back to my own quiet oasis where I could regroup and try to shake through the numbness I felt.

Then came Monday: the first day for our family to be in public since the accident. Lauren's visitation was Monday evening, and as the time drew closer, my anxiety grew. I had stayed away from people on purpose. I was not strong enough to see people. I was feeling so incredibly private about my emotions, and I was about to be the focal point of an entire room of people. Heath and I sat in the car in front of the funeral home waiting for my parents to arrive, and as we sat, I watched the building begin to fill with people. I began to breathe hard, and I just said over and over again in a near panic, "I can't do this. I can't do this." But then the strangest thing happened, except it was not some strange coincidence, it was a miracle. When I got out of my car and walked into the building, I was filled, no, flooded, with the peace that passes understanding. I am telling you, I FELT it. I went from almost hyperventilating to calmly welcoming each person I talked to that evening.

And there were hundreds of them. I had talked to maybe a dozen people since the accident, and on that night, there were people lined out the door, around the parking lot, and out to the street waiting to see and love on my family. The funeral home said they had never had such a large crowd before. It was a completely humbling experience.

The peace that filled me on that Monday night carried me through the rest of the week. It carried me to Abilene and back on Tuesday as we laid Lauren's earthly body to rest in a cemetery that used to be the farmland my mom grew up on as a little girl. The peace carried me into the auditorium of our home church for Lauren's celebration of life service on Wednesday. On the arm of my husband, I walked down the center aisle of the same church that the year before I had walked down as a bride, and the year before that, as a bridesmaid for my sister. My family filled that church auditorium three holiday seasons in a row: twice for weddings and once for a funeral.

Then, as quickly as it had all begun, it was over. Except it was far from over. The whirlwind storm had passed, and we were left with a horrible, gaping hole. As terrible as all the funeral process was, the shocking emptiness when it ended was just as bad.

The days that followed are gray, cloudy, and numb in my memory. It was not long before I had to go back to work. Bills have to be paid, so as badly as I wished I could, quitting my job was not an option. For the first week back at work, I felt like every eye was on me. Everyone knew why I had been gone, and everyone was keenly aware that I was back. People were so precious to me. They hugged me and told me how much they loved me. I had gifts and cards waiting for me at my desk when I got back. Again, I felt the beautiful outpouring of the body of Christ. When my second week arrived, however, I experienced something very common in grief. Suddenly, the rest of the world was back to normal. People carried on and went about their business, yet my heart and my world remained frozen back on November 24th. I work at the best place with the absolute best people, and I could not be more thankful for them, but I felt removed from them. It was as if I went through my days in a different dimension from everyone else. I could see and hear them, but my mind and heart were far away. Work might have been a welcome distraction for some, yet it drained me to get up and go every day. None of it seemed to matter in light of what had just happened to my family.

I went to visit Trent in the hospital once or twice a week. Aside from his deep grief, his shattered body was working hard to heal. Every step of progress he made was astounding to me, and I watched him in awe every time I saw him do something new. I had seen him at death's door, and now I was witnessing him get out of bed without help and walk around a room. He and I were able to have some beautiful, holy conversations during his days in the hospital and then his days in the rehab facility. We both knew we would miss Lauren together in a way that no one else would understand. For Christmas, my parents, Heath, and I took presents and food up to the rehab facility to share with Trent. His family was sweet enough to let us have some time alone to both celebrate and mourn with him. Again, those were special, holy times. Trent's physical healing has been remarkable—after two months in the hospital and his rehab facility, Trent walked out on his own two legs. He works so incredibly hard, and he faces his days bravely despite his broken heart. Trent is very open to share his journey with anyone who wants to hear about it. I am so proud of his courage, and I love him fiercely.

As the weeks have turned into months, I have wrestled with so many aspects of this situation. I have asked "why" more times than I can count. Losing someone is always excruciatingly hard, there is just no way around it, but there were so many things that made Lauren's loss especially hard for me to wrap my mind around. First of all, Lauren and Trent were still newlyweds. The accident occurred just three weeks before their two-year anniversary. It felt cruel that they got so little time and unfair that they did not get to grow old together. Another struggle of mine was how it happened. We were thankful and relieved to find out that Lauren had been sleeping in the car and had simply woken up in Heaven, without being aware of any of the trauma of the accident. Still, after she courageously battled illness for so long, it seemed so shocking that Lauren lost her life to something as sudden and unexpected as a car accident. I have seasons of being plagued with "what ifs." What if they had left five minutes earlier or five minutes later? What if they had stopped for a bathroom break? What if they had come to Lubbock first instead of straight to Abilene? My whole family was driving on Texas highways after dark that night. Why were Lauren and Trent the only ones who did not make it safely to our destination?

I never would have verbalized it, but I think deep down, part of me thought that my family had already experienced our fair share of trials, so we would be exempt from any further attacks. I thought perhaps there was a line around our family, a line defining "this far, but no farther." With that imaginary line being broken, my heart was thrown into a state of deep fear. It does not control me like it did in the early days after the accident, but that fear is still something I wrestle with every day. If there is no "this far, but no farther" line, then how many more people could I lose? How many other devastating blows might Satan decide to deliver to my heart?

I also grieve for the future. I mourn the happy memories my family of six will no longer get to make. I miss the vacations and the holidays we will never have. I weep when I think that I will not get to call my sister someday to share the news with her when we decide to start a family, and I will never receive the same phone call from her. I get sad and wistful knowing that I will never have flesh and blood nephews or nieces who share my genetics. I hate that my children will not have cousins on my side of the family. Sometimes, I even worry so far into the future that I think about how I am now the only child my parents will have when they age and need help. Although my parents protected me from most of the responsibilities of Lauren's funeral process, I will now bear the full responsibility of theirs someday. Do you see how easily my thoughts spiral out of control and toward despair?

Sometimes the "whys," the "what ifs," the fears, the doubts, and Satan's lies become so loud that I have to cry out to the Lord to quiet the noise and rescue my overwhelmed soul. In those moments, the One who calms the greatest of storms stops everything and calms my heart. If I close my eyes and focus as hard as I can, I hear His still, small whisper in the form of promises I have heard and read my whole life: *never will I leave you, nor forsake you...do not fear...be strong and courageous...in this world you will have trials and tribulations, but take heart, I have overcome the world...* I cling to these promises fiercely as if I am drowning and they are the only things keeping my head above water. God has sustained me through every single "why" and "what if." I can tell you story after story of God's tender care and faithful provision for my family. I simply cannot fathom how anyone endures grief without a relationship with God, support from His church, and the hope of Heaven.

I now pass through life one day at a time, or on the rough days, one minute, second, or breath at a time. I am certainly no expert on grief, but I have experienced enough of it to know that it will never fully go away. Rather, God strengthens us over time to be able to carry the weight of grief without it overwhelming our lives. Grief does not lessen us, it makes us more. Intertwined into each beat of my heart are the whispers of the names I carry with me each day. Forgetting them would be like forgetting myself; their lives and their losses have shaped me and transformed me into the person I am today. As long as my heart continues to beat, I intend to carry their legacy and extend the influence of their love—the purest, most beautiful, earthly glimpse of God's love I have ever experienced.

I struggled about whether or not it was time for me to write this chapter yet. I do not have a pretty bow to put on top of this story and call it complete because my story is far from over. I am still extremely raw in my grief. But then, as I wrestled, a still, small voice in my head suggested that was the very reason I should share my story. It inspires and encourages me to read about people who endure a trial and, through the help of God, come out on the other side. But it gives me true courage to hear people choosing to proclaim the goodness of the Lord when the night is still dark and the heartbreak is still fresh. God is good when the miracles come and the answer is yes. But, more than anything, I desperately want you to know that God is also good when the miracles do not come and the answer is no.

I do not always feel hopeful. I rarely feel strong. To be honest, I often feel weary when I think about the days ahead of me. I do not understand, and I honestly do not think I ever will on this side of Heaven. But there is one thing I know beyond a shadow of a doubt to be true, no matter what I may feel. I believe wholeheartedly in the goodness and the faithfulness of God. That truth is the manna I depend upon for my daily survival. No more, no less, just one day at a time. My favorite verse, Hebrews 10:23, says, "Let us hold unswervingly to the hope which we profess, for He who promised is faithful." I want to be like Lauren—just stubborn enough to refuse to let go of God. I frequently have to repeat my declaration of "I will still love you" to remind myself of what I know is true when my heart begins to be crowded with fear. It takes a conscious decision to cling to that hope every day, no matter what I feel, but I do it because He who promised is faithful!

Afterword

I have had the honor of working with these *Courageous Women of Faith* books from the beginning of the project. With each story I edited, I marveled at the courage and the strength of these beautiful women, and I was humbled to take part in helping to tell their stories. I spent the summer of 2015 working on Arlita Winston's chapter and reading through some of Elisabeth Elliot's works. Arlita's words about her friendship with Elisabeth touched me deeply because they reminded me of my friendship with Anabel.

After Lauren's accident, I recalled a certain striking phrase from Elliot's *On Asking God Why*: "We flew back to the air base, and I remember asking myself what I suppose thousands who are newly bereaved must ask: How is it that the sun shines today? It is as bright and cheerful as it was last week, when they were all alive." These words verbalized so clearly the bewilderment of my grief, and they gave definition to the question my aching heart had been asking. As I turned that question over and over in my mind, I discovered a passage from Hosea which brought an answer to my heart. "Let us acknowledge the LORD; let us press on to acknowledge him. As surely as the sun rises, he will appear; he will come to us like the winter rains, like the spring rains that water the earth" Hosea 6:3. The faithfulness of God is as sure as the sunrise, never to be hindered or dimmed by the broken circumstances of this world.

To have the opportunity to tell my own story alongside these amazing women is the highest of honors. I have wept and prayed and poured over their chapters, and each one has left its mark on my heart. I think of all the courageous women of faith in my own life, how they have shaped me and mentored me, and I wish I could fill book after book with their stories. Every story deserves to be told, and there is something to be learned from every journey.

The sun continues to rise each day, giving light to both broken hearts and joyful hearts. Yet the faithfulness of God shines even brighter than the sun—bringing peace in the midst of turmoil, hope in the depths of despair, and healing to any level of brokenness. May reading these stories help you find language for the deep, wordless longings of your soul, may they give you the courage to face your own battles, and may you take heart knowing the victory is already won.

About Lindsey Holt

Lindsey Holt is a native of Lubbock, Texas. Her love of words started at a very early age reading *The Chronicles of Narnia* as bedtime stories with her family. She is married to her high school sweetheart, Heath. Their golden retriever, Darcy, assumes their whole world revolves around him, and he is probably not entirely wrong. Lindsey attended Lubbock Christian University and graduated with a Bachelor of Arts in English. She now works at LCU as the Director of Stewardship in University Advancement, and she also works as a freelance editor in her free time. In her other free time, Lindsey is in progress on a Master's in English from the University of Texas at Tyler. Any remaining free time is spent with her church small group, baking homemade bread, cuddling with Darcy and Heath (in that order), reading, and writing.

Lindsey's passion lies with those who grieve. She has felt the loneliness of loss, and wants nothing more than to let others know they are not alone. Whether writing, speaking, or going through daily life, it is her prayer that God will use her as a messenger of the Kingdom.

Lindsey's blog:

couragedearheartweb.wordpress.com

Lauren, Anabel, and Lindsey

Heath and Lindsey, Becky and David Roach (Lindsey's parents) and Lauren and Trent. This photo was taken the week before the accident in November.

Sarah Maddox

Over the years, Sarah and I were friends who were involved in similar things, had lots of friends in common, and would say hi as we were scurrying from place to place with kids. It was always fun to see her and watch their family love the Lord and enjoy life. It wasn't until I asked her to share her story in our book that our friendship deepened. Watching Sarah (and her family) walk through the very difficult path of her daughter experiencing a brain aneurysm was very hard—yet, at the same time inspiring. Their faith and ability to trust God had eternal ripple effects in thousands of lives around the world. As a mom with daughters, this story was especially close to my heart.

Malori   Senior Night

A Mother's Faithful Heart

Sarah Maddox

My husband, Marray and I have three wonderful children: Malori, Peyton, and Maci. In 2015, Malori was a senior on the volleyball team at Lubbock Christian University, Peyton was playing college baseball with Southwestern Oklahoma State University, and Maci was in the 8th grade. I am sure it comes as no surprise to you—we spend a lot of our time running around in opposite directions, making it to every event we possibly can for our three children. Tuesday, November 10, 2015 is the day that changed everything for our family.

Malori's Senior Night with the volleyball team had been less than a week before, and on November 10th, we were headed out of town on a week night to watch one of her games. Peyton was working out with his baseball team, so he was not coming with us. That morning, I called Marray and arranged for him to pick up Maci from school so we could leave town in time to get to the game in Wichita Falls. Our family loves all the girls on the volleyball team so much; they became like Malori's sisters, which made them family to us. So, we liked to get there to watch them warm up and say hi to everyone. Everything seemed normal watching Malori warm up before the game. We had no idea the road we were about to go down.

The game started out a little rocky. The lighting in the gym was dim and several girls had shanked some serves, so we were a couple points behind. Malori started the game and played her back row spots, and when she came back in to serve, she served just fine, so we had no idea anything was wrong. Then, after she served, she stared missing some plays she routinely makes. However, with the poor lighting and her teammates having missed a few things, we did not think anything of it. Yet, when she missed a simple overhead pass and completely missed the ball, we began to think something might be off. Malori went to stand by her teammate, Kyleigh, and told her, "I am starting to lose vision in my right eye." Malori was so focused on losing her vision that she was not paying attention to the throbbing pain on the left side of her head. Kyleigh walked her to sideline where the trainer and Coach Lawrence checked on her. Coach motioned me over to the bench, asking if Malori ever had migraines, and I said, "No, never." So she motioned for us to meet Malori and the athletic trainer in the locker room. Marray went right away, and Maci and I started gathering our things from the stands. I just had a bad feeling; I knew something was not right because of the way she was holding the left side of her head and how she walked out of the gym. From the look on her face, I could tell how excruciating her pain was.

We got into the locker room to find Marray saying, "We don't know if we should put her in a dark room with her feet propped up and see if it is just a bad migraine or get her to a doctor." I just saw Malori rocking back and forth on the couch just holding the left side of her head. Her face looked like she was in the worst pain she had ever experienced. I know God was moving in my heart because I said, "Marray I have never seen her in this much pain. She doesn't get migraines." I asked Rachel, the trainer, "Do you think we should take her to the ER? I have never seen her like this." Rachel had never seen anything like this either, and she agreed with me, saying, "Maybe so."

Malori had had several headaches over the past three years that would randomly come and go. We thought maybe her vision was changing with all studying she did. A few months earlier, she had told me "It just feels like something is growing in the front of my head," and I told her we might want to get her eyes checked. She was trying to see her optometrist, but with our busy lives, we had not worked in an appointment yet.

Standing in that locker room, watching my daughter rocking in pain, God just put that mommy instinct in me to say, "Marray, I think she is having an aneurysm. If you will run and get the car, we will bring her out." Maci's eyes were huge as she watched all of this take place. Carrying all our things, she and I ran back to get all of Mal's stuff from the bench. Rachel and I carried Malori out because she was already to the point where she was immobile from pain and loss of vision. She was starting to go unconscious. The assistant athletic director saw us struggling to carry Malori out as she was becoming deadweight. He stepped in and said, "Let me help y'all get her to the car." Then another one of Midwestern State University's coaches stepped in and said, "Don't go to the big hospital—United Regional—because an athlete had to wait over two hours there last week. Take her to Kell West Regional Hospital, the smaller hospital." Already, at the very beginning of this trial, God was intervening.

We got Malori in the car, and were told we would have a Midwestern policeman who was going to give us an escort to the hospital since we did not know where we were going. We got in our car (Marray was driving with Malori in the seat behind him, and Maci was sitting behind me) and followed our police escort. Keeping Malori in my sight the whole time, I sent brief texts to my family and Malori's boyfriend of four years, Tyler Rogers, to let them know what was happening. All I had time to say was, "Please get on your knees and say a quick prayer for Malori. She has had to leave the game about 20 minutes into it. We think it is something going on with her brain, we are just not sure yet. We are taking her to the ER right now."

As soon as I hit send, I saw Malori start vomiting in the back seat. I jumped back there and got underneath her where she was in my lap. I was supporting her head with my left hand, and I was scooping vomit out of her mouth with my right hand. Her eyes were rolling back into her head; she was unconscious. I was scooping out the vomit, knowing I could not let her aspirate. Vomit was everywhere—all over me and her. I started kicking the back of my husband's seat. I leaned up and said in his ear, "We have to go faster. The cop is not going fast enough." I could tell that Malori's condition was getting worse by the second. Marray could not really see what was going on in the back seat, and he was hesitant to leave our escort because it was dark and he was unsure how to get to the hospital, so we just continued to follow.

Maci was beside me the whole time with fear in her face. She said, "Mom, what is happening?" I said, "Honey, I am pretty sure it is something very serious going on with her brain. Just say a prayer." Malori's eyes were rolling and her head wobbled over onto Maci's shoulder. Maci lifted it back up to help me hold up her head. I remember having Malori's head and neck in my right hand and caressing her arm, saying, "Hold on baby, God's got you. We are almost there." Then, all of a sudden, her hands just stiffened and curled up around my hands. Her legs went straight out and became stiff. Her whole body was rigid. I just leaned up and told Marray, "You have got to go." I whispered because I had heard that people with brain trauma may be able to hear things. Even if they are unconscious, they can be aware of what you are saying. I leaned up in his ear and said, "I'm not sure she is still with us. Please go faster."

Unbeknownst to us, our police escort had a dear friend who worked in the ER, so he called ahead and asked her to meet us at the ER door with a wheelchair. This was yet another example of God's intervention. When we pulled up to the ER, they were there waiting for us, but Malori's body was so stiff we could not bend her body to get her into a wheelchair. Marray and the ER workers carried her in and laid her on the table. All I thought I heard was, "Bag her." I knew I had to leave that room. They started cutting off her jersey as I walked out. I did not want to leave, yet it was getting crowded and Malori needed immediate medical attention. I knew Maci was outside crying alone, so I went to find her and give our insurance information. Marray stayed with Malori. A sweet little lady who worked there pulled me aside, said the insurance could wait, and prayed with me and Maci.

Maci took over mine and Marray's phones. She called our son Peyton, who was shopping for groceries. He stopped everything, got in his truck, and headed to Wichita Falls. What is normally a three-hour drive, he made in a little over two hours. Then, Maci called Tyler so he would not just see my text after he got out of practice (Tyler played basketball at LCU) and not know what was going on. Tyler had planned to go to the game with us, but something had come up with basketball. Maci told him we had Malori at the ER, they were working on her, and we would keep him posted.

I started giving insurance information and Malori's medical background including her symptoms of the evening. It was not long before Dr. Kamath came out and said, "I have done a CT scan, and this is a terminal condition. She has a brain bleed. She's got an AVM (Arteriovenous Malformation) that has ruptured and her condition is worsening by the second." He told us, "I need to take her across town to United Regional, or my preference would be to fly her to Dallas to Zale Lipshy to have this type of high risk surgery done. But we don't even have fifteen minutes because she's got many signs of brain stem herniation, and we don't have much time once you are to that point. I will have to do surgery here. I cannot guarantee she will survive this surgery. I cannot guarantee that she won't be paralyzed, have brain damage, or many other complications. Brain infections are a high risk for this type of surgery at this facility. I cannot guarantee any of these things—but it is what I have to do to attempt to save her life." We consented and signed. I looked at him and remember saying, "Please do what you can to save our daughter. We will be praying for you and the whole medical team out here in the lobby and praying that God will save Malori."

The little, sweet lady who prayed for me earlier came up to me after our conversation with Dr. Kamath. She told me she cuts out the scripture from the newspaper every day, and she handed me the scripture she had for November 10th. The Bible verse of the day said, "Be still, and know that I am God; I will be exalted among the nations, I will be exalted in the earth" Psalm 46:10 NIV. I still have that newspaper clipping in my wallet; it is precious to me. I held that verse in my hand for a long time that night. Throughout the night, she continually came up to us checking on us, saying, "Don't you worry, don't you fear. God has got your baby. God knows what you are going through."

After they took Malori into surgery, the three of us huddled up in complete shock, not knowing if we would talk to Malori or see her alive again. We started praying. Later, we were told that as we were praying, a nurse sprinted behind us to run to the blood bank because, when they got Malori on the table for surgery, she had no blood pressure. They were not even sure if they would be able to do surgery because Malori had lost so much blood. They gave her 5 units of blood, got a blood pressure reading after transfusion, and started surgery. Malori's brain was swelling so much from the bleed that they had to do a craniotomy: they removed the left portion of her skull, sawed it in half, and put it in her lower left abdomen to keep it viable to reuse down the road if they were able to save her. It was an old military strategy I had never heard of until that point.

The medical team worked and worked on Malori. A nurse came out about every forty-five minutes to update us on Malori's condition. She would tell us, "She is holding her own." There were probably 200-300 little things God took care of to get Malori into and through that surgery. We arrived at the hospital around 6:45 in the evening, and by 7:00, they were talking to us about the results of the CT scan and what needed to be done. Malori did not actually go into surgery until 8:00 because she needed multiple units of blood first. Tina, the nurse who met us at the door of the ER, had called over to neuro to ask if there was any chance Dr. Kamath was still there. She told them there was an athlete coming in who might need neuro care. Now, Dr. Kamath was not normally at the hospital that time of night. He had actually made travel arrangements to be in India for his mother's hip surgery, but he had cancelled those plans at the last minute. We have no doubt that God intended him to be there for Malori.

During the hours we spent in the surgery waiting room, I remember weeping out loud for the first time in my life. I have cried during sermons or certain beautiful worship songs that move me; I have had silent tears roll down my face. Yet this was a different kind of crying; I had never just wept out loud as I did during the surgery and at times over the next week. I can still vividly hear that sound—the distinct sound of my cry being different than it had ever been before. I could not even control the volume of my weeping. I am not one to ever want any type of attention. In fact, my personality is to find a corner room or table at a restaurant, and this loud weeping was like an out-of-body experience. I cried and could not control it; my heart just had to let it come out. All I could think about was if God was making that same weeping sound when he watched his son die on the cross.

While Malori was in surgery, we got word to the volleyball team about the severity of her condition. They had won the first two sets and were in the third set out of five, and Coach Lawrence told me later that she remembered thinking "If we don't win this third set, we are going to forfeit and load up to go to the hospital anyway." They won the set, and she told the team, "No ice. Get your stuff and get on the bus. Malori had a brain bleed, and we are headed to the hospital." I am told it was a long bus ride across town; the girls were in shock and in silent prayer. Around 7:45, before the team arrived, the families of the LCU players started arriving. These were all people we are close to and had bonded with over the years. We saw countless people over those hours, days, and weeks, but those first people who showed up would not leave my side at the hospital. They were rubbing my back and praying with me every few minutes throughout the surgery. It was like we were surrounded by our large, extended family.

The outpouring was incredible. People in Lubbock spread the word. Friends of friends of friends all came to support us—people we did not even know. Many came from churches there in Wichita Falls who had heard from friends who went to church with us in Lubbock. Countless people asked if they could pray for us and with us. There seemed to always be groups of people huddled up in prayer. One man who worked as a nurse anesthesiologist heard about Malori through a church email and came to the hospital to offer his services through the surgery. Normally the doctor wants 10-15 people on his crew for this type of surgery, but Dr. Kamath had to start with only three people because time was so crucial in Malori's case.

Watching Malori's teammates walk into the hospital was heart wrenching. Seeing their tears, the fear on their faces, I could tell that they were scared for their teammate, who was more like a sister to them. These girls have a special bond. Not only do they spend all their time practicing and traveling together, they also have regular devotionals and pray together. The hurt in their eyes was not just for Malori, it was for us, her family, as well. They loved on us and prayed with us. As people continued to pour into the hospital for us, the volleyball coach from Midwestern and her entire team came in. They brought us gifts: coffee, toothbrushes, water, and snacks, but more than that, they also came to pray with us.

At one point, not too long into the surgery, the nurse brought me a gallon zip lock bag full of Malori's waist-long, blonde hair. She always wore it braided in a high ponytail for her games to keep it out of the way. I just—I don't know—I had a meltdown when I saw her hair. I knew in my mind that they were bringing me this hair in case we needed it for the funeral. Thankfully, Marray and others were with me.

About an hour later, a sweet little elderly woman came up to us in the lobby. Marray and Maci were with me and the other moms were around me, loving on me and rubbing my back. Coach Lawrence had not left my side since she got to the hospital; she had lost a child of her own and could understand the anguish my heart was feeling. In front of us all, this sweet lady walked up and said, "Where is the mom of the daughter who is fighting for her life in brain surgery right now?" I said, "I'm her mom." She came and put her arm around me, saying, "Honey, I've got a brand new super-giant print, beautiful, turquoise NIV version of the Bible in the back seat of my car. I am here with a friend, I've been here for a while, and God has just laid it on my heart that when I found somebody that needed this big print, beautiful Bible that I would give it to them and bless them with it. I'm gonna run to my car because I can see that you need it right now." I thought to myself, "How in the world could she happen to know about us from a regular room down the hall, and how could she know that I don't have my Bible with me?" But the answer was simple: God knew. I have the Bible on my phone, but it is just not the same as looking at it, turning the pages, and holding God's word in my lap. He just knew I would need an actual Bible. The amount of sleep I was going to lose over the next two weeks would end up making my eyes tired and strained. God knew I needed what was called "super-giant print" to be able to keep reading his promises.

I took my new Bible to the restroom to have a little time by myself in God's word. The verse that carried me through the surgery and has carried me in the weeks and months since then is Psalm 62:1-2 NIV: "Truly my soul finds rest in God; my salvation comes from him. Truly he is my rock and my salvation; he is my fortress, I will never be shaken." These verses brought me deep comfort even in the middle of having no idea of what was happening in the operating room, and they strengthened me to go back out and be back with all of my loved ones.

Shortly after reading that verse, I remember Peyton, walking in to the waiting room. I just jumped up out of my chair and ran to hug him. We held each other and cried for what seemed like ages. I knew that the drive for him to come to us was horrible. Peyton and Malori are only 21 months apart in age, and all three of our children have always been close to each other. My sister and brother had been calling Peyton along the way to check on him, but part of me had been subconsciously watching the doors just waiting for him to get there. Having Peyton arrive was such a comfort to me because all four of us were finally together. We would receive whatever news we were going to have to endure together as a family. At this point, we knew at least that Malori was still alive, but things were still so critical. My heart not only found comfort in my family being together, but also in being able to comfort Peyton and Maci. My mommy heart was just so broken and being with them just brought some kind of peace and comfort.

About an hour after Peyton arrived, I had to just sneak off away from the crowd in the waiting room. I walked out the front doors and sat on the curb in front of the hospital. I had only been there for about five minutes when I looked up to heaven and I asked God to please spare Malori's life. I told Him I knew he was capable of miracles; I just had never personally witnessed one with a family member. I begged God for the experience of witnessing His power. "God, I just want to be able to proclaim that I have seen the power of your miracles firsthand. I know I laid my twenty-year-old daughter onto the table stiff, unconscious, with no verbal response, and no movement response— basically dead. God, I just want to witness this, and I want to be able to proclaim your power and your glory forever. If it be your will, please let her make it through this surgery. I know the odds are against her, yet I know it doesn't matter what the odds are because you are able and you can do anything—all things are possible with you. I can survive this, God, because you said I can do all things through the help and strength of Jesus. So, if it is your time to take her, I know I can do it and I will survive it—but I don't want to, and I am begging you to do a miracle."

Right as I was finishing my prayer, my mom pulled up. She had driven alone because my dad is in a nursing home with the progression of his disease. She pulled up and came over to embrace me; it was just the two of us for a few minutes. I said, "Mom, they don't know if she is going to make it. They are not sure she will survive it." She said, "Sarah, it doesn't matter what they are saying. God can do anything." I said, "Yes, I know He can," and she told me, "You just blot it out of your mind that she is not going to make it. You just hold onto the knowledge that you have— that we all know God is capable of doing anything he wants to do." Right after that, Tyler (Malori's boyfriend) and his parents drove up. I just hugged him and his parents, and God gave me the strength to try to be a comfort to him in that moment. I told him, "Tyler, we just gotta pray. We just gotta pray for God to do a miracle." After that, Tyler and his parents went inside and started engaging in prayers with everyone else in the lobby. Then, my brother and sister pulled up, and I was able to fall in their arms. We were all in tears because we are a very close family. We love each other's children as our own. With the rest of my family finally with me, I went back into the lobby and stayed close to my husband, son, and daughter. Together, we continued to wait and pray. At one point, we received a report that they had made it through what they thought was one of the toughest parts of the surgery, but there were still no promises. "She is holding her own" was all we ever heard. After each shred of news, we would gather up and pray, and then Marray would give a report to everyone else in the lobby.

After 6 hours, Dr. Kamath came out at the end of Malori's surgery, he pulled our family aside to a room. He told us, "It took me a while. I worked for hours to stop the bleed in her brain. Finally, I tried one last technique to stop the bleed with a clotting device, and somehow this time it just worked. We closed her up. I've placed two pieces of her skull in her abdomen to preserve it in the hopes that she will be able to survive these next critical 72 hours. I hope she will be able to get flown to Dallas, survive these days in ICU, and go through rehab to the point where she will be able to have the AVM removed and her skull put back together." He explained to us that the next 72 hours were very critical as to whether she would survive or not. He reminded us again of the risk of brain infection. She could end up paralyzed and we had no idea what kind of brain damage she might have.

We told him we understood and were so grateful. We hugged him, thanked him, and let him know we would thank God for him daily for staying to help us after a long day of surgery and not giving up. He told us later that he looked at Maci and saw the fear in her face and eyes, and all he could see was his fourteen-year-old daughter who was Maci's age. He said Malori also reminded him of his daughter because her physique is small and she looks so young in the face, and he hoped someday that a medical team would do for his daughter what he was trying to do for Malori in not giving up to stop the bleeding. He said, "I am going to have to wheel her through the lobby for a final CT scan to make sure the bleed has stopped. There seems to be about 150 people in the lobby with you as your support group; I may have to maneuver some of them to make a little path as we wheel her through. After we do that, I am going to let her family come back here to the holding room and see her." I responded that it would be amazing if we could just see her. He told us the plan was to get her in a stable enough condition that we could put her on a medivac helicopter and fly her to Zale Lipshy University Hospital in Dallas. Dr. Kamath had already spoken to a neurosurgeon who is considered the best of the best and who had agreed to take her on as a patient.

When we went back to see Malori, it was difficult. One minute we were watching our twenty-year-old daughter serving a volleyball, jumping up and down, and encouraging her teammates; then, we were handing her over in the ER in her stiff, lifeless body; and now, we were seeing her unconscious in a hospital bed after surgery. She was completely bald on the left half of her head, she had tubes down her throat with wires and IVs everywhere, and there was a big, U-shaped incision that went from the top of the left side of her head, all the way to the back and up under her ear like a question mark. There were bandages over the staples and the incision, and she looked as white as liquid paper from all the blood loss and trauma. I just remember thinking, "This is just not happening. This is a horrible nightmare." I could not even believe it was real; I was in shock. All I could do was clean my hand with sanitizer and rub her arm just to feel that there was still warmth and life in her. And I could pray over her. We had a prayer of thanksgiving around her

201

bed—Marray, Peyton, Maci, my mom, my brother, my sister, Tyler, and Tyler's parents. (We knew Tyler and Malori meant to be married in the summer of 2016, so Tyler's family was pretty much already our family.) We all stood around Malori and said a prayer. We asked God to continue to take care of her, to carry her through the upcoming flight, and to help her survive the transport and the next 72 hours which would be so critical.

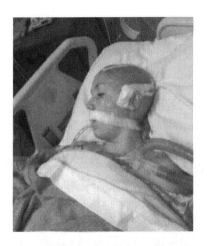

At that point, the respiratory therapist and nurse came in and said they had gotten it approved for one of us to fly with her to Dallas. I know how motion-sick I get on small planes and rides at amusement parks; I even get sick sitting in the back seat of a car. I did not want them to be tending to me throwing up on the plane. I wanted all the focus to be on my daughter. I asked Marray if he would fly with her and he said, "Absolutely, I will." We thanked everyone who was caring for her. Dr. Kamath never left after the surgery; he stayed in her room in case any complications came up. He knew that the chances of him having to take her right back into the OR during the couple of hours after surgery were pretty probable, so he stayed close. Thank God for Dr. Kamath and his selflessness throughout that whole night, not thinking of his need to rest, eat, sleep, or shower for his next full day. What a blessing! Truly, the whole medical team that stayed late and came back in and helped with the surgery was a miracle and a blessing.

At this point, it was around 2:30 in the morning, and we were blessed with the presence of my sister-in-law and dear friends, who had all arrived just before we had to start our drive. They had juggled so much with work and childcare arrangements just to come love on us and pray with us. We thanked all of our dear friends at the hospital and left to make the drive to Zale Lipshy. Yet again, God provided for us in the most unexpected of ways. A precious friend of ours had taken the time to clean up all the vomit in our car. There was no way we could have ridden in there with our empty, torn up stomachs, but this sweet angel had bagged up anything with vomit on it and had cleaned the floor mats, carpets, and seats to where we could not smell a thing. Different people volunteered to drive our various cars so we could be together without having to worry about driving. My sister is used to working nights as an RN, so she drove our Yukon with me, my mom, Maci, and Peyton. It was the most long, dreary, rainy drive I have ever experienced in my life. It was almost like a fog or a dream. We said chain prayers out loud, we cried, and we talked about all the wonderful things and wonderful miracles that had already happened and been put in place: all the wonderful people that he sent out—just vessels of comfort for us; all the prayer warriors that were with us praying—we learned of a gathering back home around the fountain at LCU; and the precious videos of prayers and singing from countless locations.

Malori arrived in her ICU bed in Zale Lipshy around 4:30 in the morning. Marray texted us that they had arrived and that Malori's vital signs were looking a little better. I could not believe it. I had been so frightened about her being transported, and to me it was a miracle that she had arrived safely and even a little stronger than before. We arrived in Dallas about an hour after Malori and Marray. Zale Lipshy has required valet parking, so we handed off our car and did not see it for many days, because we never left Malori's side. By mid-morning, our friends and family had once more taken over the hospital waiting room. The scene in that ICU lobby was unbelievable. We were camped out on mattresses, couches, and reclining chairs. There were food baskets, drinks, gift cards, and money everywhere from friends in Lubbock and people we did not even know in the Dallas area, who had heard about us. I have never witnessed such an outpouring of love.

For the first 72 hours, we all had to put on gowns and gloves before we went into Malori's room to protect her. The hospital staff conducted neuro checks every hour, and all of our family was in there every time, watching desperately for any sign of progress. We hardly slept; by the time each check was over, there was only about half an hour to briefly close our eyes before it was time for the next one. In these hourly neuro checks, they would pull Malori off her sedation and begin talking to her, asking her to open her eyes, squeeze their hands, or wiggle her toes. The first day there was no response during the neuro checks. The doctors were watching her intracranial pressure closely. They carefully monitored and controlled her blood pressure with medication and sedation. They also did a procedure where they drilled into the top of her head and placed a drain in to keep track of how much blood was coming off of her brain. We constantly watched her vital signs on the monitor. Malori started running a fever that lasted for several days. This was critical, because the fever could be a result of the trauma of brain surgery, but it could also be a sign of infection. We kept fans on her and put ice bags around her to try and get her fever down. Minute by minute, each hour slowly passed.

Early in the afternoon of the first day, we were meeting with our new neurosurgeon, Dr. Welch, when there was a knock on the door. Two nurses had come to tell me that Maci had passed out after walking into Malori's room and seeing her incision without the bandages for the first time. I walked out of the meeting room and saw Maci white as a ghost, sitting on the floor next to the door looking up at me. The nurses asked if I wanted them to take her to the ER so they could test her and treat her, but my mommy heart broke once more at the thought of having my other daughter in the ER while my twenty-year-old was fighting for her life. I reached down to hug and kiss Maci and check to see if she was okay. Her head did not feel warm, she just looked pale. I knew she had not had any food or sleep, so we decided to try having her eat a little something first before running any tests. I made sure Maci had people to be with her before returning to our consult with Dr. Welch. Dr. Welch explained to us what Malori's recovery journey would look like. We would be in the hospital for 4-6 weeks, and then 2-4 months down the road, we would have another surgery to remove the AVM. That was the first time we really realized this was going to be months and months of recovery and rehab.

On day two or three, Malori began responding to the neuro checks, but only with the left side of her body. We had no idea if she would have any use of the right side of her body, and it was not until day seven of the neuro checks that the right side of Malori's body began responding. When she would not wake up well in the neuro checks, they would give her a strong little pinch on her left side and she would lift her left arm up high. They would say, "Good, Malori. That is what we want. Let's see what you can do." The first time she opened her eyes during a neuro check, she just kind of looked around. We began to notice that she really did not acknowledge us with her eyes if we were on the right side of the bed. We did not notice at first because we were not on that side of her bed very much, because it was where the drain for her brain, the IV tower, and other machines were. We typically stood on the left side because there was more room. After several days of that we realized when one of the doctors shone the light into her eyes to check her vision that she had no peripheral vision on her right side. They asked us to start sitting by her right side to force her to turn that direction and to get her to start using her right side more often.

The hospital had rules regarding visitation in ICU, yet after a while, they gave up on the rules with us. We had the end room right by the doors entering the ICU unit, and there were usually about twelve of us at a time in Malori's room. The nurses said they had never seen anything like the number of people wanting to see Malori, and they finally said if Marray and I were okay with the visitors, they would allow it. We were never really private about any of this journey. First of all, we wanted anyone who was willing to pray for Malori. Also, as we saw the little bits of progress every day, we wanted all the glory to be given to God. We wanted any and all to see the power of His miraculous, healing hands. Anyone who wanted to go back to see and pray with Malori, we let them. We were so grateful that people would travel that far to comfort us and pray for us. People's visits were such a blessing, and the support was unbelievable.

After about four days of not leaving Malori's side, I decided I had to get a shower. I did not want to leave her, but I needed to clean up, and I thought it might make me feel better. One of Malori's nurses told me I could go up to the eighth floor of the hospital where there were rooms that family members sometimes used to shower. The eighth floor seemed so far away from Malori on the second floor, but it was better than leaving the hospital altogether, so I agreed. On my way up, I ran into a man from Cameroon, Africa who was helping me find my way. He had the most beautiful accent, and all of a sudden he said, "Stop. I feel the Spirit of God leading me. Are you the mother of the volleyball player who is fighting for her life?" It was a surreal moment for me. It seemed like he knew everything about me, but I had no idea how he would know. He looked at me and said, "Your shower can wait. We're all going to go back down to Malori's room in ICU and I'm going to pray over every cell, tissue, artery, vein, muscle fiber, organ, and every ounce of her body for God's healing and God's protection." It was amazing. At this point, we still had not talked to Malori or gotten any real responses from the right side of her body. He laid his hands on her and we all gathered around her bed to pray. It was one of the most powerful and moving prayers I have ever been a part of. I vividly remember seeing Malori's eyes flutter just a little in response to his accent. Malori has taken two mission trips to Africa, and a big part of her heart remains there. It was almost as if she knew he was from the place she has come to love so dearly. It was an incredible moment.

Several days into the ICU stay they decided that it was time to put in a feeding tube to give Malori some nourishment. This was one of my first glimmers of hope. I thought, "Thank you, God. If they are going to the trouble to give her a feeding tube, she might survive this." Things continued to progress slowly. On day seven, she moved the right side of her body for the first time. They would start pinching her right collarbone and her arm, and her right hand would come up to stop the hand that was pinching her. It was encouraging to see her moving her right side. Our main concern was obviously her survival, but as her condition became more stable, we began to think about the long-term implications for her if she never regained the use of the right side of her body. Around the same time the nurse came and got us. She told us, "I just walked in to see Malori's little hiney in the air. She was leaned over to her left side on the rail of her hospital bed, and she had already managed to pull out her feeding tube. She had her hand on the ventilator tube, and was working on taking that out next!" That moment was when I realized things were looking better. We had one feisty, little fighter on our hands. I know the nurses said it could have really agitated her airways if she had pulled out the ventilator tube, yet it was also such a happy moment for me thinking that Malori could tell that something was agitating her and she did not like it. They put the tube back in and we had to start putting big white gloves that looked like boxing gloves or mittens on her hands. Malori would wiggle and try to get them off. We eventually had to go to restraints to keep her hands tied down because she was still trying to pull the tube out. As serious as it was to keep her tubes in, it was a ray of sunshine that we still had Mal's fighting spirit on our hands.

They pulled out the ventilator tube around day six or seven. They explained that a patient gets to the point where it is a little risky to leave ventilator in because you can develop ventilator-induced pneumonia. They had decided that Malori's levels were remaining stable, so they thought it was a good time to take it out and continue breathing treatments without the tubes. We were all around her bed watching her. It was like sitting in the most suspenseful movie of our life, only even more so because we were looking at our daughter. They said, "Hi, Malori!" She slowly opened her eyes and looked at us sporadically. They asked her, "What is your name?" She said in a small whisper, "Sarah." My heart jumped at her voice, and I thought, "Okay. She can see me standing at the foot of her bed." A little time went by and they asked her, "What year is it right now?" She paused for a while and blinked her eyes. In her soft voice, she answered, "1972." That is the year I was born. We were all really fascinated by all that and thought it was interesting. At the time, I did not feel anxiety because I was so excited to hear her voice after not hearing it for a week. However, I did realize that we had a long road ahead of us. I realized there were things deep in the long-term part of her brain that she just remembers like my first name and the year I was born. I remember thinking, "We have a long way to go. There are so many things we will have to teach her again." We were happy to accept the challenge to help her get to where she wanted to be.

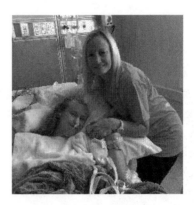

A little later that day, Peyton stood beside her and said to her, "Okay, surely you have forgotten my middle name." She just looked at him smiling a little, closed her eyes, and shook her head no. Then she opened her eyes, smiled again, and said, "Glen." He said, "No way! How did you remember that?" Peyton has always laughed about having Glen as his middle name, since it seems like an old timey name to him. Malori had not even said her own name yet, but she remembered Peyton's middle name. After that, we would get on her left side and all take turns asking, "Who am I?" She slowly responded with, "Mom, Dad, Maci, Peyton, and Tyler." She called Tyler's dad by his nickname, Harvard, and called my mom Nana. As the days passed, she started recognizing aunts, uncles, and cousins.

By the time her volleyball team came back to visit her after their conference tournament (around days 11-12) Malori knew her coaches and teammates. About three players would come in at a time with the coaches, and she would call them by name and say, "What's up? How are you?" Before they all left, they all came in the room together with our family. Coach Lawrence said, "Let's have a prayer." It was an emotional time for the team; they had gone to play in the conference tournament without one of their sisters and they had lost their game. Coach Lawrence asked who wanted to say the prayer, and Malori piped up and said, "Let me say it!" Malori prayed for their safety and their health. It was almost like she did not even realize her own condition. The Holy Spirit just took over. Malori prayed for God to help the team show His love to others, and she prayed for all of them including herself to share God with everyone they met. We were all amazed. This was a pivotal point because we got to hear Malori pouring out her heart, the same Malori who had led team devotionals and ministered to her teammates.

It was a concern for all of us, especially for Tyler, if she would remember us. Tyler and Malori had hoped and planned to be married. Tyler was so relieved when Malori remembered him and would squeeze his hand before she would even open her eyes. Then, after she started talking, she would say things to him like "Don't leave, stay here by me." Early on, we were all so careful touching her because we did not want to give her any germs. Sometimes, Tyler would give her a small kiss on her forehead before he would leave, but after a while, she began to pucker her lips wanting a real kiss from him. Tyler had to come and go frequently because he was going back and forth for school, basketball practices, tournaments, and games.

Over Malori's time in ICU, the neuro checks moved from every hour to every two hours, and then to every four hours. The medical team determined that uninterrupted rest was very crucial to Malori's continued recovery. Malori slowly grew stronger. As soon as they took her catheter out (about a week into her time in ICU) Malori began wanting to get up. She needed help with every step, and posture changes made her a little dizzy, but at the beginning of her second week in ICU, she walked 100 feet. We were so excited that she was walking even while she was still in ICU. Her physical therapist and her speech therapist visited every day.

Malori loved her physical therapy. She would say things like, "Let's get up, let's sit in the chair today, let's get up and walk." If they asked her to walk 100 feet, she would walk 200. If they asked her to walk 300, she would do 450. She always said, "Little bit longer, little bit longer." She would get her tennis shoes on and walk around the big circle in the ICU. She went slowly, and her IV poles and machines had to come along with her, but it was great to see her moving.

Speech therapy was harder for Malori. She could not recognize colors, letters, or numbers at first, and it frustrated her. I remember at one point just grabbing on to Marray's arm, leaning into him, and saying, "This is so scary." The brain is so complex and controls everything in your body. This was our driven, hard-working Malori. She had maintained a 4.0 for her whole life, acing even her hardest college classes, yet now she could not even recognize colors. As scary as it was, it also confirmed for me how amazing God is to create such complex, detailed human beings. I just thought to myself, "How could anyone question that there is a God?"

After two weeks in ICU (and a week of therapy) we got the news that they were going to move Malori to a regular room. As good as that was to hear, it was also a little bit frightening to know we were going to be leaving the incredible, nonstop care of the ICU nurses. Marray and I began watching the nurses carefully so we would know how to help Malori when the nurses were not there. Our family had gotten a room at the local Ronald McDonald house, but either Marray or I was with Malori at all times. Usually, either Peyton or Maci was there with Malori as well, and the other would be back at the Ronald McDonald house with whichever parent was there.

Just past the two-week mark, our family celebrated Thanksgiving together in the hospital. A sweet lady we had met while in ICU brought us a huge, homemade, Thanksgiving dinner. On top of that, our class from church back home had arranged for a meal at the hospital as well. Marray's family and my family all came and we all went down to a room in the cafeteria to eat together. Malori got to come down and eat with us, which was unbelievably special. We were all in awe and experienced overwhelming gratitude that we were having our first holiday since everything had happened, and Malori was there to share it with us.

In the regular room, Malori wanted to walk two to three times a day, always pushing herself further and further. After being in bed so long, she loved being able to get up and move. The night of December 10th, she just kept going and going until we thought to ourselves that she must have gone over a mile. The neurosurgeon cautioned us not to push it, and to make sure she was getting enough nourishment and perhaps not exerting quite so much. But Malori had gotten a taste and she wanted more. It became fairly normal for her to walk anywhere from half a mile to a mile at a time. We could tell how much she loved it and how thankful she was to be moving.

During this time, our family had to find a way to keep functioning with all of our other responsibilities. I took a leave of absence from work. My principal got a long-term substitute for me so my job would be waiting for me when I got back. Peyton drove back and forth a lot to finish up his first semester of college. As he was taking finals, I suddenly had the realization that I had always sent goody bags to Malori while she took finals, but I did not have anything prepared for Peyton. I ran to Walmart and got lots of treats and snacks to send to him. Despite the crisis our family was enduring, he ended up pulling through just fine for his finals. I am so thankful he was able to focus enough to finish the semester. Even after Peyton got out for Christmas, Maci still had a few weeks of school left.

Tyler's parents, my family, and our friends transported her back and forth between Lubbock and Dallas as much as was needed. Often times, Maci and Tyler wanted to stay in Dallas as long as they could, so we would put them on a 6:00 am flight back to Lubbock so they would arrive just in time to get to school. My mom moved into our house in Lubbock to be there for Maci and help take care of our house and animals. Tyler also stayed there often to help my mom keep things going. My mom would get Maci to school and to her practices, and Maci had a whole cheering section of Malori's friends from LCU who would come to watch her play. Maci's teachers and coaches stepped in and took care of her in countless ways. The way the community of God surrounded our family and carried us through that time was simply incredible.

Marray was so optimistic through the whole process. Of course, he had his moments where he would break down and the tears would flow, but he was such a rock and an encourager for all of us through this process. He would tell Malori all the time, "I can't wait until the day I hold your hand and we walk out of this hospital." On December 4, 2015, Marray's words came true: Malori was released from the hospital. We loaded up a huge cart with all the gifts and things people had brought to us. As we got to the door, I said, "Okay, let's stop. I want to get this picture." Marray said, "Yes, get this picture. I can't wait to share this picture with everyone that we are experiencing this miracle of Malori walking out of the hospital." I vividly remember that moment, and I cherish the picture and what it means to us.

From the hospital, we all went to stay in the Ronald McDonald House. Malori had therapy five days a week: occupational therapy, physical therapy, and speech therapy. She loved all her therapists, but she got the most frustrated in speech therapy—reading passages and trying to remember what she had just read. She really needed her physical therapy as an outlet between her more difficult speech and occupational therapy sessions. She would go through her therapy routines every day, and they would reverse the order every other day. We had frequent visitors at the Ronald McDonald House, so much so that we had to coordinate all the awesome people who came to see us to be sure Malori got her rest. We would get home from therapy at 4:00 in the afternoon, and then she needed to sleep. We would schedule people to visit between 6:30-7:00, and then Malori would need to get to bed to sleep. This routine went on for almost a month: from December 4th all the way to her second surgery.

We did enjoy a refreshing break from the routine to spend quality time with family over the holidays in a beautiful, spacious home. One of our many sweet, generous friends, Cathy Delaney, took time off of work from her job as an RN, went on trips, left us delicious baked sweets and Christmas gifts, and full use of her house. It was so cozy with numerous books and movies to choose from in her big den. We had Christmas with Tyler and his parents over the week of Christmas, when he had a break from basketball. Then, we spent several days over the New Year holiday with my parents, brother, sister, and their families. It was so special and having her big kitchen where we could cook holiday dishes was incredible. God really blessed us with a beautiful holiday season, in spite of all we were going through at the time.

Tyler's parents had some dear friends who let them use their condo in Plano. It gave us a place to go hang out and escape the medical scene for a few hours, somewhere that felt like home. On January 5th, the night before Malori's surgery to remove the AVM, our community gathered there: team members, coaches, friends, and family. We were surrounded by people who we knew loved us. Malori spoke a little to thank everyone. Malori said, "I hope you will all feel as much peace as I do about this surgery. I just feel God's peace surrounding me, wrapping me up in his love and mercy. I am going to be praying for y'all tonight and in the morning that y'all will be at peace about this." In the end, Malori knew that she would either wake up and see all those who love her so much or she would wake up and see God. She knew and understood that. I just remember sobbing as she talked to us in that living room. I was crying tears of nerves over the thought of another brain surgery, knowing they were fixing to cut into my child's brain again. At the same time, I was weeping tears of joy; it made my heart feel so happy that Malori was more at peace than she was scared. It was such a defining moment.

That night, after every one left, Tyler and Malori sat and talked, prayed, and cried together. The last surgery had been an emergency, so there had been no time to prepare. This time, however, they wanted to pray and be together. Aside from the serious moments they had together, there was one especially sweet moment that we now cherish. As I mentioned earlier, Malori's short term memory was not very good for quite a while. She would forget things just minutes after you would tell her. She joked and referred to herself as Dory from *Finding Nemo*. One night in early December after we had just moved into the Ronald McDonald house, Tyler and Malori sat and talked. He told her that he had bought her an engagement ring: "Mal, I got the ring. I bought you a ring." He knew he was safe to tell her because her short term memory was so bad. The night before her AVM removal in January, Malori said, "Tyler, I remember you told me you bought me a ring." He was shocked, and said, "Mal, how did you remember that? I thought I was surely safe to tell you at that point—you couldn't remember things minute to minute!" Malori's response was, "Tyler, how could I not remember that? That is a big deal for a girl!"

The next morning, we checked in for Malori's surgery and they gave us her case number. We could watch the screen in the waiting room for Malori's number to see the status of her surgery. We were only supposed to have two to four people in the waiting room with us, but we ended up having about fifty. Our church family, friends, schools, and family surrounded us every step of the way with this journey. We waited and watched her number for five hours of surgery. Then, Dr. Welch came out, and we instantly looked for his body language to see how he felt about the surgery. And there it was—he was smiling! As he came toward us, our whole clan walked toward him. I remember my mom just wrapping her arm around him saying, "Thank you so much, Dr. Welch. We have been out here praying for you and for Malori." I remember hugging him and telling him we were forever grateful for what he just did for our daughter; words would never convey our gratitude and we would never be able to repay him. He explained to us that he was able to remove the AVM without any complications of bleeding. "I feel confident I got it all, but I always do a post-op angiogram to verify that." We immediately huddled up after Dr. Welch talked to us and had a prayer of thanksgiving. It was just another miracle. Malori had survived another brain surgery.

The angiogram confirmed all of the AVM had been removed successfully. Praise God! When we finally got to see our courageous girl, she was back in a room in the ICU unit. She looked very pale and had the vomit bucket beside her in bed. The nurses said she had been using it because she was nauseated from the amount of anesthesia she had to have during surgery. It was so good to see our little warrior and just kiss her forehead, blood, bruises, and all.

It was so comforting to see that the left side of her head was not sunken in any longer. We were so relieved that the AVM, the monster that caused so much damage and heartache, was successfully removed that we almost forgot about the great blessing of her bone flap being back in its original home, protecting her brain! For two months, she carried the two stacked pieces of her skull in the lower left part of her abdomen. Once she started walking well, she was very cautious not to let anything bump the left side of her body, head or abdomen. Thankfully, God made us in such a perfect way that her vision loss and side she hit the most was the opposite side, her right side. She would only have two more weeks of guarding the left, stitched-up areas of her head and abdomen, until we would see Dr. Harold Smith in Lubbock to get the stitches removed from both areas. All of this was amazing!

Yet it was also hard for us to see her back in Neuro ICU. Peyton and Maci had been telling her for several days that she would know when the surgery was over when she could hear the song, Brainwash, by Nicole C. Mullen. They all three laughed for who knows how long, just anticipating this moment! Sure enough, as soon as we saw Malori's eyes beginning to open, Maci blasted the song on her phone while Peyton danced to the beat in his comical, celebration fashion. We had all been hoping and praying for this moment for two months!

Malori spent two nights in ICU, two nights in a regular room, and then we were released to go home. We left the hospital on a Sunday, and our whole family got to go back through Wichita Falls. We made a stop at Kell West Regional Hospital to say thank you to all the nurses and all the staff who took care of Malori that first night. When we got there, Marray pulled up to the entrance of the ER, but I said, "No, we need to go in the front door." I did not want to relive going into the ER. Sure enough, someone motioned us to drive to the front entrance of the hospital. I was grateful for that; I did not want to get out of that same car and go through the same doors where I had handed off my lifeless daughter. I wanted to stay on our current path of wellness and joy.

It was beautiful to watch Malori meet Dr. Kamath and the other people who saved her life that night. They were so familiar to us, but Malori had never seen any of them. Dr. Kamath hugged her and touched her face. He took her by the hand and walked her through the hospital. He showed her his office where he had the silhouette cut-out of her in her VB jersey that said, "Pray for Malori," hanging on the wall. He took her into the room she waited in for surgery, and he even took her to the pad where the helicopter was going to pick her up (even though it ended up being an airplane.) The staff had one of the preachers who works closely with them come in and say an amazing prayer of thanksgiving for continued complete healing over Malori. They fed us lunch and fellowshipped with us. It was so amazing; they told us story after story of how critical she really was—how they were running behind us to get blood as Maci, Marray, and I were praying and how she needed all those transfusions to get her stable enough to have surgery.

We spent three or four hours with our wonderful friends at Kell West before heading home to Lubbock. We kept getting texts from our friends and family saying, "Hey, when are you going to get here? Do you mind swinging by Greenlawn (our church) for a few minutes? There are a few people here who have been praying for Malori that just want to see her briefly." We had no idea what was waiting for us. Friends were waiting for us outside the church when we pulled up. As we walked in, we saw precious children and beautiful faces from home holding signs saying "We have been praying for you. Welcome home!" The auditorium was full of hundreds and hundreds of people there to welcome us home. (I had only been back to Lubbock one night since November.) Malori's volleyball teammates grabbed her and took her to the front, Tyler's basketball teammates grabbed him, and our friends escorted us to the front. All I could do was cry at the overwhelming love I felt. I had heard so many stories about the things happening back home: people praying, making t-shirts, and hosting fundraisers for our family. But walking in to our church and seeing that crowd of people love us face-to-face was a whole new level of amazing. Malori was able to get up and speak to the room full of people we loved so much. She was emotional and tearful as the thanked everyone for their prayers and everything they had done for our family. Then Marray got up and thanked everyone. He talked about the miracles we had experienced over the past few months. There was singing and prayer, tears and laughter, worship and thanksgiving. It was one of the most wonderful hours I have ever experienced in my life.

Let me tell you about a few of the things I learned about myself and about God through this journey. I have heard throughout my whole life that God is always with us, and He will never leave us or forsake us. I have read these words in scripture countless times. However, when you go through a storm, that promise becomes incredibly real and powerful in your life. The neat thing is, all these months later with this terrible crisis behind us, I still think about that promise daily. I often find myself talking out loud, reminding myself that God is with me and He had his hand on every small detail of our journey. He provided what we needed every moment of the way, whether that was my first sense that Malori needed to go to the hospital, keeping us calm and clear-minded to make decisions, Dr. Kamath staying to help us when he should have been leaving work, or something as simple as a giant print Bible to nourish, encourage and sustain me.

Looking back, God's provision is unmistakably evident. In March 2016, I read Dr. Kamath's notes about Malori's surgery for the first time: "I have explained to the family that her condition is grave and prognosis is very poor. Yet, they have consented to let me attempt the surgery anyway in efforts to preserve her life. We will be in contact with UT Southwestern Zale Lipshy neuro surgery team to take over care as soon as surgery is over and she is stable enough to fly." When I read these words, I had an emotional meltdown. We experienced this traumatic journey, but our hearts were in shock for a good deal of it. To look back, remember how close she was to death, and see what a true miracle it is that we have Malori with us today, I can do nothing but pour out my wonder and thanks to God.

Through Malori's weeks of recovery in ICU, Satan worked his hardest to throw his fiery darts of despair, fear, and anxieties at us, and it was only through the Holy Spirit, hours of prayer, and the word of God that we were able to combat those attacks. I wrestled with fear every hour of every day. I would wake up terrified in the middle of the night and just have to see her to believe that she was still breathing. I would watch her walking around in the hospital, and I would worry that she would fall and hit her head. For about six months, my sleep patterns were very sporadic, and I would wake up every morning and ask myself if all of this really happened or if it has just all been a terrible nightmare. I am slowly getting back into a more restful, peaceful sleep routine. My time in scripture and my quiet time with God were my only source of protection against this hurricane of a storm that hit our family. My life was changed in the best way possible by this tragedy. I crave that closeness with God now. My prayer life has also been deeply changed. I will never discount a single prayer that went up on Malori's behalf. James 5:16 NIV tells us, "The prayer of a righteous person is powerful and effective." When I say I will pray for someone, I mean those words to my very core. I keep a prayer journal to remember who I am praying for and to see God's work through my prayers.

I cannot tell you how much I have wrestled with the question, "Why?" I find it hard to understand why this had to happen to Malori. She always works so hard to be kind and considerate to others, she never let a day go by without quiet time with God, she was a blessing to everyone she encountered, and she had her whole life ahead of her: graduation, PT school, marriage, and more. I am not the only one to wrestle with this; Peyton even told me he just kept asking "Why Malori and not me?" the whole time he was driving to meet us at the hospital. After being home in Lubbock for a few months and settling into a routine of taking Malori to her rehab appointments, I brought it up one day. I asked Malori, "Do you ever wonder why this didn't happen to someone who never really tried to do the right thing and might have needed more of a wake-up call than you did? Malori thought about it for a while and said, "Mom, perhaps it may not have had the same effect if it had happened to someone like that. God let this happen to me for a reason and we just have to trust that." I was blown away by her answer.

The biggest blessing in this journey has been watching Malori's heart for God stay as strong and constant as it was before this happened to her. She could not believe how many people were praying and turning to God for "little ole Mal." The way her tragedy brought others to God in prayer, others closer to God, and families stronger and closer, just made her so happy, that it was almost unreal to her daddy, brother, sister, and me. How could she be so joyful while struggling to recognize numbers, letters, colors, and learning to walk steadily again? How could this make her so happy when she had to fight to remember words she wanted to say and get them to come out of her mouth properly? For many days, she could not even recall her own name. The truth is, she always had an inner peace from God dwelling within her and never felt alone or afraid. She found great joy in being constantly surrounded by her family and friends who loved her the most. She was able to relax and let God be at work in what was happening. This blessed our family, Tyler, and his family beyond measure, and we are forever changed by this journey. Naturally, Malori still has her moments of frustration, like her loss of independence by not being able to drive because of her loss of peripheral vision from the

AVM rupture. But even through the frustration, she remains grateful for the blessing of life and the gift of being able to walk, exercise, talk, get married, have a chance at graduating from LCU, and just have the opportunity to live a normal life outside of driving. On April 14, 2016, Tyler proposed to Malori at the Rip Griffin Center at LCU where both of them had spent their college athletic careers. That was such a special, joyful night. Malori's volleyball team and Tyler's basketball team were there to celebrate with them, along with both their big families.

Malori and Tyler got married on July 29th, in the presence of 500 wonderful friends and family at Autumn Oaks Event Center. They both love the outdoors! It was so special and emotional because we were so amazed that this day could even happen. We thought it was so neat that they asked one of their mutual favorite professors, Andy Laughlin, to marry them. Malori now jokes with Andy that his A&P exam she took the morning of November 10th is what caused the AVM to rupture. He and his wife are beautiful mentors to them, and every prayer he said before the wedding and every word he said during the wedding was so perfect and so meaningful.

Malori continues to see her sweet OT, Dawn, at Vision Center of West Texas weekly. She is making great strides there, and Dr. Riley explained that active therapy is always better than passive therapy. We will never give up hope for full vision return, and we won't stop praying for complete healing. Malori has now completed Physics, Physics lab, and Exercise Testing and Prescription from her Fall 2015 courses. She has four more to go, and is currently working on Anatomy and Physiology. She is also teaching a PE class at LCHS, where her amazing father-in-law is the President, for part of her internship. She will attain three hours of internship and just work on completing last Fall's classes during this Fall 2016 semester. Then, she will only need 13 more hours and a medical mission trip to Peru to graduate. God is good!

I have always felt pain in my heart for people who lose a child or have very sick children, like a different level of heartache. I have said multiple times, "I just don't know how people live through the loss of a child," and have said "I don't know how parents have the energy to keep on keeping on while caring for sick children day in and day out." But I never imagined that I would find myself in this position, and I would never have dreamed that I would have the strength to endure it. I think back to those vivid, nightmare moments, Malori stiff in my arms in our car, Maci looking at me with such fear in her eyes, and I honestly wonder how my mommy heart survived them. How could weak-stomached, soft-hearted me endure that without screaming or passing out? How could our family survive that night and the many critical days that followed? How did we go through the many months of caregiving and watching Malori struggle through the mentally challenging parts of rehab, while having great joy in watching her sail through the physical therapy side? How did we have the strength to send her back into surgery for the second time? How could we deal with the sadness of her losing her right side peripheral vision and not being able to drive again? There is only one answer to these questions: God! God sustained us through countless hours of prayer and time in His word, and He surrounded us with family and friends to love us, support us, pray for us, and hug us through this storm. God spared Malori's life that night. He turned our fears, doubts, and anxieties into incredible joy and gratitude. All the time now, Malori says, "God is so good. He is always working for our good."

"You turned my wailing into dancing; you removed my sackcloth and clothed me with joy that my heart may sing your praises and not be silent. LORD my God, I will praise you forever." Psalm 30:11-12 NIV

Sarah and Malori at the wedding

Maddox and Rogers families with Dr. Kamath and his
wife at Malori's wedding

About Sarah Maddox

Sarah Maddox is the daughter of a preacher and a teacher, and has a younger brother and sister. She is thankful to have such wonderful relationships with her family and all of her in-laws. Sarah is happily married to her high school sweetheart, Marray. They have spent 28 years of their lives together. After graduating from high school, Sarah ran track and cross country at ACU, then transferred to Texas Tech to be in Lubbock with Marray. They both feel so blessed to be raising a family in Lubbock, the most loving, caring, generous, and supportive community. She now works in the library at Legacy Elementary, and Marray was blessed with the opportunity to partner up with two of his good friends and start a business called Physical Therapy Today back in 2003. Marray serves as a shepherd at Green Lawn Church of Christ, where he, Sarah, and their three children enjoy being an active part of a wonderful church family. Malori is 21 and married to Tyler Rogers, who Marray and Sarah thank God for daily. Malori is working hard to finish her ESS degree at LCU and has high hopes of graduating in the Spring or Fall of 2017. Peyton is 19 and is pursuing a business management degree while playing baseball at SWOSU in Weatherford, OK. Maci is 14, and is a freshman at Frenship High School. She has big dreams of playing basketball in college one day. Sarah feels blessed to have a loving, faithful husband, three children who seek to serve the Lord, and an amazing son-in-law who loves the Lord and their daughter unconditionally. Malori, Peyton, and Maci all gave their lives to Christ in baptism at the age of 14. These three days were among the happiest days of Sarah's life. Her favorite scripture which she loves to cling to is found in Psalm 62:1-2 NIV. "Truly my soul finds rest in God; my salvation comes from him. Truly he is my rock and my salvation; he is my fortress, I will never be shaken."

Sarah, Malori, and Marray at Mal's Wedding

**Photos of wedding courtesy of Courtney Hill Photography in Lubbock, Texas.

Rose Johnson

Rose and I have not known each other long, yet I feel like she has been my friend forever. I was initially drawn to her as we both are passionate about college students, helping them to grow and develop. We enjoy working together in order to fuel that passion. Before I met Rose, others had shared with me details about her remarkable gifts and talents as well as a little about her story. I had only known her a week when I asked her to be part of our book; I just knew in my heart it would be powerful. As much as Rose is passionate about her students, an even deeper passion is her faith in Jesus Christ. You will be blessed richly by the way she shares in an authentic and candid way. Rose knows what it means to be a disciple of Jesus Christ, especially when it is hard. Her ability to think of others in the midst of hardship challenges me to want to be better. Rose's story encourages me in my faith journey, and I know will do the same for you. She is a special blessing who God brought across my path. I am grateful.

Be Still and Know I am God

Rose Johnson

I thought I was going to Lubbock Christian University to play volleyball, but God had other plans for me. After suffering a knee injury and having reconstructive surgery, I decided not to pursue volleyball, but still stay at LCU because I felt God had brought me here for a purpose. The very next semester, I met Leron. He was kind and funny, and he had bravely faced so many obstacles in his life, including losing his mother at a young age and suffering many lingering health problems from a car accident when he was five. Somehow, even with all that hardship, Leron was still full of life. While we were dating I was focused on school activities and getting my degree. However, the longer we dated, the more I began to realize that there was not a single area of my life in which I did not want Leron to be present. When he asked me to marry him in the fall of 1992, I said yes.

My mother loved Leron. Her own two sons, my older brothers from other fathers, refused to have a relationship with her. My mom did not become a Christian until they were older, and many of her life choices caused them pain and resentment toward her. Leron quickly became like a son to her. He had grown up without a mother, so he and my mom hit it off in a very special way. I loved that for both of them. We all joked about their close relationship because my mom would call me, check on me briefly, and then ask to talk to Leron.

Leron and I were married on May 15, 1993. We were living life and doing what many newlyweds do to make ends meet. We were both working several jobs and going to school to finish our degrees in social work. Life was moving right along for a few months, but in October, we could tell something was not right with Leron's health. We assumed it was related to many of his health problems he had struggled with at times over the past few years and all he needed was another round of treatments. However, the doctors told us we needed to consider a liver transplant. This came as quite a shock to us. We were young, barely making ends meet, and we were still in school. We did not have good insurance, and we were required to have $250,000 before they would even consider the transplant. My mom kicked into gear to help us because Leron was hers now, too. She travelled across the country to churches raising money. LCU and the Lubbock community got involved and had all sorts of fundraisers for us. Even 7-11 stores in Lubbock had jars for Leron for people to donate. It was amazing how many dear friends loved and supported us, letting us borrow cars, helping us with hospital visits, and encouraging us. These people were deeply woven into our lives and remained so for years to come. It was quite the ordeal and adventure.

My mom knew a person who knew a doctor at Baylor Medical Center in Dallas who specialized in liver transplants. Through this connection, we were able to see him for a second opinion on Leron's situation. After this second opinion, they determined Leron did not need a liver transplant, but rather needed a specialized series of treatments. So we began treatments. It was such a relief not needing a transplant. However, we had to go back to Baylor Medical Center every month for the treatments, which could be pretty daunting.

After a while, some things were just not adding up. Leron was not feeling well and was experiencing pain in his treatments, yet they could not tie some of his symptoms back to his liver issues. We had to figure out what was going on. After a series of tests, they finally discovered that he had a mass on his left kidney. It had nothing to do with the car accident when he was five or any of the other health issues he had experienced for years. Because of all the scar tissue from his many previous surgeries, it was very difficult to navigate around his organs. When they went in to remove the mass, they saw there was only one path to get to the kidneys, and the only kidney they could access safely was the left one—the one with the cancer. I was so grateful that they could reach the kidney and remove it. After that surgery, we were able to resume the treatments for his liver. The treatments and the trips were not pleasant, yet we made it through and wrapped up his treatments by the fall of 1994. They told us he was good and all was well—he would be able to live a normal life.

We carried on with our lives, working to find our passions and establish our careers. Leron was working at the Children's Home of Lubbock and Buckner's Children's Home. As I finished a second degree in Psychology, I did an internship with the school district that turned into a job after graduation. The school was very accommodating and allowed me to have Mondays off so I could continue working on my Master's in Social Work at UTA in Arlington. I would fly early every Monday morning to Arlington, rent a car, go to school all day, fly home on the last flight, and get up to teach school on Tuesday morning. I had the routine of my life running smoothly and I was almost done with my master's, but then, without planning to, we got pregnant. As happy as we were about the new life that would be joining our family, it changed all of our plans. Suddenly I was too sick to fly to school, and I was disappointed to have to put a halt to finishing my degree. Then, five months in to the pregnancy, I lost the baby. It was so incredibly hard. I grieved, Leron grieved, and my mom grieved. Leron and my mom talked often about it, but I did not want to talk. It seemed pointless and too painful to talk when there was nothing I could do to change the situation.

After losing our baby, school was not something I could just jump back into—emotionally, I was just not ready. I began doing some consulting work with companies, and eventually one of my clients ended up hiring me, throwing me into the corporate world. Over these years, I moved up through the company into the position of Vice President.

Leron and I were okay with not having our own children. I was working in my corporate job, and with Leron's work at children's homes, we decided we would foster at some point. In 1999, we were surprised to find out we were pregnant again. We were delighted. On December 31, 1999, our first son was born. Interestingly, my brothers also had their first kids in 1999. As my brothers became parents, their hearts began softening a bit toward my mom. Their hurt was still not completely healed, yet they were slowly allowing her in to have a relationship with her grandkids. We were all living spread out over the country, and my mom was the glue that helped us all stay connected. When the grandkids were all under the age of one, my mom organized a trip for us at her favorite place called Kalaloch Lodge at Olympic National Park near Seattle. That became such a special place for our family to get together every year.

Three years later, our second son was born. I was still breastfeeding our second son when I began not feeling well. I could not think what could possibly be wrong. Finally, Leron suggested I might be pregnant again. Sure enough, I was. I was not happy—being pregnant again was not part of the plan! I finally went to the doctor to find out how far along I was. At my ultrasound, the nurse said "Hold on a minute." They left the room, and someone else came in, looked, and left again. I was beginning to get nervous, and I finally said, "Hold on, what is going on?" They said, "Well congratulations, you are pregnant with twins."

I began laughing hysterically; apparently, that is how I deal with shock. Leron, on the other hand, turned pale with shock. We could not believe we had a three-year-old, a newborn baby, and now I was pregnant with twins. I called my mom and she was ecstatic. I, however, was very nervous. I was already over three months pregnant when we found out, and I could have really used all nine months to wrap my head around the news. It was a blow to my system because it was nothing like what I had planned. I just kept thinking, "How am I going to do this? I am still trying to get used to having two children while working, and now I am going to have four." The girls were born a month early, but they were still at good weights and healthy. It was actually like having triplets—three in diapers and breastfeeding two. There were days I did not know how we would get through this, but God was with us, and we managed to keep putting one foot in front of the other.

With our family having grown to six people, Leron and I sat down one day and decided that one of us needed to get a second job, or one of us needed to stay home with our children. We could not afford to put four kids in daycare. If I left my job in the corporate world, I would have to start back at the very bottom and work my way up again. Leron, however, would never have a hard time getting back into his profession. So, even though it was very uncommon at the time, we decided for Leron to stay home for a while. We agreed to try it for six months at a time to see how well it worked. For the first six months, Leron loved it. He was such a patient person, and so many of his characteristics made him a wonderful stay-at-home-dad. He had such a strong and courageous spirit to take care of the kids and allow me to stay on my professional journey. After the first six months, he decided he was good to do another six months. After the second six months, Leron was feeling a little discouraged that he was not contributing to our family financially. Yet, when we did the math again, we realized we were saving a lot of money by not paying for childcare. Leron stayed home for another year, and by the time the girls were two years old, we had more options. Leron went back to work being a full-time social worker in the school system in the fall of 2006. This was a crazy time for us as any family with four small children would be, but with God's help we managed to get through pretty well. Things seemed to be looking up.

In January 2007, Leron began not feeling well. We just thought we needed to do the treatments like before. What I did not know at the time was that my mom was experiencing a cancer relapse from a few years before. Leron and my mom were close, so he knew about her cancer but kept it to himself to keep me from worrying. He had to come clean and tell me about my mom's cancer in order to ask me to keep his health problems a secret so it would not worry my mom. Now, I was worried about both of them, but I thought we would work it all out as it had before. In April, we went to Baylor Medical Center for Leron's appointment, and they told us he needed a liver transplant. We had plans to go to Kalaloch that summer with my family as we did every year, so we decided to wait to tell my mom about Leron until our family time in July. At that point, Mom's cancer had come back really aggressively. When we got to Kalaloch, Mom was thrilled. She was very sick and had lost all her hair, but she was so happy to be with everyone. She was scrapbooking, sharing pictures, and telling stories. She did not have much of an appetite, and she was feeling worse and worse, so we took her to the hospital. We had planned for her to tell me stories about our family—to share the family history I would need to know. She also still needed to update her will. There were so many things we were planning to get done. Yet, on Friday, July 13, 2007 at 6:00am, my mother passed away in the hospital. The night before, I had decided to stay the night with her. I held her hand all night and felt her take her last breath early in the morning. With Leron by my side, I held her hand until noon, I just could not let her go.

We were supposed to travel home on July 14th to get Leron to Baylor Medical Center by the 16th to begin the assessment for his transplant. However, all of that had to change while we made plans and arrangements for my mom's funeral. My brothers and I, along with one of my mom's long-time friends, planned the service for her.

Finally, I was able to get home, and we started the week-long process to get Leron's liver mapped for a transplant. After looking at Leron's condition, they said at this point a transplant would be too risky, and they could not help us. Shocked, I asked them what our other options there might be, and they said they would present our case to a leading expert to see if he would accept Leron as a patient. One thing led to another, and we were offered an appointment with this doctor in Dallas. When we met with him, he told us, "When I talk to patients, I tell them there is risk of death. In your case, I need you to know that death is not just a possibility, it is a reality." He wanted to be sure we had a very clear reality of what was at stake. When he asked if we had any questions, I said, "I want you to understand three things. One, we are very clear of the risks of this surgery and of this transplant. We are very well aware this could lead to death. But if you don't do it, it certainly leads to death. We choose the chance at life. Two, as much as we respect who you are, the role you play in the transplant world, and the skills you have been blessed with, we worship our God and we are about Him leading us. So, we are praying that you will use everything he has blessed you with to help Leron and our family so our children can have their Daddy. Three, we know you are a man just like anyone else and you put your pants on one leg at a time like everyone else, but you are the one who has been put before us that will give us an option that we cannot get anywhere else. So, we are asking that you use what has been given to you to help us. If it ends in death, that is okay. All I ask is that you give your 100% to try to help us." Later, the doctor told me that the words I shared with him are what made him decide to do the surgery.

The reality about a liver transplant is that the organ comes from a donor who is facing death. In other words, one must die so another can live. I wrestled constantly with knowing my prayer for my husband to live meant I was praying for someone's death. That was so hard for me. Death is a part of the deal with the transplant. I was constantly having to remember that, but I was never to the point that I would stop praying for my husband to have the opportunity to live. So many things have to line up for a transplant to happen: someone has to die, then the family has to consent to give the organ, then if all the markers match up, you have to hope the surgeon can be reached for the transplant to occur within six hours. There were times that a liver was passed up because all those things did not align for us. In the meantime, they gave Leron medicine to try and maintain his health. One of the other requirements of a transplant is that you have a caregiver with you for at least six months after surgery in Dallas. So, I went into planning mode regarding what to do for the kids. We decided it would be best to leave the kids in Lubbock, and dear friends of ours helped to organize the care of our children and make sure all their needs were being met. God provided a city of angels to care for my kids during that time. Families, and some complete strangers, took my children into their homes. Some provided for needs like new clothing or shoes, while others helped to transport them. Another way God took care of us was in our insurance coverage. Through a rare opportunity, my company had somehow signed up for an insurance policy that covered a transplant. They did not pay extra for the coverage; it was just a bonus available for that year only. It provided money for me to travel, and it covered some transplant expenses. That policy was only offered for one year, but it was the exact year we needed it for Leron. God continued to open door after door until everything was ready for Leron to get a liver.

In September, we got our first call to come for the transplant. Our kids were three, four, and seven. We said goodbye to everyone and headed to the hospital. We got there and began the twenty-four-hour preparation process. We were so excited. Leron was so ready to get his liver and move on with life. However, there is another factor in the liver transplant process: two people get the call for one liver. Both patients go through the prep process, and at the end, they decide who the best match will be. At the end of Leron's prep, we got the message that the liver was going to the other patient. We were so devastated! I just wanted to say, "But we are right here! We are ready!" But those moments just come with the territory when you are waiting for a transplant. So, we went back home, retrieved our children, and continued to wait.

In late October, we got our second call. It came late at night, so there were no flights for Leron to catch to get to Dallas. A close friend offered to drive Leron. Our goodbyes were quick—they had to hit the road in a hurry to get to Dallas in time for the transplant. I stayed behind to get the kids situated and took a flight the next morning. Leron began going through the twenty-four-hour prep again, but this time the wait was longer. Finally, at 1:30 in the morning on November 1st, the liver came. Our friend and I were there with Leron, and that moment felt like a TV show. We saw a person walking in with a cooler, and we knew it was the liver. I kissed Leron as they wheeled him away for his new liver. In my heart, I was actually really hurting for the family who lost their loved one in order to provide the liver for my husband. I was so grateful he would be given a second chance at life because of their gift. What is sweet is that November 1st is my mom's birthday, so we joked about how she was in heaven tapping God on the shoulder saying, "You know it would be really great if my son could get a liver on my birthday."

We knew it would be over an eight-hour surgery. A few close friends came during the surgery and a few members of Leron's family came. I remember one of the many doctors assisting with the surgery coming out and telling us everything went well. We got to go to ICU to see Leron, and it was so amazing. There was already a noticeable, physical difference, much like when an adult comes to Christ and you can see a distinct change in them. Leron knew he had been given life and given it abundantly. He was so excited and thankful. People would come in to see him, and he would point to the picture of his kids, saying, "These are my kids and I am going to get to be their dad." He kept saying, "I know what the gift of life is!"

Leron was doing well and recovering according to plan. However, after a few days, he began having trouble. They ended up taking him back into surgery and discovering that the hepatic valve in the liver was not working. If we did not get things fixed quickly, the liver would fail and Leron would die. It was so discouraging; we had worked so hard to get a liver, and now we needed another one. Leron was moved to ICU, and his case became a very time sensitive issue. The transplant specialist from Leron's first surgery was gone, so another doctor from the surgery took over the case. He was making phone calls trying to find Leron a liver, and once he found one, it was time-intensive to take all the protocol steps to claim the liver for Leron. They had given Leron some medicine to sustain him until the liver arrived. We only had a twelve-hour window, and we were getting to the end of that time. I was praying over Leron in ICU before he went back into surgery. Those who saw me praying knew I was praying for Leron to live. Although that was true, the conversation between God and me was more about a defining moment in our relationship. I had arrived at a fork in the road in my journey with Him. All of my prayers had been pleading and begging for a particular outcome, not just in this moment, but in many moments prior: for my mom to live and not die, for my husband to live and not die, for my kids to have their grandma and their daddy, for me not to be alone, and so much more. As I was standing over Leron in the ICU praying, it was clear to me that if God chose again to take another one I loved away from me and my children, if I begged God to save my husband and He did not, I knew I would experience anger and frustration and turn my life away from Him. If I truly wanted to be a disciple and really follow God, I knew I must praise Him in all things and give glory to Him in all things—in life and in death. So in that moment, my prayer became about dying to self and submitting to Him, to be still and know He was God.

The doctors were getting a little frantic. They could not wait any longer to remove Leron's failing liver; they were fighting to keep him alive until the new liver landed. I remember watching them wheel Leron down a long hallway to an elevator, and right as they got in, the doctor waved and called to me that the liver had landed. I was so grateful! From that point on, I took things one moment at a time, just reminding myself to be still and know. There were a lot of complications even after Leron's second transplant. He ended up having twenty-six additional surgeries in the next forty days. I had to sign off on every surgery. One evening while preparing for yet another surgery, a matter-of-fact doctor pulled me aside to tell me Leron's likelihood of survival was minimal. I stepped into his personal space and replied, "You don't get to be God in this situation. You are going to do whatever you can do to save him. If he dies, that is fine because that is between me and God, but you don't get to make that determination. So, I hope you are fighting for him and not relying on the fact that you think this is a lost cause." I was angry! If my husband was in there fighting, then every doctor needed to be fighting, too. I did not care what the odds were; nobody got to make the decision to quit. That doctor looked at me a little surprised as he processed what I said. Later, we joked with our friends that none of Leron's doctors wanted him to die on their shift because they did not want to have to answer to me.

Those forty days Leron was in ICU were some of the most overwhelming days of my life. Every moment was life or death for him. In the meantime, I was still dealing with the processing of my mom's will, my job, and our kids were far away in a different city where I could not see them or take care of them. I missed them desperately, but I knew I needed to be with Leron. Managing all these things and emotions, one might think I would lose my mind. But God carried me from moment to moment. I am normally an avid planner, but during those days, I felt like I was completely blind from one minute to the next. I had to wait on the Lord to show me exactly what I needed. He became my daily bread; I relied on him completely to help me make every decision ranging from getting a cup of coffee to making decisions for my kids back home in Lubbock.

Our dear friends brought our kids to the hospital so we could all celebrate Christmas. We were overjoyed to be together as a family. In March, Leron was finally moved to a rehab facility. We had to continue going back and forth to the hospital as we discovered holes in his body that needed to be closed. They had opened him up so many times during his stay in ICU that there were parts of his chest where there was not enough skin to close him back up, so the doctors had to be innovative about how to help Leron heal and recover. As I helped to care for Leron and dress his wounds, I could literally see right through him, and I knew he would never be the same.

As the months passed, we continued to fight. Every day was a fight to be heard, every day was begging not to be reduced to a limited box of knowledge in how to handle this very complex case, every day had to be conquered. I did not walk around angry, but I went through every day ready for battle to fight for my husband. I became Leron's best nurse, keeping track of what he needed and explaining his situation to every new doctor and nurse. It was very lonely to fight this battle without my partner by my side. I knew Leron couldn't fight for himself while he was physically fighting to heal. He needed to concentrate all his energy on getting better. Through all of that, God continued to lead me one moment at a time, giving me exactly what I needed and nothing more.

Every day, I was profoundly aware of my opportunity to show God. In the midst of rolling up my sleeves and doing battle, I remembered that to be a disciple of Christ, I must honor and glorify Him in everything I did. Leron also had a wonderful opportunity to witness to those who cared for him. They could tell something was different about him, and it was beautiful to watch his ability to have peace of mind in the midst of his difficult circumstances. His impact on the people around him was powerful. In the midst of the storm, we knew very well who we were serving and who had control of this. Even when we had bouts of anger, hurt, and frustration, we never got stuck in a place where we blamed God or turned away from Him. I do not recall a single moment of our journey that was easy, but we clung to God as our anchor.

In June, eight months after Leron's transplant, I was given an ultimatum from work saying I needed to get back. I was a full-time nurse for my husband, but I was also in a position at work where I was having to prove my competency to be able to keep my job. The doctors prepared us as best as they could to send Leron back to Lubbock. We were so thankful to be back with our children after being separated for eight months, but everything else about being back in Lubbock was still a struggle. The doctors in Lubbock were not able to give us the help or resources we needed, I was fighting to keep my job, and trying to care for Leron. Our children had been through significant trauma of their own by being separated from us, and Leron was so sick when he came home, that in many ways they did not recognize him as the Daddy they knew. Being home in Lubbock did not mean that our crisis was at an end.

As God and I were walking together through this, I would say to Him constantly, "This is just too much. It is too much." People would quote the scripture "I can do all things through Christ who strengthens me," to me to encourage me, but it was actually discouraging. Hearing those words was like fingernails on a chalkboard to me. I was overwhelmed, and I just kept praying, "This is too much." Finally, I felt God tell me, "It is too much for you. All things are possible because I give you strength. It is me, my strength, that makes things possible." That realization was an "aha" moment for me. I finally understood the true promise of that verse. We were never meant to have the strength to do these things alone; it has always been about God and how He provides strength for us. To be still and know He is God. It gave me so much encouragement to understand that truth from God, and it helped me to be at peace with the knowledge that His strength would carry me. One of our favorite scriptures became "The joy of Lord is my strength" Nehemiah 8:10 NIV.

Trying to live a normal life being back home with Leron was hard. He was too sick and weak to be able to work, and every three months we had to go back to Dallas for a week-long evaluation. It took constant work for both of us to learn how to navigate our situation. I was unexpectedly let go from my job in a round of layoffs. With all of the trials we had encountered by this time, I had a peace when I lost my job. I was not in a panic because I knew God would continue to provide for us just as He had been doing. After a few months, I had the opportunity to go work for a large university. The university gave me wonderful professional opportunities, and it had wonderful benefits with no pre-existing condition clauses, so it was a perfect fit for us. God yet again showed me how He was taking care of us down to the smallest details.

Our life began to settle down. Leron still had many health challenges, and I was his nurse, changing his dressings for two to three hours each day. He was physically half the man he used to be, but we were so grateful to be together as a family. Leron could not work, but he was eventually able to drive, so he was able to help with transporting our kids to and from their activities. It was on our bucket list to take the kids to Disneyland, so for Christmas in 2010, we were able to make that happen.

We did all of the usual wound care for Leron while we were there, but he was feeling good enough to enjoy the trip. We have countless blessings and cherished memories from that trip; God was so good to bless us with that time as a family. That was our last family trip.

By August of 2011, Leron was not doing well at all. One of the things that happens when you get a transplant is you take the anti-rejection medications and they are incredibly hard on the kidneys. They hit Leron even harder because he only had one kidney. A colleague and friend of mine was a doctor, and he was helping us get Leron set up for the treatments he needed. That connection was a huge blessing. Through all of Leron's health issues, we had been waiting for years to have a doctor in Lubbock who would be willing and able to help us with our special situation. After looking at many options, it was determined that Leron had to start a special type of dialysis for his complex health issues. This treatment required even more care for Leron. I rolled up my sleeves and learned the ropes for another level of patient care. Nurse Johnson just received more responsibility and another struggle.

For the next year, Leron struggled through his dialysis. He was in and out of the hospital more and more. He suffered some strokes and had to start walking with a cane. Different issues kept popping up. I was watching him deteriorate right before my eyes. He was a size XL before his transplant, and by that point, I was shopping for youth XL for him. He was just a skeleton. It was hard to watch. He could not really function with the kids, and he could not stay awake, so his driving privileges were revoked. His quality of life was not good. I could tell I was losing him. I wanted him to fight and he wanted to fight for his wife and his children, yet the man was tired. It broke my heart to see him so weary.

In November 2012, we reached the 5th anniversary of Leron's transplant. It was a very big deal, so we celebrated. But Leron was still not doing well. By mid-November, we made the decision to put him on hospice. However, we did have a wonderful Thanksgiving: we spent time with friends, and Leron ate his fill of wonderful food. We also spent time putting up decorations for Christmas and shopping for presents. It was the perfect weekend.

Right after Thanksgiving, I noticed a sore on Leron and asked the hospice nurse to come and check on it. She came over to our house and took a look at it. He had to stand for her to see it, but he was too weak to stand on his own. I remember just standing with him, holding him in my arms. I was looking over his back, and the nurse was looking at his sore. When she looked up at me, I knew without words that his body was breaking down. There was no fix for that. But I knew I could make him more comfortable, even if that was all I could do. Later, I remember we were sitting on the couch and Leron was holding my hand. He asked me, "Is it okay?" I knew what he meant. I responded, "It's okay—just be free." I knew my husband was dying, and he was so sweet to ask me if I would be okay. I was giving him permission to let go.

I called friends and Leron's family that week saying they should come see him because the doctors did not think he had much time. On Sunday, December 2, 2012, the kids said goodbye to their daddy as friends came to pick them up for church, but I stayed with Leron. His respiration was changing, and I could tell we were near the end. I just sat with him, holding his hand. I stepped out of the room to make a phone call, and I remember just taking a sudden intake of breath. I just knew—I ran back into his room and he was gone. As much as I did not want him to go by himself, I know he did not want to leave me. I knew he had probably waited for me to walk out of the room. I was only gone for a minute. And he was just gone...

Leron passed away at 10:30 on a beautiful Sunday morning. With just two phone calls, word spread, and within ten minutes my house was full. That was a big deal to me. I did not want him to be left alone. With all the people there, I made sure there was someone with him in his room at all times until the funeral home came to get him. That first night our kids just wanted to have a group devotional at our house. Dear friends filled our house to the brim, and we just sang and sang devotional songs. As we worshipped, I thought to myself, "Mom is thinking this is way cool." I knew she was saying, "I am sorry for your hurt, Rose. But I am getting my boy Leron, and you are all singing with us." The thought of Leron in heaven being loved on by both of his moms, and holding our child, could not help but make one smile. I admit, I was jealous, but was so happy for all them to be together. I was so happy Leron was free and feeling the love. We sang just as we had the night we sang my mom into heaven. Even in the midst of our grief, we celebrated Leron's life that night in our home. I was determined to give God glory in all circumstances.

Then, I began the work of making arrangements for Leron. I tried my best to involve his family and honor them through the service. I did not call my brothers. Our lives had drifted apart after my mom passed away and had not been in contact for over a year. As I made preparations and decisions for Leron, it hit me: I had no family left to help me. With my husband gone, it was just me and my kids. However, with the showering of love and support we received, even in those feelings of loneliness, God showed me that I had a family in Leron's family and in the friends who were surrounding me and lifting me up.

Leron's service came a week later on Saturday. I wanted as many people as possible to be able to come. I was surprised and honored to see how many of Leron's medical team, teachers, co-workers, and friends took the time out of their busy schedules to come to his service. It spoke highly of the relationship they had been able to build with him. Leron's family traveled from all over, and they were incredibly moved by how our church family loved on us and took care of us. I was so proud to see the impact Leon's life and faith were having, even in his death. The kids (ages 12, 8, and 7 at the time) had decided they wanted to talk at their dad's service, and they all wrote out what they wanted to say about what their daddy had taught them. The funny thing was they all shared that he taught them to chew their food twenty-two times before they swallowed. It delighted my heart to hear them bring that up. What they did not know is that their dad told them that so he could get a little bit of quiet at the dinner table. If they were chewing that much, they could not talk non-stop. It made me smile to think about such a funny memory with our family. After the kids, I got up to speak. I knew it was important to Leron that I share with all those that came how much we loved and appreciated them. We wanted them to know we had seen the glory of God through them. We had seen God's face through them. We had received love beyond our imagination through them.

With Leron's passing, I have had to work as hard as ever to provide for my family. Challenges have come with certain jobs. I find myself praying the same prayer I prayed as Leron was being wheeled into surgery for his second transplant. I do not pray that God will give me the outcomes I want, but instead I pray that I would be still and know that He is God, no matter the outcome. Since Leron's death God has provided me with a variety of jobs. Some would be considered entry level and others more managerial. In each job, I have worked very hard to be willing to serve Him during my time in the various roles. So, I move forward each day in faith. I have to remind myself what my purpose is. After being attacked by storm after storm, it is easy to forget my true identity. My purpose was not to be a caregiver to Leron, and my purpose was not professional success in a job. At the beginning and the end of each day, my purpose is to be HIS and to display Him to the world, no matter what I am called to do along the way. It is that simple. The job I do does not matter, but how I reflect Christ does. Currently, I am working to be a mom to my kids while also providing for them financially. I will do whatever it takes to make sure we have a roof over our head and food on the table, even though it means I have two or three jobs. Yet through all of that, I sense God telling me, "You are mine. Everything about you matters to me, Rose." In this lonely season of my life, God's love for me is my refuge.

Through the dark times and trials of my life, I have felt a profound responsibility to show who I serve. I have wrestled with hurt and frustration on a regular basis, yet I have desired nothing more than to remain faithful and honor God no matter what comes my way. Leron was a beautiful example of remaining a faithful disciple, and his impact was tremendous. People all around are watching all the time: doctors, family members, friends, and coworkers. It is in our darkest moments that we have the highest responsibility to witness to those around us.

The hardest part of my journey is the feeling of being alone: the loss of my mom, the loss of a job, the loss of my husband, my lover, my best friend, my better half, and now, taking on single parenting. Although I know God is always with me, the feeling of loneliness never goes away. Yes, you move forward, but every step you take to live your life, you take with the constant companion of loss. Loss does not mean you can never be happy, but it never truly leaves you. Every special, hard, joyous, frustrating, happy, sad, and neutral moment is experienced in the presence of loss. All these moments I want to share with my Leron. I miss him.

Interestingly enough, the richest blessing of my journey has been to know I am not alone. You see, every moment experienced in the presence of loss is also experienced in the presence of my Savior. God never leaves me or forsakes me; He is my comforter, my everything. He dwells within my soul. I experienced God's unconditional love for me through the way my mom and husband loved me, and now, in their absence, I know and feel His love more than ever. Scripture tells us that "because of the Lord's great love we are not consumed, for his compassions never fail" Lamentations 3:22.

Each day, I continue to trust Him by claiming and proclaiming my commitment to Him and our relationship. I seek Him every day. Every day is a treasure hunt to see what He has to show me. He does things for me all the time that leave me with no doubt that He is present. I cherish those love notes from God. Knowing He loves me so much that He will carry me through every step of my journey brings me pure joy. I focus on the truths I know, and I testify to the faithfulness He has shown me time and time and time and time again. Truly, "the joy of the Lord is my strength and my shield; my heart trusts in Him, and He helps me. My heart leaps for joy, and with my song I praise him" Psalm 28:7 NIV.

Finally, I close with the thoughts Leron and I shared with those who came to celebrate his life at his service. May you have much peace, comfort, and joy on your journey called life. May you listen to the nudges from God that will guide your next steps. May you know to honor and glorify Him in ALL things. Those of you that have been on this journey with us, our love for you is deep. And always remember, God is good all the time, and all the time, God is good.

About Rose Johnson

Rose Johnson is a mom to two boys and two girls. She is passionate about her love for God and seeking Him daily. Her professional opportunities allow her to work with young people and guide them on their journey. Her limited free time is spent supporting and watching her kids play sports, participate in school activities, and spending time with them any way she can.

Tonya Carruthers

Tonya and I also have Pure Hope Foundation in common. She has a heart for young women who have been through tragic experiences. She is going to make a huge difference to the women that PHF serves. I also was drawn to Tonya because she is a highly successful professional in the human resources world. She has worked for large - corporations being promoted quickly through the ranks because of her talent. I plan to have Tonya speak to my business students at the university in the future—she has much to offer. As Tonya shared her story with me, I was heartbroken over what she had experienced. Her courage to share her story makes me want to be brave. It also is such a powerful illustration of God's ability to redeem our broken places and create something new and beautiful. Tonya's life is making such a difference in this world.

Beneath the Mask

Tonya Carruthers

I remember well the day my life changed forever, the day my mom married my step-father, Vegas. One day I was living surrounded by my extended family, the next day we were picking up and moving to a new state. My biological father disappeared from my life at that point. There were no custody battles, no attempts to visit; he simply had nothing to do with me. As a very young child, all these changes were difficult, but I had no idea what kind of nightmares lay ahead of me.

I spent a lot of time with my extended family before the move, but the move became a force of isolation in my life. Vegas was not close with his family, and we did not keep in contact with any family except my mom's parents. My brother, my mom, Vegas (who I came to call Dad) and I all came to depend on each other and do everything together. When Vegas started his own cleaning company, we were the only workers he had. As a family, we worked all hours of the night, and then my brother and I would get up the next morning and go to a full day of school. As the business grew to become successful, both of my parents became very invested and respected in the different communities in which we lived. About a year after we moved to Texas, we had a one-year-old baby girl show up at our house. My brother and I were told that Crystal was going to be our little sister. We were young enough that we did not pry or ask any questions, we just accepted what we were told.

I vividly remember the first time Vegas sexually abused me: I was five or six years old. I remember lying on the floor of my parents' room and seeing him coming over to me. I remember feeling the pressure of his body and not being able to breathe because of the pain. I was so confused because he was hurting me, yet he was telling me in a calm and nice voice that everything was okay. He told me to just relax and I would like it. So, the pain I was feeling did not make sense in my head because he was so comforting. This was my dad, and I loved him. Over the next couple of years, things like this happened once every other month or so; I said nothing because I didn't know life was supposed to be any different.

When I was about eight, I began to realize something was wrong and that I did not like what was happening. I told my mom. True to her nature, she cried, acted shocked, and said we were leaving to go live with my grandparents. I was so excited and relieved; I even had a suitcase packed and ready to go. But then my mom said we were going to wait and talk about it. I was confused as to what there might be to talk about, but it quickly became clear as she told me. She was not sure if we would really go because she could not financially provide the nice lifestyle we were currently living. I told her I didn't care about that, I wanted to go. But she brushed me off and told me we should just talk about it because I did not want to ruin the good life we had for the rest of the family. This excuse became the basis for all of my mom's decisions; everything was about her, and everything ultimately came back to material things and money.

So, we talked. My parents and I were in the bedroom. I was sitting on the bed crying, and my parents were calmly talking about what was happening. It was like they were having an everyday, normal conversation. My dad said he was sorry and it would never happen again. I felt sick. I kept saying over and over again, "No, no, no," but my mom would not listen to me. She said, "See? It is going to be okay now. It is not going to happen again, so we are not moving."

But of course, nothing changed. Once everything was out on the table with my mom and she did nothing about it, my dad became filled with boldness and arrogance like never before. The frequency of the abuse increased until it was almost a daily occurrence. He had no fear of consequences anymore; he was safe to do whatever he wanted. I felt betrayed by my mom. I saw that my parents were liars, yet I still loved them. These emotions plagued me for years into my adulthood because I could not understand how I could hate someone and love them at the same time. I was miserable and I did not know what to do. From time to time, we would have more family discussions. Promises would be made, and then they would be broken. The people I loved most in the world repeatedly broke my heart, my spirit, and my trust. Over time, I developed survival skills and put up barriers to protect my heart, though I could do nothing to protect my body.

As I got older and entered my teenage years, I became more defiant and tried to fight back against the abuse. He began to beat me when I tried to fight him. I was so small; I could not put up much of a fight. I still have scars on my backside from the different materials he would use to whip me. Each day when I look in the mirror, I see the scar above my eye where he once punched me while wearing his ring. He began taking pictures of me posing naked in different positions. Over the years, his perversions only progressed. Because I was small, natural penetration was not easy for him. He began exploring other techniques and various items to use to penetrate. Later in life, I found out that I had developed an infection from something he used on me that would probably prevent me from ever having children. This was yet another piece of my life I felt he had taken from me, another instance where evil triumphed. Through all of the abuse, he continued to talk to me like everything was normal. He would tell me that he was teaching me how to be good at what men really wanted sexually.

During those years, I was painfully aware of the sound of his footsteps in the hall. I would cry when I heard him coming. He typically came to abuse me in the early mornings after my mom left for work and while my siblings were still asleep. School was my only escape. Summers were horrible for me. Most kids look forward to getting out of school, but I hated it because I was home alone all day. Because my dad owned his own company, he had the flexibility to be home a lot. My mom's job would take her away for weeks at a time, which allowed my dad to have free reign with me.

I was living in two completely different worlds. In the mornings, my dad would come to have sex with me, and then I would get ready and go to school, where I learned to wear a "mask," faking my emotions and pretending my life was perfect. After all, who would want to admit to living such a life? I felt completely unworthy of love, alone, and disposable. As a teenager, I never viewed myself as pretty. I thought I was ugly and there must be something wrong with me. It was the only thing that would explain the abuse.

My mom was the only person I had ever told, and she did nothing to protect me. If my own mother did not care about what was happening to me, why would anyone else? Telling the truth had gotten me nowhere, so I just learned to fake my way through life, building walls and protecting my heart.

I strove for perfection in school and athletics because they were the only areas of my life in which I had any control. I was a Straight-A student, and I thought if I worked really hard and excelled in academics and sports, I could get scholarships, get out, and never look back. That was my one and only goal.

I hit a pivotal point in my life the summer before I became a senior. My brother had just left to go to college, so this was the first time I was living at home without him. I do not remember what made my dad so angry, but one morning he called home and told me, "You'd better be ready when I get home." That meant that I would be in his room with my clothes off, ready for him. In that moment, I thought to myself, "I cannot do this anymore. I can't live this way. I can't keep doing this." I had considered ending my life several times before; many nights I sat on the kitchen floor with a knife to my wrist or my stomach, but I could never bring myself to pierce the skin. This morning was going to be different. I made up my mind to end my life. I went to my mom's medicine cabinet and took every pill I could find, about 200 pills in total. After a while, my body began to reject the pills. I started throwing up, and my sister heard me. She came in, saw all the bottles, and called my mom at work. She told my mom, "Something is wrong with Tonya. She took all these pills, what should I do?" My mom's response was, "I don't have time for this. I don't have time to play on my phone," and she hung up. Fortunately, Crystal decided to call 9-1-1. The paramedics came and took me to the hospital to pump my stomach. A social worker came in to talk to me, and I told her I did not want to talk to my parents. All I could think about was what a failure I was, and what a failure my life was. Eventually my mom came to see me. It was just the two of us in the room. She acted emotional until she reached my bedside. She leaned over and asked me, "What did you tell them?" That was her first response. Not "I can't believe you did this, are you okay?" not, "I love you, I hear you crying out for rescue," but "What did you tell them?" At that point, I realized there was no escape for me. I was doomed to a horrible life. My parents created a story that, because I was under so much pressure from being an honors student and an elite athlete, I tried to take my life. No one questioned it. On the outside, my family was perfect: supportive and involved in the community, in a good school, in a good neighborhood, and lots of money.

Shortly after that, school began and I entered my last year of high school. I was on a path to get a full-ride scholarship to continue my passion for sports medicine. For two years, I had been working as a trainer for our football team. All of the guys on the team knew my brother and feared him. Between my brother, my dad, and my low self-esteem, it was certain I would never get the chance to date. This year was my first year without my brother at the same school, so I thought there might be a possibility.

Many of my friends at school did not have a car, so I often gave them rides. During two-a-days, I was giving one of the guys a ride to meet the group to go eat at Wendy's. He asked if we could swing by his house so he could get something he had forgotten. When we got there, he invited me inside to wait out of the heat. I did not think anything about it and followed him inside. I was sitting on his couch waiting when he came out of his room naked. I was completely shocked and caught off guard. He came over to me, overpowered me, and raped me. When he was finished, he got up, handed me my clothes, and left to get dressed. I was still stunned and in complete shock at what happened. The only thing he said to me was, "Let's go." So, we went to Wendy's with our friends and acted like nothing had happened. I was an expert at faking, so I was used to it by that point. In my mind, I was devastated, disgusted, confused, angry, and hurt. My heart was crying out, "WHY?" But, just as I did at home, I did not tell anyone what happened. I simply assumed it was normal, that it was how men treated women, and I just needed to get used to it.

A few weeks later, my brother came back in town to visit from college where he was playing football, and was working out in our high school gym. I had the reputation as the girl who no one had conquered yet; most of my classmates had already been sleeping around. Because I was being molested by my dad, sex with anyone was the furthest thing from my mind. As my brother was working out with the team, he heard the guy bragging about his conquest of me. My brother was livid. He came home and yelled at me, calling me a slut and saying he was barely out of the house and I was already sleeping around. I tried to defend myself. I told him that I did not sleep with him, I had been raped. My dad cut in at this point and declared girls only say that when they have done something and been caught. I felt so lost and betrayed. I did not know where to turn. The only sexual encounters I had experienced were awful and unsolicited. In that moment, my mindset changed. I decided if sex was so important to people, that I wanted to control it. From that day on, it would be on my terms; I never wanted to be controlled by sex again. I would be the captain of my life going forward, no one else.

For the rest of my senior year and into college, I used my body in a horrible way. I had no respect for myself, but I felt like I was winning because for the first time in my life, I was in control. Sadly, if a guy actually liked me and wanted something more than sex, I pushed them away. I did not want a real relationship because it would require me to open my heart for true feelings. I thought as long as I kept from caring for anyone, I could not get hurt. I trusted no one, and I surrounded myself with huge walls and barriers. I was living with a heart full of hate and it was eroding me from the inside out.

When I graduated from high school, I had many scholarship offers to run track. I decided I was going to accept a full-ride scholarship at a university in North Carolina. But again, exerting his control over my life, my dad called the coach in North Carolina and told them I was going to a local school instead. I abided by that decision for a week, but then I finally hit my breaking point. I was an adult and could make my own decisions. My dad was not going to control me anymore. I withdrew from school, walked away from my scholarship, and moved in with a friend and her mom. I told my friend about all of the abuse and that I simply could not take it anymore. Before I made a quick get away with one bag of clothes, I asked my sister if she was being abused. She denied it and said I was crazy. Her reaction made me feel like even more of an outsider. What was wrong with me? Why was this happening to only me? I left that day and never looked back. That was the day the constant dread of daily abuse left my life. It never happened again.

I felt completely liberated. I no longer lived with people telling me what to do or oppressing me. My parents came to my friend's house to get me the day I moved out. My friend's mom met them at the door and told them she knew everything. She told them they could either leave or she would call the police. My parents left but in one last effort to control and manipulate me, they took my car with them.

During the few months I stayed with my friend, I used my new-found freedom to make a series of terrible choices. I had plenty of people in my life willing to let me use them. There was always a purpose behind every guy I slept with: one did my hair and eyebrows for free, and another let me use his car. One night, I had been out late partying and realized I left my keys at home, so I could not get back in the apartment. I went home with a guy I knew from the party and just stayed at his place that night. The next day when I got back to the apartment, I could tell my friend was mad and her mom was disappointed in me. I was ashamed of myself. I remember looking at myself in the mirror and asking, "Is this the life you want? If you continue down this path, your life is going to amount to nothing. Or, you can pick yourself up, work hard, and move forward." In that moment, I knew my life was supposed to be more. It had to mean something; I just had no idea what it was. However, I did know my current lifestyle was not the right choice because I felt more empty and worthless than I did when I was being abused by my dad. That day, I called my grandparents in Plano and asked them if I could live with them. They came and picked me up within the hour.

I enrolled for the next semester at a community college close to where my grandparents lived. The second week of school, I met a guy who I began running into on campus from time to time. For a while, I could not even remember his name, but over time, Daryn and I became friends. One day, we were hanging out in a group. All of a sudden we went from a group conversation, to a conversation with just the two of us. We had an instant connection and discovered we had many things in common. When the rest of the group began to disperse, we were nowhere near ready to leave. We were pretty much inseparable from that point on. I still had so many barriers in place, but I was enjoying his company. I thought we would have a nice summer together, but I did not see it going any further than that.

Over the summer, I reconnected with a coach at one of the universities that had offered me a full-ride scholarship for track. I made plans to attend in the fall, only to discover Daryn had decided to go to the same school. We had not even talked about it. We went to school together and continued dating. One weekend, we went to our hometown and his parents' house to meet up to go watch his little brother's high school football game. While riding with several members of Daryn's family to the game, Daryn's Uncle Marcus, a pastor, was asking me questions to get to know me. Then, he asked me, "Tonya, if you died today, would you go to heaven or hell?" Without hesitation, I answered, "I would go to hell." The entire car went silent. Daryn was looking at me in shock, and I said to him, "What? You would go too; you know what we have been doing." Everyone was stunned, except for Marcus. He calmly asked me, "Well, do you want to go to heaven?" I said, "Sure, but I am not good enough." Marcus told me that it was not about being good, but about opening my heart to God and receiving salvation from Him. He asked if I would be willing to do that.

I had always thought being a Christian meant you had to know the Bible from cover to cover, you went to church all the time, and you had to be a good and innocent person to get in. I was none of those things, so I never imagined that Christianity could be for me. I never dreamed it would be so simple. That day in the car, I accepted Jesus Christ as my Lord and Savior without a grand audience, not in a church, and without angels coming down from the heavens. Later, as I thought about myself and my commitment, I did not see any miraculous change, so I asked Daryn if I was supposed to feel any different. I did not understand the process that had begun, but from that moment on, I had a deep thirst within me to know more about God and Christ.

I knew nothing about God growing up. We never went to church as a family, and we did not associate with anyone who went to church. Jesus and God were foreign concepts to me. I had heard of them, but not anything in-depth. Sometimes when I heard my dad's footsteps coming down the hall, I thought about praying, but I thought God must not love me because He was not protecting me. Looking back, I know God was with me. I cannot count the times I was in the kitchen late at night with a knife in hand, thinking about killing my parents. God saved me from those thoughts each and every time. God was so many things to me even when I did not know it, which is why He is so amazing. I love that God saw me and loved me when I could not see or love myself.

Daryn and I dated for a couple of years before we decided to get married. During that time, I had absolutely no contact with my parents. I had found that the best way for me to cope with the pain and anger was to cut them out and move forward with my life. Even my siblings and I had lost contact. My brother had moved away for college, and was no longer involved in any part of our family. None of us were even present at his wedding. My junior year in college, he decided to attend the same university as me. Because of that, we were able to become involved in each other's lives again and begin rebuilding our relationship.

We heard about a big family event and my brother felt that we should go support our parents. I was uneasy about going, but I would have Daryn and my brother there with me, so I decided I could do it. Daryn drove us, and my brother and I got deep into a conversation about our family. My brother began to give me a lecture about my rebellious attitude toward our family, and I just felt in my heart that it was time for him to know. I could not be silent anymore. I turned around to look at him in the backseat and interrupted him, "What are you thinking? Mom and Dad are not the perfect parents you think they are. Dad abused me all those years." My brother got quiet. He asked, "What do you mean? He was touching you?" Then without going into too many details, I explained to my brother what my life had consisted of growing up. He turned to Daryn and said, "You have to turn this car around. I cannot go see them, or I will kill Dad." We turned the car around and spent the whole way home talking through things. The more I told my brother, the more he said things made sense. He remembered being sent outside to play or go to the gym, but I was never allowed to leave the house. He was able to understand why my character had changed the way it did. It was a God-given moment to be able to finally tell my brother the truth. We bonded in a way we never had before. It was a long time before my brother had any relationship with my parents after he found out the truth.

I began to reach out to my mother and my sister with some encouragement from Daryn. He believes very strongly in the importance of family. I wanted to be able to be involved in my sister's life and support her in her school athletics. As hard as it was to be around my family again, I tricked my mind into believing I had forgiven them. I was a Christian at this point, so of course, forgiveness came with the package, right? I began to repair my relationship with my parents at least on the surface. During this time, they had adopted my dad's nephew, DeMarcus, whose own parents did not want him. I wanted to be a part of this baby's life, even if it was just to protect him from the life I had.

The day Daryn and I got married was a beautiful day, yet I was riddled with many different emotions. I believed it was time to move forward with my life and start claiming things that were stolen from me as a child. Marrying Daryn was giving me a family I never dreamed I could have or deserve. His parents treated me like the daughter they never had, and his brothers filled a void left by my brother. I was hurt by the fact that my brother did not come to my wedding, but I also understood. I wanted my wedding to be perfect, so I played the dutiful daughter and made peace with my parents. It was such a strange feeling to have my dad walk me down the aisle; it was more for ceremony than anything else. However, despite all of the horrible things he did to me, I still loved him, so I really wanted to include him in the wedding. I had convinced myself that I was over everything. I felt like my wedding day was an opportunity for a new beginning in my life. I got to marry the man God had provided for me. I got to make a new life with him that would be untouched by the horrors of my past.

Life was as normal as possible over the next year and a half. It certainly was not perfect, but Daryn and I were at least cordial to my family. I spent a lot more time at my parents' house once we had our son, Daryn II. It made it easier because there were two baby boys in the family, and babies make spending time together fun. However, it was not long before my world came to a screeching halt once again. While my family was on vacation, my sister called me crying at 2:00 in the morning. She told me she could not take it anymore. I asked her what she meant. She said, "Dad and I had a fight earlier, and he pushed me down the stairs, grabbed me by the hair and pulled a chunk out." I was stunned. I asked her, "Where is mom?" She told me mom was in the kitchen making pork chops; she had not done anything to stop it. I told her to call our grandparents to come get her and, as soon as I was home I would come pick her up. When we got home, my sister came to live with us. She began to share with me that my dad had abused her consistently since the time I left home. I was devastated, angry, and overwhelmed with guilt. All the feelings of hatred I had lied about and convinced myself were gone, came boiling up once again.

About a week after Crystal came to live with us, I came home from work to find her crying uncontrollably. When I asked her what was wrong, she said, "I really want to tell you something but I know you are going to lose it. I don't want you to freak out and be mad." Inside I prayed, *God, what else can you lay on me that is worse than what I have already experienced? I don't know that my life can get any crazier.* I was panicked on the inside, but I remained calm on the outside. Daryn was by my side supporting me. I told my sister, "Just tell me. I promise I won't freak out." She hesitated, and then said, "Well, DeMarcus is really mine. I had him going into my sophomore year. Mom and Dad hid it and covered everything up because dad was having sex with me." I was in horrified shock. I prayed to God again, begging Him, *You have got to hold my tongue. Keep me strong. How do I help her?* I asked my sister how it happened, and she told us the whole story up to how my mom forged the birth certificate in the hospital to cover everything up.

After we finished talking, I had to go outside. I broke down crying in Daryn's arms. I did not know how to handle this information, or what God wanted me to do with it. I did not know how to respond. I decided to call my parents. When they answered, I said, "There is no point in lying to me, I know the truth. I am coming to pick up DeMarcus because he is not going to live with you anymore." My mom said, "What are you talking about?" I told her my sister had told me DeMarcus was her baby and Dad was the one that got her pregnant. My mom coolly responded, "Well, we don't really know who all she was sleeping with at the time." I was floored. I asked, "Do you really hear yourself? Shouldn't the bigger problem here be that it is possible DeMarcus could be your husband's?" My dad cut in and arrogantly said, "What are you going to do about it?" I told them we needed family counseling, but they blew me off. I told them DeMarcus needed to live with me, and I would come pick him up in the morning, but when I showed up, they would not answer the door. At that point, I felt that I had no choice but to go to the police to protect DeMarcus. It was one of the hardest decisions I have ever had to make; I would much rather have fixed my family and broken the cycle of dysfunction, but my parents had no intention of changing.

The next day, we went to the police to press charges. We were there all day and all night giving our statements. A few days later, my parents went in for questioning. By that evening, my grandparents called me yelling and cussing. They could not believe I would lie about my parents and get them arrested. I was surprised, I had no idea my parents would be arrested. My grandparents continued to accuse me of lying and making my sister lie as well. I was very hurt. My grandparents had been more of parents to me than my own had been. For them to accuse me and refuse to believe me was crushing. That was the beginning of the whole family ostracizing us. My parents were bailed out by one of my aunts. The police could not find DeMarcus because my parents had taken him to an aunt in another city before they were arrested. As soon as they got out of jail, my mom began to spin and weave stories to my whole family to make me look hateful and crazy. Only one person in my entire family, my cousin from Florida, called me to get the real story and believed me. Everyone else believed my mother. We were disinvited to our own family Thanksgiving dinner. When my grandfather relapsed with cancer, the family lashed out at us even more.

It was not until my grandfather's cancer got very serious that he requested to see my sister and me. When we got there, he handed Crystal an envelope containing her original birth certificate and social security card. My grandfather was Crystal's real father. He had an affair years ago, and to cover up Crystal's birth, he got my mom to take her in as her daughter. When Crystal showed up as a baby out of the blue, my mom was actually taking in her own sister. This convinced me deep down that brokenness and deceit ran as a vicious cycle in my family. It was not until the end of his life that my grandfather made the effort to be honest about his past mistakes. When I heard this news, I thought to myself, "Wow. Our family will just continue down this path because we are being held in bondage by generational curses." But thankfully, that is not true for me and my own family because we have accepted Christ. We live as new creations who are no longer under the curse of sin.

Our lives were in utter chaos at that point. My dad had confessed to everything. His mentality was that Crystal and I had belonged to him, so he was at liberty to do whatever he wanted with us. His lawyer, however, intended to plead not guilty. Both of my parents had charges filed against them and were awaiting their trial. My grandfather passed away from cancer. I accepted an out-of-state job. Looking back, I see without a doubt that our move to Arkansas was God's way of protecting us from being so close to all of the turmoil and trauma. When we moved, we only had each other. We had to learn to be a family unit who depended on God and on each other. Our time away from Texas brought healing and strength to our marriage and our family.

My sister, however, went down a path very similar to my mother's. She married a man who is just like my dad, and she had two children with him. She became a victim of domestic violence and ultimately left her home to live with another man. Because we were in Arkansas at the time, I was not aware these things were happening until I got a call from Texas CPS. They told me that my nieces, whom I had never met, were found home alone, malnourished and covered in ants. Unfortunately, due to the fact that Daryn and I were living in a different state, we were unable to get temporary custody. Crystal signed her rights to her daughters away, as well as DeMarcus, so they are all living with non-relatives.

While we were in Arkansas, my dad was sentenced. He decided to plead guilty, so there was not a trial or any need for us to testify in court. My brother and his wife watched my dad's confession, but I decided against it. They told me he was arrogant and unapologetic. A search warrant had produced pictures and videos he had kept all these years of my sister and me. If there had been a trial, that evidence would have been enough to put him away for life. As it was, he got thirty years in prison with a minimum of fifteen years. My mom, on the other hand, was given probation. That was a hard pill for me to swallow. I felt that she was just as guilty as my dad and should have spent time in prison. The day we heard the verdict of the case, I was hit with all sorts of emotions: excitement, relief, anger, sadness, guilt, vindication, and loneliness. I do not think there is any child who would rejoice at having put his or her parent away in prison, but I knew my dad needed to be where he could no longer hurt anyone. When the verdict came out, the rest of my family felt foolish. Some of them apologized, and others were so embarrassed that they kept silent.

Forgiveness has been a huge obstacle for me to overcome in my life. I have exchanged a few letters with my dad in prison, but I have never gone to see him. My children know that because of the decisions he made, he will not be a part of their lives. I have struggled to forgive my mother perhaps even more than my father. Despite his arrogance, he at least admitted what he did, and he is now reaping his consequences in prison. To this day, my mother will not admit to any blame or responsibility. She only says we should not dwell on the past. I have had to work through issues with my extended family after they accused me and isolated me during the investigation.

For a while, I would believe I had reached peace with my circumstances. Then I would hear something as simple as my parents' names, and my insides would be consumed with fury and hatred. I began being legitimately sick and suffering from a lot of stomach issues. I was literally making myself sick from the inside out from all the hate I was carrying. Finally, one day, God hit me square in the face with my own sin. He spoke to my heart that no one was above forgiving others because Christ made the ultimate sacrifice to forgive us for our sins. At no point in scripture does it say, "honor your father and mother if they are good parents, or if they did not abuse you," it simply says, "honor your father and mother." Without forgiving them, without finding a way to honor them, I cease to look like Christ.

I had to learn to practice forgiveness with boundaries. Just because I forgive does not mean I walk blindly and carelessly. I try to act with a spirit of forgiveness and a spirit of love toward my mother. She is allowed to have a relationship with my children, but she knows that it will always be on my terms. My children will never be allowed to be alone with my mother, but she is welcome to come see them at our home.

The longer I live, the more I understand that forgiveness is a journey. There were so many times I would say, "I forgive," but the concept stayed in my head and never traveled to my heart. I would think to myself, "I am good. As long as I don't have to see them, interact with them, or hear their names, I am good." I thought I had forgiven them, but then one little reminder would bring all of my bitter feelings rushing back to the surface. God works forgiveness into our hearts, not our mouths or our minds. Our hearts cannot lie to us or fool us into believing we have found forgiveness. We have to pray to God, asking Him to peel back the layers of our brokenness and renew our hearts. Let me tell you, it is HARD. It is a daily decision to follow Christ and give your burdens over to him.

I look back at my childhood, and I remember being a little girl praying desperately in my room as I heard the footsteps coming down the hall. I did not even know I was praying, and I certainly did not know the God to whom I was praying, yet He was watching over me. There are many names of God, but my favorite is El Roi, which means "God who sees me." He protected and strengthened my mind so I could survive. He kept me from taking my own life, or from killing my parents. I did not know who He was, but He knew every hair on my head and heard every cry of my heart. 1Peter 1:6-7 HCSB says, "You rejoice in this, though now for a short time you have had to struggle in various trials so that the genuineness of your faith—more valuable than gold, which perishes through refined by fire—may result in praise, glory, and honor at the revelation of Jesus Christ." This is such a comforting scripture for me; it allows me to live in joy and be grateful for the purpose of my trials.

I would never have gotten to this point in my life without the foundation of my relationship with Christ. Accepting Him as my Lord and Savior was the best decision I have ever made. Because of the presence of God in my life, I learned to nurture my relationship with Him rather than feed my own hatred. I learned to keep my eyes on His faithfulness rather than falling into a self-centered, victimized mindset. If you look at me on the outside today, you would never guess what happened in my past. God is a redeemer and a restorer. He restored my life in ways I never thought possible and has shown me His vision for my life. God has blessed me with a professional career I do not deserve. He has opened doors no man can shut, and I have been at companies and in positions I was not supposed to have. God has given me a family with a husband who has a heart for God and who leads our two boys (who I was never even supposed to be able to conceive) and teaches them how to be kingdom men. For all the times I felt lonely and abandoned, God has given me the parents I never had in the form of my in-laws. They love me as if I was their own daughter. He has surrounded me with friends who are truly like brothers and sisters to me. The Holy Spirit has given me the voice I was without all those years, and it has allowed my test to become my testimony and my pain to manifest as my purpose. I am no longer ashamed. I am blessed that God chose me and trusted I would use my life as a living testimony to bring girls and women to Christ. I serve a God that can do the impossible. There is nothing he cannot do, no one he cannot save, and no one he cannot love.

About Tonya Carruthers

Tonya J. Carruthers, first and foremost is a servant of God who was placed on this earth to speak life and truth. She is a Human Resource Professional, Diversity Strategist, and Inspirational Speaker who loves to invest in people. Tonya has the ability to see things strategically and speak with the wisdom God provides. She helps people use what they have to get where and what they want. She works daily to help people find purpose and be positioned for greatness.

She holds a Bachelors in Business Administration and Human Resources from Texas Women's University. Tonya also serves on the Advisory Board for Pure Hope Foundation.

She is a faithful wife to Daryn Carruthers and devoted mother to sons Daryn II and Micah and is blessed to help raise her nephew Jaden.

Melissa Keyt Quayle

I first knew about Melissa when I heard her speak at a leadership conference – and then got to spend some time with her at another leadership retreat. She is one of those people that you feel like is your best friend after only a few minutes. Her love for the Lord is infectious and draws you in. She makes me want to be better. With so much positive feedback from the first book related to Melissa's story, we decided to publish her story in this book as well. Without any spoilers, know that someone in Melissa's story agreed to write their story at the end of her chapter. Even if you read her story in the first book, I know you will be so encouraged by reading it again. It is just another example of how God mends our broken hearts and makes all things new.

Will You Believe Me for the Impossible?

Melissa Quayle

My once upon a time began over thirty years ago when I left my home in Arkansas to attend Lee College in Tennessee. It was there that I fell in love with my college sweetheart, Perry. Following college, we worked together in full time ministry for twenty-five years. After 10 years as an associate minister, we were heading to LaGrange, Georgia to start a new full-time pastorate.

I don't know about you, but sometimes I just have to have a whining session with God. He is a big God and he can handle it. Taking this new ministry position meant we had to leave behind our home, our church, and even some of our family. Our daughter, Tiffany, was a sophomore in high school, and our son, Matthew, was a senior. Matthew would be staying behind to complete his senior year. Let me tell you, as a mother, I was not handling that well. So, in my whining session, I was open and frank with God about how I was feeling. "God, I feel like Abraham. I feel like you are asking me to lay everything that I love on an altar and sacrifice it. You are asking me to leave my church, my friends, and my family. Asking me to lay my *son* on the altar and give him up–asking me to put a knife to everything that I love and leave everything that is familiar." And God answered me so sweetly. *What did I do for Abraham?* "You gave him a ram." *Everything you need will be in that ram.*

So we made the move. Perry had seemed to be a little under the weather for the previous several months; he had developed a cough, but the doctors accredited that to allergies. We went to see a specialist, and an x-ray revealed something in his lungs. They felt fairly certain it was a chronic disease known as sarcoidosis, but they wanted to do a biopsy to be sure. Because Perry was under the anesthesia, I met with the doctor after the biopsy. I'll never forget walking into that room by myself and seeing the doctor sitting there, pale, with his head in his hands. "I don't know how to tell you this Mrs. Keyt, but your husband has stage-3 lung cancer." It was like an out of body experience. Cancer hadn't even been on the radar. All I could think was, "This really can't be us. He's never smoked a day in his life." The doctor went on, "Does your husband take bad news well?" I could tell that he did not plan to be the one to break the news to Perry. So, the task fell to me. As we were leaving the parking garage, Perry asked me what the doctor had said. I told him that we would talk about it later, and he stopped me, saying, "No, I want you to tell me right now." So, I had to tell the love of my life that he had stage-3 lung cancer. That was eight days after our first Sunday at our new church.

On our way home we called Perry's mom to tell her. Some dear friends of ours that had become almost surrogate grandparents to our kids were at our house when we told the kids what was happening. Dan, our adopted grandfather, spoke a profound truth to our family in that moment. "You know what? No matter what name this has, we know that everything has to bow to the name of Jesus." So we made the decision as a family that we were not going to walk in fear. I remember looking at my kids and saying, "I am so thankful that God trusts us enough to walk this journey." My wonderful mother-in-law told me she understood exactly what I meant, but if I said that in public, people would think I was crazy. But I meant it. I still mean it today; I just say it through a lot more tears now.

One of our first questions was why God would bring us to minister to a new church only to have Perry be diagnosed with cancer. We believed with all of our hearts that this situation was just going to be another way for God to receive glory. I was adamant about how we were going to approach the situation. I told people, "If you can't stand in faith with us, I do not want you calling and speaking doubt or fear to my husband." Perry joked with the church at one point, "You'll have to excuse my wife. She is a bulldog/rottweiler dressed as a poodle." The church, even though we were new, prayed with us, stood with us, and believed with us. So, we held fast, rock-solid in our faith, believing that Perry was going to be miraculously healed.

Perry had never smoked, and there was no history of cancer in his family. It truly made no sense, but God had promised me that he would provide everything I needed in that ram. So, you had better believe that this girl began studying Abraham. I had heard his story preached all of my life. I had studied about him, and even taught about him before. Yet, I needed to know more about him. How in the world could a man take a knife and sacrifice his own promise?

Romans 4:19-21NIV Without weakening in his faith, [Abraham] faced the fact that his body was as good as dead—since he was about a hundred years old—and that Sarah's womb was also dead. Yet he did not waver through unbelief regarding the promise of God, but was strengthened in his faith and gave glory to God, being fully persuaded that God had power to do what he had promised.

Faith is not ignoring the facts. Faith is when you believe God with undaunted perseverance, despite the fact that everything around you is telling you something different. You see, I never denied that my husband had cancer. But I believed the truth much more than I believed the facts. The truth to which I held fast was my faith and my trust in God.

Genesis 22:1-2 ESV Some time later God tested Abraham. He said to him, "Abraham!" "Here I am," he replied. Then God said, "Take your son, your only son Isaac, whom you love, and go to the region of Moriah. Sacrifice him there as a burnt offering on one of the mountains I will tell you about." Abraham was human just like us; he had feelings and emotions. He had this promise that God had given to him, and now God was telling him, *I want this son that I have given to you back.* Imagine. You never even asked for this promise. Remember, God is the one that told Abram, *Go out and look at the stars in the sky. As many stars as you can see, so shall be your descendants.* Abraham never asked to be the father of many nations, but God chose him, and now God is asking for that promise back.

The January before Perry's diagnosis in September, I was sitting in a special time of worship with my head bowed, minding my own business. Then, out of nowhere, I vividly heard God ask me a question: *Will you believe me for the impossible?* It wasn't loud, but it was loud enough that I literally looked up to see if anyone heard it. Nobody was looking up except me. I was so excited; I felt like I had been hand-picked when he asked that question. The next morning, reality hit me. In order to believe in the impossible, I would have to be in an impossible situation. I just had no idea what lay ahead of me.

During Perry's chemo, we were living in LaGrange, and his treatments were in Cobb County, which meant we had to drive quite a ways for every treatment. This was when gas was over $4 a gallon. There was one month during that time that we spent over $1800 for gas for our car. Our old house still had not sold, so we were maintaining two homes. And to top it all off, I was away from my son. So, I was getting a little panicked. I thought maybe God needed reminding of everything we were dealing with. As I started to pour out my problems to him, I said, "God, what are you doing? This makes no sense to me, it makes no sense!" Then he said a phrase to me that still to this day brings tears to my eyes. *Melissa, I thought you said you wanted to look like me.*

Genesis 22: 5 NIV [Abraham] said to his servants, "Stay here with the donkey while I and the boy go over there. We will worship and then we will come back to you." This is my favorite passage in the whole story. Abraham was my example when I was desperate to know how to walk this walk of faith. Even though God was asking for his son, he still responded with *we will worship.* You see, he loved God more than he loved his promise. When Abraham said *we will come back*, he was saying "God you have asked for my promise, yet I am still going to worship you. Somehow, I will still come back with my promise." When Isaac asked Abraham, "Where is the sacrifice?" Abraham told him that God would provide. He was looking eye to eye with his promise, and he said that the Lord would provide.

During Perry's illness, I can tell you that the man walked a life of worship. When the pain was too great, he would have to try and sleep in our recliner, so I would lie on the couch to sleep. If I woke up at any point, I would look over and see him with tears streaming down his face, listening to music on his headphones and worshipping. In the fourteen months following his diagnosis, Perry only missed one Sunday of preaching. As the chemo destroyed his body, we were in and out of the hospital all the time. Many Sundays, I would have to get him dressed in order to get him to church. Some days, he was so weak that he had to sit in a chair to preach. He had a banner made for our church that said "Don't let what's wrong with me stop me from worshipping what is right with Him."

I can't tell you how thoroughly I believed my husband would be healed. I was convinced he was going to live. We were building a house with the contingency of selling our house back in Cobb County. I would take him out there and prophesy what our future was going to look like. I told him that someday we were going to be out there with all of our grandbabies. We had picked out all the cabinets, granite, and carpet. I had scriptures picked out that we were going to write on the floor of each room. I was convinced that he was going to be healed. I remember being on the phone with my brother; he was the only one for whom I did not feel that I had to be strong. I was crying and telling him how tough things were, yet, I can vividly remember telling him, "Barry, the good news is that at least I don't have to worry about being a widow." I was convinced.

On November 26, 2008, I was still so convinced that Perry was going to live. Even when we were in ICU, the kids and I were around praying and singing healing scriptures. At 8:30 that morning, when they said that Perry was going to be moved to hospice, I told him, "You and I both know that you are walking out of hospice." I was thoroughly convinced. I was lying in bed with him when he began to get really bad. I had become very close to the ICU nurse, and she had asked if I wanted her to stay. She was on the right side of me, and I was next to him in the bed when he quit breathing. I asked her, "Is this it?" and she told me yes. But even then, I wasn't asking if he was dead. I believed he was going to come back; that's how convinced I was. He didn't come back.

I remember sitting in my son Matthew's lap, crying with Tiffany, my daughter, right beside us. I don't know where it came from – I can promise you I am not this big, or this spiritual – but something in my spirit rose up. I got up and got back up on his bed and said, "God, you are the Alpha and the Omega. You are the Rapha: the healer of all things. You are Jehovah Jirah: my provider. I will declare this: from this day forward, as for me and my house, we will serve you." I don't know where that came from, but looking back on it now it was as though I had to draw a line in the sand, saying, "Devil, you will not have my children. You will not have my family. You will regret the day you ever touched my family, because we will touch the body of Christ. We will absolutely let people know that you can be crushed, you can be broken, your hopes can be devastated, and you can still come out on the other side." I am so aware that the way I worship is the only way I have remained sane; it is the only way I still have breath in me. In God's presence is the fullness of joy, even in the midst of the greatest of sorrows. I am so convinced of that.

The days after Perry went to be with the Lord consisted of simply putting one foot in front of the other, just getting up every day and doing the tasks before me. We had sold our home in Cobb County the Labor Day before Perry died. So, when he died, we were living in a rental house as the home we were building was being finished. Matthew was off at college. I had to get out of the contract for the house and find a place for my daughter and me to live. So truly, Tiffany and I were homeless when Perry died. The only thing that sustained us was just total belief in God that he would take care of us.

My children will tell you that they both dealt with a lot of shock and disbelief initially. Tiffany especially was really wrestling with fear, a struggle that I had dealt with all of my life. I was talking to her about how God did not give us a spirit of fear and how perfect love casts out fear. Then God began nudge my heart, and I was thinking, "Yes Lord, I know that perfect love casts out fear, haven't you been hearing me talk about this with Tiffany?" He spoke to me. *No, you have got to know me; I am perfect love. If you know how much I love you, you will walk anywhere I ask you to walk.* If we know his perfect love, we know we can trust him. My love for my kids cannot compare to the love of the Father. He impressed upon my heart that there is no way he will fail to provide us with what we need.

Every event throughout the first year is difficult to maneuver. Sometimes you put pressure on yourself to do things the way your loved one would have wanted. Or, you make a really big deal about keeping things exactly how they were before in honor or in memory of your loved one. I went through a lot of confusion at first. I knew in scripture it says that Jesus bore our grief, so I didn't know if I was supposed to be grieving or not. Then I would have someone call me and tell me, "Melissa, you have got to grieve, or it will show up somewhere else in your body physically." I am a firm believer that the Holy Spirit teaches us things, so I simply began to pray, "I need you to teach me how to grieve."

People with the best intentions would say things that made the ache so much worse. I had so many people say to me, "I know what this feels like." I even had someone send me a sympathy card that said, "I know what this feels like; I lost my dog." All I needed was for people to tell me, "I am sorry. I have no idea what this feels like, but I am so sorry." I needed them to let me have my grief. One of the biggest things that strengthened me and encouraged me was a group of women in my life who had also lost spouses. I was the youngest of the group at age forty-five, but our common experiences bonded us. I would call them and check on them. Pouring my love and encouragement into other people helped me to get my mind off of myself. But I couldn't do that every day. Some days I just didn't have the strength.

When Perry and I got married, we became one. When I lost him, I became a half-person trying to live as a whole person. Every evening when the sun went down, not only did it get dark physically but also there were moments that I just wondered how I was going to keep going. I didn't have a sounding board anymore; I didn't have someone to talk to when I was trying to help my kids. It was the little things I missed. Not just the intimacy, not just not having someone to touch me, but hearing him say "Do you have your jacket?" I missed the feeling of security when he placed his hand on my back to support me and having someone to help me put on my coat on as I left a restaurant. People think the first year is hard, the first Thanksgiving, the first Christmas, trying to make new memories on each first holiday without that loved one, and it is. But, I will tell you that the second year was worse. That was when reality hit. Every holiday was no longer a dress rehearsal. This was my life now. I was alone more than I was with someone. There was one holiday season three years after Perry died that I sat on the couch and watched Christmas movies for the whole month of November and half of the month of December. I just didn't have any get up and go. I gave myself permission to do this because I understood that all I was capable of doing on those days was lying on the couch and watching those movies, and that was okay.

I had always heard that a widow would need to allow the Lord to be her husband. I would try to tell myself that and believe it, but I wanted real arms. The enemy would magnify what I didn't have; he would make me feel like a perpetual third wheel or like a round peg trying to fit in a square hole. I had spent the last 25 years of my life being married, and all of my friends were still married. I just didn't fit. People would look at me with concern and pity and say things like "Wow, if that were my husband, I would never marry again," which was easy for them to say as they went home to their husband. Or, I would have someone say "You know, Jesus will be your husband, and that should be enough" and that same friend would go home to her husband and go away on a special trip with him. But I just had to keep telling myself and reading in scripture that God is the one who said it is not good for man to be alone.

Tiffany was a junior in high school when Perry died, so we had about a year and a half before she went to college. During that time, my kids and I really bonded to each other. Mathew was only a few hours away at college, and he would come to visit often. We were already an incredibly close family, but this experience drew us even closer together. I experienced deep loneliness when the kids moved away. It is a horrible feeling to see the worry in your children's eyes when they are leaving you, to watch them wrestle with the heavy knowledge that no one will be there with you once they back out of the driveway. I struggled with the loneliness, but at the same time I was overwhelmed with concern for my kids. No kids at the ages of eighteen and twenty should have the burden and worry of feeling responsible for something that is not their responsibility.

Genesis 22:9-13 NIV When they reached the place God had told him about, Abraham built an altar there and arranged the woo on it. He bound his son Isaac and laid him on the altar, on top of the wood. Then he reached out his hand and took the knife to slay his son. But the angel of the LORD called out to him from heaven, Abraham! Abraham!" "Here I am," he replied. "Do not lay a hand on the boy," he said. "Do not do anything to him. Now I know that you fear God, because you have not withheld from me your son, your only son." Abraham looked up and there in a thicket he saw a ram caught by its horns. He went over and took the ram and sacrificed it as a burnt offering instead of his son. So Abraham called that place The LORD Will Provide. And to this day it is said, "On the mountain of the LORD *it will be provided."* When God fashioned that ram, he fashioned it with horns so that it would be caught in the thicket. It was specifically designed to be a provision for the father of many nations. God's provision for us is powerful.

I can tell story after story of God's provision for us after Perry died. This is one of sweetest to me. I remember telling a friend that I couldn't keep sleeping under the same bed spread. I didn't want to spend a lot of money, so we went to Sam's Club. I saw one for $185, and even though I didn't need to spend that much, I decided it would do. I went to the check out, and the lady at the cash register asked how I was doing. I told her I was thankful and blessed, and she said the same. She scanned the bedding and it came up $36.01. She said, "Girl, that is the favor of God." I touched her on the hand and said, "You have no idea, you have just seen a ram in the thicket." I carried that receipt in my billfold for a while, because it serves to remind me of God's provision. The receipt read "COMFORTER $36.01." It was like a love note straight from the Father to me.

I was making my bed one day, when God asked me a question. *Do you know why I picked out your bedding?* I said "No sir." *So you would know you are resting beneath my provision.* I am not making this up; I am not smart enough to make this all up. God wants us all to know that we are resting under his provision. Abraham and Isaac were walking that road of obedience up one side of mountain, while their provision was walking up the other side. God wants us to know that he provides; Psalm 34 talks about him being our deliverer, close to the brokenhearted. How many of us are guilty of trying to deliver ourselves? We try to get ourselves out of our situations, out of our circumstances, and all the while God is asking us like he asked me that morning during worship: *Will you believe ME for the impossible?*

About a year after losing Perry, the Lord spoke to my heart. *You need to embrace your singleness.* It made my stomach drop. I knew marriage was in my future, and so his words confused me. He went on to say, *Be the best you can be.* I began to start trying to make myself a better me. When I would pray over my future spouse, one of the scriptures I would pray was to make me a suitable helpmate. I knew I had prayerfully been a helpmate suitable for Perry for 25 years, yet, I knew my future husband would have different needs with different things in his life.

I was single for a total of 5 years after Perry passed away. I knew in my heart that I would eventually get married again, and I had talked with my kids at length about it. Tiffany embraced the idea more than Matthew at first, but after Matthew fell in love and got married, he had a better understanding of what I had lost. I was probably ready to start dating about two or three years in, but I didn't want to go out on a date just for the sake of dating. I wanted to be sure it would be with someone who was compatible with me. I went out on a few dates, but it was just not a fit. It was very discouraging, and I often felt that I would just rather be at home. The enemy tried to convince me that finding someone at my age that had the same beliefs that I did and who would love my kids the way I needed him to was impossible. But then my daughter-in-law told me about someone that her aunt Jeanette knew, and told me that they wanted to introduce us.

Jeanette's father was a pilot, and had been hired by a man named Mike to give him some flying lessons for a specific kind of plane. Both being strong believers, the men connected during their time together. As soon as Jeanette heard about Mike, she instantly thought of me. So, of course I trusted my daughter-in-law and Jeanette, and I let them contact Mike for me. He was a little apprehensive at first, because he had had some bad experiences with set-ups, but he went ahead and emailed me. That very same morning as I was working out, I just really had an amazing time with the Lord. Through serious tears and sobbing, I felt like it was the first time I was able to celebrate the Lord as my true husband. I just worshipped him. I said through tears, "Lord, you are the greatest husband I could have dreamed of, the greatest husband I could have asked for." The timing of it all was incredible, and I know without a doubt that it was all God's doing.

Mike poured his heart out to me in his email. He was a retired newspaper publisher. His wife had died of cancer several years before, and that had caused him to lose his faith and become an alcoholic. During that broken time of his life, he had remarried, but that marriage had ended because of his alcoholism. He told me that he was nine years sober, that he had a great love for God, and that he may even sound like a zealot at times. I laughed and thought, "Wow, you don't know me yet. You just wait." We emailed back and forth for a while and then had a live phone call. After that, we talked pretty often on the phone and skyped. I felt like I was falling in love with him even before I ever met him in person.

Mike flew to Tennessee to see me and meet my kids. I had been very open with my children about Mike, and in our early dating stages I had forwarded all of Mike's emails on to my kids to read. Tiffany and Matthew joined us for the first dinner of his visit. My children are so much a part of me that it is like they are an extension of my own heartbeat, so it was very important that they be included in the process. We had plans to all fly up to Ohio to spend a weekend together. Mike was showing me his plane, an old style, open cockpit Waco biplane. He and I were in the front cockpit, and I saw a plaque on the plane with letters and numbers. I asked him what it was and he told me it was the call letters of the plane. I said, "You are kidding. That is my birthdate and my initials." It was like another one of those precious love notes from God. It was like he was saying, *I've got you. I've had you this entire time.*

Mike asked Matthew and Tiffany for their permission to marry me before he asked me. He told them that he didn't want to ever replace their dad, but that he would like to be whatever they wanted or needed him to be in their lives. Mike and I had flown to Arizona so that I could meet his mom and get her approval. While we were there, we would go out on morning flights. One morning, we were flying over the Sedona mountains and talking about what heaven was going to be like. He asked me, "Would you live with me in heaven as my wife?" and took a ring out of the back seat of the plane. So, we got engaged flying over the Sedona mountains.

We got married on August 31, 2013. It was an amazing outdoor wedding; my son walked me down the aisle, and our kids were the ones who stood with us as our attendants. It was a beautiful day, and we spent it surrounded by some of the most important people in our lives as we began this amazing endeavor.

I like to call Mike my Boaz. I had a list of things I wanted to find in a man before I would remarry. I wanted someone who would be able to travel with me and work with me. At my age, I knew that would be difficult to find, but Mike was retired at an early age. He travels with me, and we minister to people together. We talk to people about preventing disease, staying healthy, and keeping their bodies strong. Another important reason why Mike and I work so well is because we both know how it feels to have lost someone. All of our children have lost a parent. When I made my list of what to look for in my Boaz, I figured there were some items on there that were wishful thinking. Kind of like as a kid when you circle all the things you wish you could have out of the Sears and Roebuck Christmas catalog, even though you know there are some things that you will never get. But once again, I underestimated God's incredible provision. Not only did I get everything on my list, it's like I got the whole catalog.

I never dreamed that my once upon a time would take the twists and turns that it did. I'm not the same woman that I was seven or eight years ago, but I praise God for that. I am not going to tell you that it did not rock my world when Perry died. He was not at my son's wedding. He was not at my daughter's. He will not be there for our grandchildren. But, every trial that I have been through, that my family has been through, God has used to his glory. He has strengthened me to be a voice in the wilderness for others who are struggling. God has faithfully sustained me and provided for me every step of my journey, and he continues to fulfil his promises to me daily. I don't know what kind of crushing you are going through. It may be way tougher than my crushing. But I can promise you, I am a testimony that God will love you and will never leave you. He will heal those broken places. When you are facing an impossible situation you are either going to stand in faith, or you are going to stand in fear. In fear, you are convinced you cannot pull through. In faith, you are confident in God to control the situation, because he is I AM, our perfect love who casts out fear. *Everything you need will be in that ram.*

About Melissa Quayle

Melissa was born and raised in Blytheville, Arkansas and left home after graduating from High School to attend Lee University in Cleveland, Tennessee. While at Lee she met her husband, Perry. After graduating she and Perry spent 25 years in full time ministry in Michigan, Texas and Georgia until Perry's death in November of 2008. After her husband's death she returned to Atlanta to raise her two children and then moved three years later to Cleveland, Tennessee to help care for her aging father. In 2009 she started her own business with the Juice Plus+ Company. In 2013 she met her present husband Mike. They married later that year and together they operate their Juice Plus+ business and travel extensively for their businesses and pleasure. Melissa is a frequent speaker at church and women's events to inspire audiences wherever she travels with her Christian messages of faith and hope. Today, Melissa lives in the Chattanooga, Tennessee area with her husband. She enjoys spending as much time as she can with her children.

Mike Q

I knew a lot about Mike before I met him. Melissa and I had stayed in touch and I was always grilling her about the new developments related to the new man in her life. It was so fun getting updates – from how it was going exchanging emails to the big day when they would actually meet. We all became involved in Pure Hope Foundation, and that is where I got to know Mike even better. I would hear parts of his story and knew I wanted to share it with others. Mike has such a heart for those in recovery and also those who don't know Christ. His ability and willingness to relate to people is remarkable. I am so blessed to have Mike and Melissa in my life!

You Can't Make This Stuff Up!

Mike Q

Have you ever been overwhelmed by God's ability to weave things together in such a magnificent way that you are left saying, "you can't make this stuff up!"? I have said that many times over that past several years. Three years ago, the Lord amazed me by revealing the tapestry He had been weaving out of all the pieces of my life, and He continues to exceed any hope or dream I may have for my life. Let me explain.

I am a pilot and have been flying for many years. In 2012, I purchased a new Waco, a newly-manufactured replica of the popular 1930's era open-cockpit, bi-plane. It was beautiful and powerful and unlike anything I had ever flown. Because of its design, specifically being a conventional (tail-dragger) landing gear design, I had to hire an instructor to become certified to fly her.

The factory gave me the name of one of their instructor pilots. Jerry is an Air Force veteran and retired from US Airways. I was asked by the airplane manufacturer to bring the airplane to Palm Springs for display during an annual airplane fly-in. I agreed and emailed Jerry to see if he would instruct me on a long trip to southern California. He was delighted. We joined another company Waco and departed for a three-day trip to Palm Springs.

I had rented a house in Palm Springs for our stay, and I got to know Jerry quite well during the five days we were there. Each morning, I would notice Jerry on the patio with his Bible, reading some cards. I was intrigued and asked what the cards were. He explained they were his favorite "life" scriptures.

I had always had an interest in the Bible but was quite ignorant of its content. I was a believer and was hungering for a chance to know the Lord. Jerry and I spent several days talking about Christ and scripture, and each day I wanted more. I grew up as a believer but never had a real relationship with the Lord. I knew there was more, but I never had mentors to encourage me to embark on a relationship. Jerry had re-ignited my quest to know the Lord better.

Soon the fly-in was over, and I found myself back in my home town of Fort Wayne, Indiana getting ready for the holidays. Knowing that I would be visiting family, I called Jerry and offered to fly to his hometown in western Ohio and buy him lunch. He agreed, and I was excited to get to see my new friend and talk more about the Lord. I jumped in an old Piper Warrior airplane that I had bought for just such a trip. We met for lunch and continued our conversations about family and flying, politics and patriotism, and, of course, the Lord. It was a delightful lunch, and before I left, Jerry asked me stay and meet his daughter and son-in-law.

Tony and Jeanette came into the restaurant before I left. They were wonderful people and were filled with joy. Jeanette mentioned that she had someone for me to meet if I was interested. I was single, and it seemed that nearly everyone in my life was trying to set me up on a date with a friend or sister or someone they knew. I had been on many blind dates, each one worse than the one before. So, when Jeanette asked, I offered a firm, "no thank you!"

Over the next couple of months, I had little instruction time with Jerry due to the winter weather, but we managed to talk frequently on the phone and through email. A new item added to our conversations was the fact that Jeanette still wanted to know if I wanted to meet her friend. Jerry seemed a little put out making that offer, but I am sure he had promised his daughter.

The winter passed slowly. I was working on a project in southern California and spent much of the winter there or visiting my elderly mother in Arizona. I would hear from Jerry often, and we would talk about continuing my training when the winter weather allowed. He also followed up each call with 'the' request from Jeanette.

Out of the blue, Jeanette called me one evening and was asking questions about Butler University in Indianapolis. She knew that a couple of my kids had graduated from that school. She and Tony were interested in finding out more for their son who was thinking about attending there after graduation. I answered her questions and gave her a recommendation. Before we ended the call, she asked again about me meeting her friend. This time I relented. I thought to myself that I could always use another friend. I told Jeanette to email me her friend's contact info and I would get in touch with her.

On March 28 of 2013, I sent an email introducing myself to a woman that I would fall in love with before even meeting her in person. The night I composed the message, I suddenly felt like a teenager with butterflies in my belly. I also felt a calm like I was about to meet someone that I already knew. I figured I would not hear anything back. I was wrong.

The next day, I received the sweetest email reply from Melissa. I learned a little about her in that note, and I asked her to send more information and maybe include a photo of herself. I received a photo of a gorgeous woman and her beautiful adult children. I was quite intimidated by her beauty. On top of that, I was quite intimidated by the fact that she was a licensed minister. She was from a very Christian past and was the widow of a pastor. Together, they had been in full time ministry for more than 25 years. I was not from a Christian past, although I had hungered for a relationship with the Lord for many years. I longed for more knowledge and understanding about the God who had saved my life so many times.

During my correspondence with Melissa I made sure I was honest and completely transparent about my past. I was in my late fifties and a retired newspaper publisher. I had grown up in Indiana and led a fairly normal life. At least that is what I thought. I also wanted her to know that I was a devout Christian. As I continued to share things about myself, the most painful thing in my life kept surfacing in my mind, and it was time to make sure Melissa knew everything about me. I knew I was falling for her, and I felt the same was happening to her. I needed to share the last important thing about me, the fact that I was a recovering alcoholic. Just the thought of telling her frightened me. Most people bristle at the word "alcoholic," let alone invite that person into their lives. My mind was spinning as I typed the words in the email I was composing. Suddenly, I found myself transported back in time, re-living my painful past. I was about to tell Melissa about all of it. It went something like this:

"My name is Mike Q! I am an alcoholic!" I have introduced myself that way in Alcoholics Anonymous meetings for much of my adult life. I wonder how many times. Hundreds? Thousands? I don't really know, but I do know that today I am sober and have been since August 15, 2004. I have had stretches of sobriety before, but depending on my own strength has always failed me eventually. This time feels different because I have a new teammate helping me. I have put the Lord at the center of my recovery team and my life, and every day I am more grateful for His involvement than I was yesterday. But it was not always that way.

My twin sister and I are the youngest in my family. My two brothers were eight and ten years older than us. After a short, early life in Arizona, my father moved us in the early 1960's to a small, farming community in northeastern Indiana. He had purchased the local newspaper and became its new publisher. My mother was a homemaker and had lots of friends. We were the quintessential nuclear family of the 1960's.

My sister and I attended a small, rural school. My sister was always cute, blonde, and popular. Me—not so much! I was always small. I was the kid that was always picked last for the kickball game or the basketball game or for any sport. The other boys in my class were athletic. I was considered a nerd and was told that most every day. I so badly wanted to be popular like the other boys.

I grew up as many little boys do with a great love for my dad. I idolized him! He was a giant of a man to me. He was smart and honest. He was a lover of America, a proud patriot and a veteran of the United States Marine Corps.

He was highly respected by everyone who knew him, and I wanted to be just like him.

My dad was not a very affectionate man. As a little boy, I looked forward to a seat on his lap or a hug and a kiss good night. But that all ended on my seventh birthday; he told me that I was a man now, and men shake hands. I was confused and devastated by this change. I cried myself to sleep on that birthday and for many other nights after that. Every time I shook his hand for the rest of his life, I felt sorry for him and the little boy he had forced to grow up too soon. Despite this, I continued to love and adore my dad for the rest of my life. He was my inspiration in so many things and was my hero. I wanted to follow in his footsteps.

Growing up, I always went to work with him on Saturday mornings. It was our special time together. He would take me out to breakfast and buy me silver dollar pancakes. He frequently taught me things about life on those wonderful Saturday mornings. At his building, he would give me a chore to do like cleaning out a storeroom, or cleaning up the back alley and loading dock area. For this, I would receive a small monetary compensation of a half dollar or even a dollar. But it was his verbal praise for of a "job well done, Michael" that I always craved.

My parents had lots of friends, and they entertained frequently in our home. As in most social situations alcohol was served. I never asked what it was, but I was told never to drink it. When the adults would go into the dining room for dinner, I would investigate the leftovers of the appetizers and the smelly stuff in the cocktail glasses. I would think to myself, "they have fun drinking it, why shouldn't I?" I would finish all of the drinks left over and then be half sick as I ran upstairs to hide. Every time I did this, I got sick to my stomach, but I would continue to do it each time my parents entertained. This repetitive, destructive behavior would reappear many times in my life

On Sunday mornings, our family attended a small Episcopal Church, and I loved it. The priest was kind and always took a moment to talk with me. I became more and more involved in the church and was confirmed after a year of classes. I was then allowed to receive communion and drink the awful wine they serve with it. I became an acolyte (altar boy) and would have to attend practice once a week. For the first time in my life, I was not being seen as a nerd. My parents seemed proud of me, the priest treated me like a good kid, and my friends in the church seemed to think I was cool.

One Saturday morning when I was eleven, I had to be at the church to help the priest and the altar ladies prepare the church for an Easter celebration. That morning in 1967 would change my life forever, and the change was not for good. I found an open bottle of wine about half-full in the corner near the trash that had been tossed out. Without even thinking about it, I took the bottle and went to the restroom where I drank the whole thing. I remember feeling triumphant, that I had gotten away with something. Shortly thereafter, my dad picked me up, and I began feeling sick on the car ride home. My dad kept saying he smelled something funny on me, so I told him that I had eaten some Easter candy. I got home and ran around the fence to the backyard and vomited. I had no idea what I had just started.

Later that summer, I was able to spend a couple of weeks with my grandmother who lived near Indianapolis, Indiana. Nana was a devout Christian and she loved the Lord. She never raised her voice and always had a hug for her grandchildren. Nana took time to teach me to love. She taught me more about God than any other person in my life. As the years went on and my use of alcohol grew, I always felt as though I was letting God and Nana down.

My junior high years were quite cruel to me. My sister was very popular and would be invited to things that I would not be. My grades suffered as I spent every waking hour trying to figure out how to be one of the popular kids. No matter what I tried, nothing was working for me. I prayed every day to be cool. I asked God to help me to be. But in my mind, He never showed up.

The summer before I was to enter the 10th grade, my father offered to let me attend a boarding school. I thought it was my chance to start over and be normal. I applied, and that fall I was accepted to a prestigious military academy in Northern Indiana. I remember the two-hour drive there and thinking that my life was going to change and things were going to be wonderful. I did not realize that the change I needed was internal, not external. I spent the first year of my military school experience as a plebe getting hazed by the older guys and laughed at by the athletes in my company. I spent most afternoons after class by myself on the campus somewhere wishing I had never come. I would call my parents on weekends asking to come home.

My roommate introduced me to marijuana. The high that I felt took me away from myself and made me cool, or so I thought. So, I started smoking pot and even drinking a little every chance I got. Each time I did, I felt an immense amount of guilt. I felt that I had disappointed God, my grandmother, my parents, and probably my entire family. I promised God that I would never do it at again. I made a promise to myself never to be that weak again. But the following Friday night, I would find myself doing it again, and I could not stop. My feelings of guilt were soon enough replaced by a magical euphoric high—and the cycle began.

I finally graduated from high school and happily left those miserable days behind me. The thought of going to college was exciting for me. I chose a small college in southern Michigan for one reason. In 1974, Michigan had an 18-year-old drinking age, and in October of that year, I would be legal to buy and consume alcohol. My new college roommate was a fellow alcohol enthusiast who dabbled in drugs too. Upon meeting, our first major college decision was to walk into town and buy some beer. That decision unfortunately set the tone for the next four years.

I spent three and a half years drinking and doing drugs. College life was a party. I attended classes when I had to and barely scraped by with my grades. I spent many weekends traveling throughout the state of Michigan finding new spots to party. Once again, my life was spinning out of control, but this time I knew it. I never attended church. I rarely prayed and God was not a part of my life. I felt empty most of the time. I felt that God had abandoned me because of the way I was living my life.

Looking back, it is clear that I was hopeless. And without God in my life, how could it be anything but hopeless?

I decided I could not go on this way anymore. So I did what I did best; I decided to run away from the problem. I quit college with only one semester left. I had no plan. I prayed every night for God to help me. I couldn't figure out who I was praying to and what I was praying for. All I needed to do was to get away and start my life over "again." I moved to Arizona to a little town where my father owned a newspaper, and I went to work for him. Life was good. No parents around. No stress. No one to judge me. Yet, once again, I had no friends. For the next several years, my alcohol intake would go up and down depending on my emotional needs.

A year later, I met a wonderful woman, Cindy, who had two darling boys. Her husband had abandoned her and the boys, and she was trying to put her life back together while staying with her mother in Phoenix. After dating for several months, I asked her to marry me. We had a small family wedding at my parents' house and then moved our little family to Phoenix. We set up house in a suburb. I was happy and content. I was married to a beautiful woman and had two little boys who adored me. Life was great, and I did not feel the need to drink, except for the occasional beer by the swimming the pool. We attended church as often as we could. I tried to instruct my kids in the Lord, but many times felt unequipped to do so. I also felt things were still not right between the Lord and me.

Just as quickly as things had improved in my life, they fell apart. Work pressures and family pressures led me back to abusing alcohol. I spent more and more time away from my family working. I would stop at local bars after work. And after arriving home after midnight intoxicated too many times, my wife gave me an ultimatum—stop drinking or get out!

I accepted the ultimatum and entered my first alcohol rehab in Phoenix. I worried about what my family would think, especially my dad. His opinion of me was so important to me, and I thought he was embarrassed by my problem. When I got out of the thirty-day program, he wrote me the kindest letter about how he understood alcoholism and was there to love and support me. He related to me that many of his friends had ruined their lives or even lost their lives to alcohol. He said that he was proud of me for tackling it head-on. I still have that letter. For the next seven years, I remained sober and toughed it out through many difficult situations both involving work and family. However, the biggest test came when my wife was diagnosed with cancer.

This devastating news came as pressures at work and a growing family had nearly brought me to my knees. Despite the ups and downs of my spiritual life, I had always believed myself to be a Christian. Now, I leaned on the Lord heavily as my wife faced leukemia and as my children watched their mother's health slowly erode. Each day I would end up on my knees asking God to intervene.

After four years of research, treatments, and blood transplants, Cindy's health became critical. She lay on a hospital bed dying. I asked our priest to come in and give her last rights. I held her hand and prayed openly. Several nurses joined in and by early morning, she was still hanging on. I was alone with her as she slept. I was exhausted and slept lightly with my head on her bed. I felt her stir. I also felt a calm that I had never felt before. I opened my eyes and saw Cindy with her eyes open and that familiar twinkle in her eye. She asked if there was any breakfast. I began to cry and prayed again to thank the Lord for restoring her. She said that she had never felt better. Had she been cured? Did she win the war? Or just the battle? I did not question anything and was able to take her home a couple of days after.

I felt that my need for alcohol had been replaced by a need to talk to God every day. For the next couple of months, Cindy felt better. Then, one day she felt so weak that she could not sit up. The doctor said that she needed another blood transplant or she would not live long. Cindy underwent chemotherapy for six weeks while we waited for acceptance to a new transplant program in Durham, North Carolina. She survived the chemo treatments, and we prepared to leave for the transplant program. She kissed the kids goodbye. Both of us knew she would probably not be coming home. As we drove out of the driveway, she began to quietly cry. She told me that God had different plans for her. Tears filled my eyes. I knew it too. I prayed quietly on the entire 15-hour drive to Durham. We spoke very little, but we knew what the other was feeling as we traveled to North Carolina.

More chemo. More radiation. More prayers. More tears.

Finally, the transplant was complete, followed by many stressful days of critical blood counts and other ominous results. She was losing weight and had very little energy. I spent every day by her side until midnight and then return to my apartment to complete work for my job and to write updates to our family. I would go to bed each night crying and praying. Each day, I felt in my heart that she was losing this most important battle. The thought of her dying overwhelmed me. I felt each day that I could not handle things. I needed something to help me.

Late one night, I went to a nearby liquor store and bought a bottle of vodka. I took it back to the apartment and placed it on the table. I sat down with a glass of ice. I stared at the yet-unopened bottle. A voice in my ear kept telling me it was ok and that I deserved a drink. Looking back, I know it was the enemy. He found his way through my armor and encouraged me to drink, so I gave in. By the next morning, I had consumed most of the bottle and passed out. The feelings of guilt overwhelmed me, and I knew I had to hide this behavior so that Cindy would not worry. I was successful and she never knew.

Over the next few days, I prayed and started to negotiate with the Lord by telling Him I would not sin or drink anymore and I would live a righteous life if He would let my wife live. The next day, I arrived at the hospital and Cindy was up walking and feeling normal. The Lord came through! Blood tests revealed her cancer was gone. The doctors said she would be released to live in the apartment but would have to visit daily for platelet infusions and other treatments. I thanked God for His healing powers and made plans to return home to see our kids for the fourth of July. Cindy's sister would come and stay during my absence. I went home and celebrated with the kids with a trip to the pizza parlor. I felt like I had been pessimistic and that Cindy was now past the danger point and had been healed.

The next day, I went to the grocery store to pick up some things for dinner. Walking down the liquor aisle I also found a bottle of vodka. I bought it without even thinking about it. That night, ignoring the promises I made to God, I had my own celebration in the privacy of my bedroom after the kids had gone to bed. The more I drank, the guiltier I felt. I could not stop and drank the entire bottle. I woke in a haze. The enemy had hooked me again.

I enjoyed a routine for the next couple of weeks with my kids and Cindy's parents who were there to care for the kids while we were in North Carolina. Each night, I would retreat to my room where I would empty another bottle of vodka and pile on more and more shame. Then, everything changed. I received a frantic call from Cindy's sister telling me that I needed to return immediately. Cindy had collapsed in the clinic and was in critical condition. My mind swirled in confusion. So many things to do. My sons were gone with friends. Cindy's parents had planned a short trip. I needed to be back at my office. What was I to do with my teenage daughter?

As quick as I could, I made arrangements to leave again and decided to take my daughter with me. She could hang out in the apartment while I went to the hospital. We landed at the airport in Durham at midnight and took a taxi directly to the hospital. I asked my daughter to wait in the waiting room while I found Cindy's sister and got a report. I entered Cindy's room and saw a woman whom I did not know. She was on a ventilator and unrecognizable due to the fluid in her body. I was crushed. What was going on? I had no answers!

I took my daughter to the apartment and tried to explain things to her. I told her to get some sleep and I would be back shortly. She asked me if she should pray. All I could say was that would be best. I spent the rest of the night in Cindy's room. I prayed quietly at her bedside as I had done for the past several years. I prayed for her not to suffer. I tried making deals with God to spare her life. Her condition worsened through the night. I prayed while I lightly stroked her face. I had the overwhelming feeling that she would not survive this. She would drift in and out of consciousness over the next 24 hours. I divided my time between going to and from the apartment checking on my daughter and updating my sons and the rest of the family. I received a medical update every 15 minutes from the medical staff. Between all of this, I would retreat into an empty office and pray. I was begging God to spare her life and making more and more promises. I was not eating and was living on coffee.

The next morning, Cindy was now mostly unconscious but still in acute pain as evidenced by her moans when touched. I kept hearing a voice in my heart to say goodbye, but I could not do it. I kept pleading with the doctors to reduce her pain and suffering. She would open her eyes every so often, and I could see that she was pleading with me to let her go as we had talked about for that past several years. I was losing my wife. I knew what I had to do. The awful decision was supported by her sister and her wonderful nurses who had seen this situation so often. I called my daughter back at the apartment. She was so strong and courageous. I hung up the phone and collapsed on the floor in uncontrollable tears.

After I composed myself, I called the medical team together and told them it was time to let her go. I needed some time to talk to her and to pray. At 7:30 PM, I ordered the ventilator removed. I asked for a priest to come in and give her last rites. I prayed for God to take her home. He listened. Cindy died in my arms a few minutes later.

Cindy's sister, my daughter and I left for our home in Indiana the next morning. The three of us were quiet for the most part, except for intermittent stories of Cindy's wonderful life. Once home, Cindy's mother was already preparing to feed everybody. I had already pre-planned her funeral so we waited for friends and family to gather. I was numb. I was exhausted.

I went to my room that first night home with a bottle of vodka in my hand. I was angry at everyone. Mostly, I was angry at God. In my mind, God had forsaken me. He took my precious wife from me. I kept these feelings to myself and would make them worse when I drank. This was just the start of a tailspin that my life would take over the next 10 years. Cindy's death never became any easier. I cut off any form of relationship with the Lord. I quit my job. My life was under the control of the enemy. I was on a road leading me to destruction. Little did I know, God still had hold of me and would show up in a most glorious way.

In August of 2004, I was visiting with my family in Santa Barbara, California. Little did I know; family time was not the only thing on the agenda. After lunch one day, they gathered in my mother's room and invited me to come and chat. It was an intervention. After lying to my family for the past ten years about my drinking, they called me on it, and I was caught. That evening, I ended up at the

Betty Ford Center. Once again, I was not the cool kid. I felt like I was an embarrassment to my family, and now I was in a place where they could hide me away.

I was resistant to the rehab at first, but I came to realize that I was a sick man. My health was horrible, and my liver enzymes were off the charts. I had never really mourned my wife, and I had lost my relationship with God. Maybe this place was where I should be. I navigated the routine of the recovery program, keeping things surface level much like I had done in Phoenix years earlier, but my small recovery group saw through my fake work and called me on it. My counselor worked me over to find the roots of my shame. I started work on accepting the 12 steps of the AA program. The first step, which is typically the hardest (admitting that I am powerless over alcohol) was easy for me. In my troubled past, I would often stand at the bathroom mirror and ask the man in the mirror, "Why can't you stop?"

The second step was easy for me, too. I knew that a power greater than me could restore me to sanity. It was the third step that baffled and made me resistant to the program. The third step was to make a decision to turn my will and life over to the care of God. What God? The One who abandoned me in my time of need? I couldn't do this step and was told that I could not move on or leave the program until I did.

Sleepless nights followed. I was miserable. The thoughts of Cindy's death came roaring back into my memory. Late one night, I spoke to one of the center's spiritual counselors, Patrick. He was a former Benedictine Monk and also a recovering alcoholic. I told him of my dilemma. For once, I did not feel judged. He listened and told me he had the same feelings years ago. I told him that God was probably mad at me and had discarded me much like I had Him. Patrick chuckled and simply told me God did not work that way and encouraged me to get on my knees and ask for His help again.

For the next few nights, I did just that. I got on my knees and asked Him for forgiveness and direction. Nothing became easier. I was losing my faith again. Was God finished trying with me? The next day it was extraordinarily hot—not a cloud in the sky or a breeze of any kind. I was frustrated. I walked out to a small pond on the campus. My emotions were boiling to the top. With tears streaming down my face, I literally fell to my knees and shouted out, "God, where are you? I need you! Please help me! I can't go on without you!"

Right then, in the midst of a hot, dry, windless afternoon in the desert, God showed up. A cool breeze came across the pond making ripples in the surface. The cool breeze nearly knocked me over. A peace came across me, and my heart was filled with an indescribable joy. I felt in my heart a voice saying, "I've always been here. I would never leave you!" I cried uncontrollably for several minutes and then sat by that pond for another hour. Although it was 116 degrees, I sat in the coolness of God's joy. I realized that He was always with me. While I know that the depths of sin I walked in would not have been what God wanted for me, I know now that if I not walked there, I would not have come to the knowledge that He is my savior.

As my memories faded, I was drawn back to thoughts of Melissa and her sweetness toward me. She read my story and still invited me to Tennessee. A few weeks later, I was on an airliner bound for Chattanooga to meet this precious woman whom I had fallen in love with over the past few weeks. The palms of my hands were sweating as the plane touched down on the runway. As I walked off the plane my heart and my thoughts raced. "What if she doesn't like me? What if she really doesn't want a recovering alcoholic in her life?" What if's started flooding my mind.

I looked up and saw this beautiful woman just past the security area waiting on me. She was jumping up and down and unable to contain her excitement. Was she looking at me or someone else? The doubts continued. A few feet from me and our eyes met. There were no doubts anymore. We embraced as though we had known each other for years. Tears filled her eyes. I, too, was choked up at the thought of this divine meeting.

Our first "date" consisted of dinner at a local restaurant talking about things that we had only written back and forth. We prayed before our dinner in public; something that I had never done as I was told it offended people. Now, I really did not care. God was in the center of my life to stay. All I could think was that I was being accepted and loved by this woman whom I barely knew. She was well aware of my past, and she was okay with it. She told me the story of the death of her husband of more than 25 years. I thought it was so awesome that she was still in love with him. I understood that because I was still in love with Cindy. Only two people who had gone through that hell could understand and accept the love one has for a deceased spouse. I felt like I had known her my whole life.

After checking into my hotel, we drove a short distance to her house where we talked into the wee hours of the morning. It was hard to leave her, but I did only to return a few hours later for breakfast. Our stories continued and we made plans for me to meet her grown kids the following evening for dinner. I had offered to make dinner for everyone. As that meeting grew closer, my nerves began to take over again. I knew Melissa liked me, but all this could go south if her children did not.

First, I met her eldest, her son Matthew and his beautiful wife, Kayla. We exchanged pleasantries and I think all of us were a little nervous. The nervousness ended when Melissa's daughter, Tiffany, came. Melissa always referred to Tiff as sunshine in a small package. This could not be truer. Tiffany's boyfriend, Nate, came with her. All of us were at ease with one another quickly. The most important thing to me was that Melissa had shared everything about me with them. They accepted me with all of my faults and dark history. I was at peace. Before my visit was over, all of us agreed we should meet in Ohio so I could meet Kayla's family and see Jeanette, who was responsible for all of this joy.

We arranged to meet at Jerry's farm. Jerry has a grass landing strip at his farm that was perfect for me to land in my Waco. In order for me to have another lesson to continue my certification, Jerry flew his plane to my home town and we jumped in the Waco and headed back to the Dayton area. We were met on the grass runway by Jeanette (our cupid) and her husband, Tony. Later that afternoon, we were joined by Melissa and her kids, who had just arrived in town, and I was introduced to the entire family. It was a wonderful experience, albeit an intimidating one.

I was struck by the Godliness of this family. I was humbled by their deep relationships with the Lord. I found it wonderful that Jesus Christ was in the middle of all of these lives. They had a relationship with the Lord that I had never known. They knew scripture and prayed devoutly. This was truly the family that I had hoped for so long, and I wanted to be a part of it. I felt at home, like I had known these wonderful people for my entire life. I was questioned by each of them and felt like the inquisition had gone well.

As the weekend was winding down on a beautiful Sunday afternoon, I asked Melissa if she would like to go on a short ride in my airplane. She never hesitated, we were shortly airborne with Jerry as our pilot. Flying over the area was awe inspiring and having my new girl at my side in the tight cockpit was heartwarming. As we banked over the farmland of western Ohio, I noticed Melissa kept starring at the instrument panel with an uneasy look on her face. Thinking she might be afraid, I asked if she was nervous. She replied that she was not, but pointed to the plane identification plate and asked what it meant. I answered that those numbers were the plane's tail numbers, the identification of the airplane. She had a nervous look on her face and elbowed me firmly in the rib cage, exclaiming, "That is my birthdate and initials!" The tail number was N835MK. We are still not sure what the number five is for, but it was clear to me at that point: the

Lord had arranged this new relationship and was pointing out to me that He was the orchestrator. Goosebumps covered my body and a warmth fell over me as we flew back to Jerry's strip.

The wonderful weekend was over too quickly, but my love for this woman was growing. I knew in my heart that we were meant for each other. I needed Melissa to meet the important women in my life: my daughter and mother. Since Cindy's death, my mother and I had become extraordinary close. She was not only a mother to me but had become a wonderful friend too. I visited her often in Arizona, where we shared many hours of conversation and family fellowship. As she aged, my visits grew closer together and lasted longer. I worried about how she would take me introducing a new woman into my life.

Perhaps the most special woman in my life was my beautiful daughter, Jamie. She and I had been very close as she grew up. She loved animals as I did and had a zest for life that was most like mine. She was fifteen when she was with me the night her mother died. That experience further cemented the bond between us. In an instant, I had become both her father and her mother. I hurt for her as I knew she would be spending the most precious times of her life without her mom—graduation, college, marriage, babies. During those difficult times, Jamie and I had become best friends.

A quick trip to southern Indiana for Melissa to meet my daughter's family was a heartwarming success. Jamie found a mother and Melissa was gaining another daughter. My granddaughters fell in love with her and started calling her Mimi by the end of the visit. Melissa was a natural when it came to being a grandmother. The Lord continued to weave this tapestry of love in our lives. I kept thinking, "This can't be real." I prayed on the flight home to Atlanta thanking God for His blessings. As our plane touched down, it was time to plan our next adventure. I invited Melissa to travel with me to Arizona to meet my mother and to celebrate her 91st birthday. My mother and Melissa immediately hit it off. My mother always loved the south, and here she had her own southern belle with whom to chat, and possibly a new daughter-in-law to join the family.

A couple of days later, I asked Melissa to join me on an early morning flight over the beautiful red rocks of Sedona, Arizona. The sun was coming up as we took off. As we headed to the northeast and at 5,500 feet over the famed red rocks I asked Melissa to marry me. I reached into the back seat of the airplane where I had hidden an engagement ring and presented it to her. She was so overcome with surprise that I had to ask a second time to get the answer that I was seeking. God was smiling on our relationship and our engagement. Why wouldn't He? He arranged all of it!

That night I prayed. I thanked the Lord for all He was doing in my life. I was overwhelmed with His love and forgiveness. I had abandoned God after Cindy's death. I had abandoned Him during my wild days of drinking. But I now knew that God had never abandoned me. I had thought, with all of my drinking and hard living that He might not be interested in me anymore. I was so wrong. From the day I had put Christ in the center of my life at the Betty Ford Center and let Him have all of me, the Lord continued to overwhelm me. My Savior was indeed in control.

Melissa and I were married later that summer in a storybook wedding on a hot August evening in north Georgia. During that ceremony, it was evident that Christ was in the center of our marriage and our family and our lives. We prayed together and received communion together. This beautiful woman was purely a gift from God. I have never loved anyone as deeply as I do Melissa. This beautiful tapestry the Lord had woven is inspirational. Since then, our lives have increased in His glory. Our children are part of one family and could not get along better. The blessings the Lord has bestowed are unbelievable. Not only did I fall in love with a beautiful woman, she helped me rebuild a relationship with my Lord and Savior, a relationship that has filled my life with love and joy. God is the cornerstone of our lives. I do not have many regrets in my life. The one that I do have is running away from the Lord during the hardest times in my life rather that running to Him. He has His arms around us today. Melissa and I could not be happier.

And I say once again, "You can't make this stuff up!"

About the Mike Q

Mike grew up in northeastern Indiana. He attended Culver Military Academy and Hillsdale College, where he majored in communications and journalism. He spent most of his professional career as a newspaper publisher in Arizona and Indiana. Prior to that, he spent many years as a firefighter and paramedic in the metropolitan area of Phoenix, Arizona. Today, he enjoys operating a Juice Plus+ business with his wife and being a grandfather. He is a member of the Pure Hope Foundation Board of Trustees and spent many years serving on the Betty Ford Foundation Board of Trustees. Mike and his wife, Melissa, together have five grown children, three granddaughters and a grandson. Mike is an avid pilot and enjoys traveling with his wife in the couple's plane and spending time with their family. The Quayle's live in the Chattanooga, Tennessee area and are members of the Westmore Church of God in Cleveland, TN.

Kathrine Lee

Similar to Melissa, I had heard Kathrine Lee speak at a leadership conference and was immediately drawn to her. A few years after first hearing her speak, I found myself sitting in her home in California as we were both being filmed for a training video. Her humble, warm spirit welcomed me into a special friendship that continues to bless me richly today. We both marvel at how God has woven our stories together in very profound and meaningful ways. She has taught me much about what it means to be in love with Jesus Christ and be willing to serve Him with all of your heart, even when it is hard. She sharpens me as a Christian, wife, mom, teacher, and leader. I still kinda scratch my head in wonder that we are friends since she literally has thousands and thousands of people who love her and are her friends. She also is a bit famous—being on the Oprah Winfrey show multiple times. God knew I needed Kathrine. Just another way God provides for me in such sweet, tender ways.

Since the profits of the first book and this book are all going to the Pure Hope Foundation, we thought it would be helpful for all of you to read the story of how it came into existence. We would love for you to become part of the story by praying for the foundation, volunteering, donating, or simply commenting on FB words of encouragement. Those of us who have been part of the story so far have been absolutely blown away by what God is doing! It is such an honor and privilege to be involved with Pure Hope. We would love to share that feeling with all of you!

The Pure Hope Foundation Story

Kathrine Lee

My name is Kathrine Nadine. Early on I felt it was a special name because Kathrine means pure and Nadine means hope. And I knew that God had that name Pure Hope reserved for something special. I have been blessed to spend the last 20 years in many business opportunities and have had many different companies and even curriculums that I created and was teaching. But nothing seemed worthy of that calling and name Pure Hope – until now.

The Pure Hope Foundation was established to address the horrible impact of human trafficking on individuals and societies. You might wonder how I came to this point. After all, this topic is not exactly a common one around the dinner table. My journey to this point has been a long one, full of challenges and joys. However, the full story of that journey is for another day. Right now, I would like you to know about the Pure Hope Foundation, why it is important, and where we are going with God's help.

Several years ago, I was on an airplane traveling to a speaking engagement. I had planned to work on the flight, and had my books and other materials with me in my lap. My seatmate, a very dashing business man, kept wanting to talk to me, so I abandoned my work to speak with him. You can imagine my surprise when I asked him what he did for a living and he proceeded to inform me that he owned the second largest pornography company in the world. Long story short, we had the most compelling conversation. He told me later that he had seen the faith-based books I was working on and the conversation was to set me up to victimize me and shock me. He had been waiting for me to judge him and be shocked. But through the grace of God, I was able to remain calm while the conversation took me to a place I had never been. By the time we landed, I had been able to make him think about what he was doing. He even told me, "Kathrine Lee, I don't think I am going to be able to sleep quite the same again." I was grateful to God that I was able to have some impact on him, because believe me, that conversation had an impact on me. Those moments planted the seed of this legacy in my heart.

The idea for the Pure Hope Foundation did not spring full-grown at that moment. It is still not full grown to this day. Over the years, there have been many starts and stops, successes and things that have not worked out. But through that process, I have learned that our purposes are revealed over time. We can see them unfolding right before us, and the journey is the blessing. Despite the considerable challenges, the Pure Hope foundation is in place and is working. The foundation has four purposes: **F**ighting human trafficking, **R**estoring survivors, **E**mpowering advocates, and **E**nding demand—**FREE**.

I have learned that trafficking in the United States is the second largest criminal industry and the fastest growing. It will be number one soon. As I met with the FBI and Homeland security I asked why is this the case? And they said you can sell a drug once—yet you can sell a girl over and over. There is so much money in it. Some say this is a victimless crime. Nothing is further from the truth. I personally think it is also growing so fast because we are not talking about it. Members of law enforcement encouraged me to start speaking and getting the word out. As communities begin talking about it and become equipped to have the eyes to see and recognize it is going on, the criminals will decide to go to a different place. Shine the light on what is going on. We want to be very careful not to create secondary victimization by sharing details that people will replay in their minds, yet want to provide enough information to be aware. There are dedicated people working to save these women (there are males in the same situation, too, though the number is much smaller). Yet – where will they go when they are rescued? These in front line ministries who actually contact and physically rescue the girls are underfunded and overworked. Their programs help the girls to heal for about 6 months to 12 months. Yet when the girls finish the program, 80% go back to being trafficked. They need more time to heal.

To address this need, our goal is to create second-stage homes and programming for survivors coming out of those first months of rescue. I can see it in my mind, almost like a movie – a ranch. It will be a place where women who had been in the jaws of sex trafficking could be brought to be restored and be revived to the abundant life they were meant to live. Not out of slavery into the wilderness, but out of slavery and into a promised land. With rare exceptions, survivors desperately need continued healing, restoration and life skills training before they are ready to safely re-enter society. Pure Hope Foundation will continue the great care that began with our partners in first-stage safe house programs, and add a myriad of therapies and training to help the young women prepare to live and thrive independently.

At that ranch, we will also serve front-line workers by hosting retreats to offer rest, revival, and equipping for those who serve this population. Front-line workers are physically and emotionally drained because their job is so hard. They are chronically short of funding, so they work long hours in often-times unsavory even dangerous surroundings. Without rescuers, there is no rescue, so we need a place for them to rest so they can continue their important work.

A very strong way to fight human trafficking is to end the demand. To address that need, Pure Hope Foundation will host men's events to build strong men and address the issue of trafficking at its source, rather than from a symptomatic approach. When men stand in their rightful roles, families are strengthened and children are protected. I learned that pornography is the rocket fuel to trafficking. The average age of a boy exposed to pornography is 8 years old, probably not in print, but most likely in videos. And even grown men who would never intentionally click on pornography accidentally come across it as it pops up from different ads. It instantly shifts something in their brain and they are addicted to it. Men all the way into their 80's are addicted and share how they carry the shame of being caught in the jaws of pornography. We hope to raise up the hero's heart in men again, so they can be men who would lock shields together to protect our daughters. Men will grow stronger together.

We are not there yet. The journey has not been short, nor the way straight. However, God has helped us every step of the way. The dream of the ranch where important work can be done is still strong. We have found the place— 1,018 acres. We do not own that ranch yet, but we have met with the owners, and they are walking in faith with us as we work through a capital campaign to purchase it. We are all watching and waiting for what God is going to do. We personally purchased a few acres right next to the ranch as we continue to trust that God is leading us. But we are not waiting; we have already taken our first step. We purchased a house in a small town nearby where we can begin serving women. We can help the few and provide them with our programs and services to help their healing. We are learning as we go and are developing a better understanding of what will be needed when we own the ranch and have many, many women to serve. In one year we have been able to purchase this home debt free, hire key staff, get curriculum, programs, and services in place. And now young women are being served. God is good!

About Kathrine Lee

Kathrine is an internationally recognized speaker and has touched millions with her message of hope and transformation. She has worked with companies such as Boeing, Disney & the Saddleback Church. You may recognize Kathrine from one of her appearances on the Oprah Winfrey Show or by reading her story in O Magazine

Kathrine is a highly sought after life and business strategist. She is the Founder & Co-Creator of The Ultimate Source, a faith-based personal development system that teaches practical application of essential life skills. It was designed so that anyone can experience the abundant life God designed them to live. The Ultimate Source creates a deeper personal connection to God and His Word; therefore, producing more complete satisfaction and fulfillment in life. For more information, go to www.theultimatesource.org .

Kathrine is a National Marketing Director with the Juice Plus+ Company. The freedom and flexibility she gained through her alignment with this company has afforded her the opportunity to establish the Pure Hope Foundation where she currently serves as CEO. You can learn more at www.purehopefoundation.com .

Kathrine and her husband Michael live in Texas and have three wonderful children.

Be watching for the full Pure Hope Story in Kathrine Lee's new book that will be out in 2017 by liking the Pure Hope Foundation Facebook page or signing up to receive the newsletter at the Pure Hope website.

Afterword

The process of completing this book has been an incredible growth journey for me and has drawn me even closer to my Lord and Savior Jesus Christ. I continually marvel at the way He is so tender and caring to my friends during their darkest moments and walks with all of us on our journeys of faith. If you have questions regarding who this Jesus is—or if you are not really sure what it means to have a personal relationship with Him—I would like to talk with you and share all that He is to me and wants to be for you. No judgment – just a conversation between friends. That is the remarkable thing about Christ – there is nothing you could do that would make Him love you less. And there is no better place to be than in a relationship with Him.

Let's talk.

kathy.crockett@outlook.com

And I am convinced that nothing can ever separate us from God's love. Neither death nor life, neither angels nor demons, neither our fears for today nor our worries about tomorrow—not even the powers of hell can separate us from God's love. No power in the sky above or in the earth below—indeed, nothing in all creation will ever be able to separate us from the love of God that is revealed in Christ Jesus our Lord.

Romans 8:38-39 NLT

In Gratitude

One of the key things I have learned from this journey with the authors is that some of our richest blessings are the communities who support us. When I was in the John Townsend program he would continually teach us that healing comes in community. That is something that has not come naturally to me – to reach out for help. Yet I am so grateful I have communities who support, love, encourage and challenge me.

The first is my family. My husband Steve, who gives me incredible support in all my adventures, and whose deep faith encourages me. His love helps me believe I can do things that I would otherwise not do. Calley and Maddy— my amazing daughters who cheer me on and bless me immeasurably. And my mom, Dr. Lynn Huffman, she has been my mentor, encourager, challenger, wise counsel, and safe place my entire life. The rest of my family bless me as well.

The Sunset Church in Lubbock, Texas is another community where we have dear friends who we do life with. It is the place where Steve and I met and where we have chosen to raise our children. Our church is full of people who love Jesus Christ and yearn to draw closer to Him each day. We are not a perfect people, yet try to live authentically for Him.

The Lubbock Christian University community is special to my heart. I have served there as a business professor since 1997. College students are some of my favorite people. Their desire to learn and grow is contagious. The opportunity I have to pour into their lives is a blessing. I have such rich memories with former and current students travelling to places like New York, China, Italy, Colorado, and Atlanta for experiential learning. I look forward to many more memories. I am also grateful for my colleagues who serve alongside me in this ministry.

I have been part of the Juice Plus+ Company since 2001. I still marvel at times that God would bless me with this group of people. I wasn't looking for another community – and certainly never dreamed it would grow to thousands of people who I have met over the years. This community of servant-hearted people inspires me to be better each day. Our work of helping others is meaningful. The abundance God provides has allowed us to support causes we care about. Even helping to found non-profit organizations like Pure Hope Foundation. I have met some of my dearest friends and spiritual mentors in this community. It is as if God placed an unexpected, beautifully wrapped gift in my lap – and I continually get to pull more blessings from it each day.

My deepest gratitude is for Jesus Christ. His love for me and desire for my good is often more than I can even fathom. My hope is that my life can be a gift right back to Him as I share what He is to me with others.

~Kathy

About Kathy Crockett

Kathy Crockett, PhD, is Professor at Lubbock Christian University where she has served since 1997. Her teaching areas include marketing, management, and leadership.

She graduated from Texas A&M University and then completed graduate work at Texas Tech University. She has completed formal training from the Center of Creative Leadership related to Women in Leadership and Executive Coaching. She also completed a year-long leadership coaching program with Dr. John Townsend. She has been a facilitator for the Franklin Covey seminar entitled Great Leaders, Great Teams, Great Results.

Kathy has worked with the Juice Plus+ Company since 2001 and is currently a National Marketing Director. She and her team are focused on marketplace ministry and supporting causes such as the Pure Hope Foundation.

She develops customized leadership trainings and seminars for students, non-profit organizations, and corporate groups globally. She is also involved as a speaker at churches including women's retreats, ladies Bible classes, and servant renewal seminars. Kathy works as an entrepreneur in corporate leadership training, executive coaching, and wellness programs. One of her favorite programs is called Women in Leadership. She has served on various boards and is currently on the board for the Pure Hope Foundation.

Kathy has been married to the love of her life, Steve, for 21 years. They have two daughters, Calley 18 and Maddy 17 who bring much joy to their lives. They are members of Sunset Church in Lubbock, TX and are involved in missions and youth ministries.

Steve, Maddy, Calley and Kathy Crockett

Made in the USA
San Bernardino, CA
09 June 2020